The Soviet Social Contract and Why It Failed

Russian Research Center Studies, 86

The Soviet Social Contract and Why It Failed

Welfare Policy and Workers' Politics from Brezhnev to Yeltsin

Linda J. Cook

Harvard University Press
Cambridge, Massachusetts
London, England
1993

Library of Congress Cataloging-in-Publication Data

Cook, Linda J.
The Soviet social contract and why it failed : welfare policy and
workers' politics from Brezhnev to Yeltsin / Linda J. Cook.
p.   cm.—(Russian Research Center studies ; 86)
Includes bibliographical references and index.
ISBN 0-674-82800-3 (acid-free paper)
1. Labor policy—Soviet Union. 2. Working class—Soviet Union.
3. Soviet Union—Social conditions—1945–1991.   I. Title.
II. Series.
HD8526.5.C64   1993
331.1'0947—dc20
93-19068
CIP

To the memory of my friend and colleague
Bruce Philip Cooper

Contents

Tables

Figures

Acknowledgments

The idea for this book began at the Workshop on Political Control of the Soviet Economy, held at Yale University in March 1989. My first thanks go to Peter Hauslohner and David Cameron, who ran the workshop, and whose excellent critique of my paper suggested much of the research strategy employed herein. Many other individuals and institutions contributed intellectual, moral, and financial support during the writing. I want to thank especially Harvard University's Russian Research Center, and its former director Adam Ulam, for a fellowship which allowed me to devote many months to full-time writing at a critical stage. I much enjoyed the Center's collegiality and, with special thanks to Susan Gardos, its excellent research facilities.

Research for this book was supported in part by a grant from the International Research and Exchanges Board (IREX), with funds provided by the Andrew W. Mellon Foundation, the National Endowment for the Humanities, and the U.S. Department of State. Both IREX and the Center for International Studies at Brown University funded indispensable research trips to Moscow. There I was fortunate to be a guest of the Institute for the Study of Employment Problems, and I want to thank its director, B. V. Rakitsky, as well as Vladimir Kosmarsky and, most especially, Lena Vinogradova for her extraordinary help and hospitality. Nikolai Popov and others at the All-Union Center for the Study of Public Opinion provided valuable information and materials. Numerous labor specialists gave freely of their time and expertise, and I am grateful to them and to the freedom and openness which makes such scholarly cooperation possible now.

Many individuals gave me valuable advice on this project in response to talks at the Russian Research Center and at Brown's Center for Foreign Policy Development; others read drafts of the manuscript. I would like to thank the following for their comments and suggestions: Eric Nordlinger, Timothy Colton, Tom Biersteker, Mark Kramer, Stephen Shenfield, Darrell West, and Eric Goldhagen. The support of a few individuals has been especially critical, both in the writing of this book and otherwise in my professional and intellectual endeavors; I extend my deepest thanks to my graduate adviser, Seweryn Bialer, and my present colleagues Walter Connor, Tom Gleason, and Nancy Rosenblum. It goes without saying that none of the individuals or organizations named above is responsible for the views expressed in this book.

Three research assistants, Innes Gumnitsky, Alexander Vacroux, and Tamara Juswigg, provided invaluable assistance at various stages as well as some much-appreciated camaraderie. My brother-in-law, Steven Tribble, graciously contributed the computer artwork. Heidi Kroll patiently explained to me some economic concepts. My editors, Julie Hagen and especially Elizabeth Suttell at Harvard University Press, have gently prodded me through final revisions and improved the manuscript in various ways. My thanks go to all of these people.

Some portions of the present work have been published in earlier versions: "Brezhnev's Social Contract and Gorbachev's Reforms," in *Soviet Studies,* vol. 44, no. 1, 1992; "The Politics of Soviet Enterprise Insolvency," in *Soviet Union/Union Sovietique,* vol. 17, no. 3, 1990; and "Lessons of the Coal Miners' Strike of Summer 1989," in *Harriman Institute Forum,* vol. 4, no. 3, March 1991.

The writing of this book was, for the most part, a labor of love. However, it did require a degree of forbearance from my family and friends. I especially appreciated Laurinda Bedingfield's empathy on the matter of the notes. To Dan, who has constantly encouraged me to keep inching along and has shared his love and his joyful approach to life, I give my warmest thanks. To Dr. Bessel van der Kolk, for his wise counsel and support during these years, I am grateful. Finally, deepest gratitude goes to my parents for their unfailing support in this and many past endeavors.

My friend and colleague, Bruce Philip Cooper, died before the book was properly begun, but our conversations about Soviet politics, distributive justice, and so much else inform its pages (though often,

I'm sure, in ways he would not have liked). I am grateful to have known Bruce, and for his brilliance, his courage, and his faith in me. My dedication fulfills a promise, and makes a small tribute to the memory of a life rich with promise which could not be fulfilled.

The Soviet Social Contract and Why It Failed

The Social Contract Thesis and Conceptions of State–Working Class Relations

The Soviet political economy presents us with a paradox: its working class was until recently politically quiescent and organizationally weak, denied rights to form independent trade unions, to organize political parties, indeed to engage in effective or meaningful political participation. Yet Soviet workers seem to have gotten from postwar regimes major policy goods—full and secure employment, rising real incomes, and socialized human services—which have remained inaccessible to the best-organized labor movements in the industrialized world. How can we explain this paradox?

The explanation most generally accepted among Soviet specialists, including, for example, Seweryn Bialer, George Breslauer, Walter Connor, Peter Hauslohner, Ed Hewett, and Gail Lapidus, is that the post-Stalin regime and its working class made a tacit agreement to trade social security for political compliance, a "social contract."[1] The Stalinist regime had relied heavily on coercive controls over labor, as over society generally. Soviet workers were paid little, the wage structure was highly inegalitarian, and workers had no legal right to leave or change their jobs. In 1956, when Khrushchev removed the harsh legal restrictions on workers' mobility as part of his overall de-Stalinization of the political system, he also initiated new labor and wage policies that provided incentives and basic welfare, then codified these into a set of policy commitments which the Brezhnev-Kosygin leadership subsequently adopted. These commitments constitute the regime's side of the hypothesized contract.

Basically, the regime provided broad guarantees of full and secure employment, state-controlled and heavily subsidized prices for essential goods, fully socialized human services, and egalitarian wage policies. In exchange for such comprehensive state provision of economic and social security, Soviet workers consented to the party's extensive and monopolistic power, accepted state domination of the economy, and complied with authoritarian political norms. Maintenance of labor peace in this political system thus required relatively little use of overt coercion.

The social contract thesis purports to explain much about Soviet social policy outcomes and workers' political behavior. Though many Soviet specialists assert that such a tacit agreement existed, however, the thesis has not been subjected to systematic and critical examination. Moreover, competing explanations for both social policy and working-class quiescence coexist in the literature, and many social scientists outside the Soviet field find the thesis problematic and unconvincing.[2]

Perestroika raised new questions about the social contract thesis. The reform program threatened central provisions of the hypothesized contract, including employment guarantees, price controls, socialized services, and egalitarian wage policies. The Gorbachev leadership's agenda included wage reform designed to increase differentials, price reform that promised to reduce state subsidies and weaken price controls, industrial restructuring that threatened job security and stability, and proposals for privatization of social services.[3] But while reform policies did erode Soviet workers' social and economic security, the leadership eschewed measures that would have cut deeply into the old guarantees. The reform period also brought a dramatic rise of labor unrest and political activism. The unconstrained voices of Soviet workers could be heard for the first time and constituted an important new source of information about their political values and economic demands.

I wish to make a critical examination of the validity of the social contract thesis, and to assess its utility in explaining social policies and labor politics under Leonid Brezhnev and Mikhail Gorbachev. To carry out this examination, I must first specify the theoretical implications and empirical requirements of the hypothesized contract and consider some competing conceptions of regime-worker relations. I will then look carefully at evidence from the Brezhnev polity to determine how well it fits the requirements of the thesis, and consider whether Gorbachev's policy-making was constrained by the contract, in spite of his efforts to break free.

Theoretical Implications

The concept of the social contract, as it has been used in the Sovietology literature, denotes an exchange between regime and society in which each party tacitly committed itself to deliver political goods valued by the other.[4] The regime, for its part, consistently provided certain policy and allocational outcomes; the society, in turn, gave political consent and compliance. The thesis therefore implies two central, controversial claims about the Soviet polity: first, that the regime was constrained; and second, that popular compliance was consent-based and contingent.[5]

Under the terms of the social contract, the Soviet leadership was strongly constrained in its policy-making: it had to provide employment security, broad social welfare, and increasing income equality to fulfill popular expectations and to buy compliance and legitimacy. With these goods it satisfied basic material needs and justified its claim to be socialist. The contract thesis is based on the assumption that what the Soviet state delivered was precisely what its society most valued, that is, that party and people shared a conception of distributive and social justice that gave central place to material welfare and egalitarianism. It further assumes that the state must deliver these goods (in preference to pursuing other goals) or sacrifice legitimacy and risk open discontent. It implies, finally, that the Soviet regime needed popular acceptance and quiescence, or at least that it was willing to pay a high price in constrained policy and allocational options to achieve these goals. Seweryn Bialer wrote of the Brezhnev leadership in the late 1970s: "The responsiveness by the leadership to certain aspirations . . . can be described as an anticipatory reaction with regard to workers, that is to say, a response not to their actual behavior but to the leadership's fear that if the interests of the workers [were] not sufficiently considered, their behavior might [have] become disruptive and dangerous . . . Only at this price [could the party] continue to . . . withhold much of political freedom, and preserve political stability."[6]

The social contract thesis also implies that societal compliance was contingent on the regime's provision of comprehensive economic and social security. Soviet people, in other words, consented to the power and governance of existing party and state institutions because they were at least minimally satisfied with the substantive outputs of those institutions.[7] The society's acceptance of political authoritarianism, including prohibitions against political challenge, organized protest, even effective political participation, depended on the state's provision of accustomed benefits. If the state failed or ceased to deliver these benefits, the people would, according to the thesis, withdraw their ready consent and compliance and turn to political challenge or other expressions of discontent. In *Soviet Labour and the Ethic of Communism,* David Lane wrote that "consensus [was] maintained through a combination of social and welfare benefits coupled to the provision of employment . . . The welfare state and full employment [were] linchpins in the loyalty/solidarity/commitment system and the political support system."[8]

Soviet specialists have applied the social contract thesis variously to the regime-society relationship, the regime–working class relationship, and sometimes ambiguously to both.[9] It seems, however, that the thesis cannot be applied to the whole of the regime-society relationship; it breaks down at critical points for the intelligentsia, the non-Slavic nationalities, and the rural population. Even in the midst of the Brezhnev period, significant strata of the intelligentsia and the nationalities rejected the legitimacy of the established political order. Many intellectuals opposed authoritarianism on normative grounds, engaged openly in dissent, and sought procedural guarantees of legal and political rights. Many ethnic groups aspired to greater autonomy from Slavic political domination. Neither of these groups was exclusively oriented to substantive or material outputs; some of their members gave primacy to political values (specifically, liberalism and autonomy) that were not offered by the social contract. The rural population, meanwhile, remained residual claimants on the welfare state (though they received a great deal more than before) and had little capacity for collective political challenge.[10]

The thesis does, on the other hand, seem to apply in the case of Slavic blue-collar workers. Such workers were politically conformist and were the major beneficiaries of the welfare state. Moreover, they formed the core of the Soviet industrial labor force. Their strategic position in industry gave Slavic workers at least the potential for collective action that could have damaged or paralyzed the economy. Slavic blue-collar workers would seem to offer the strongest case for testing the hypothesis of a regime-society deal, and I will confine my arguments largely to this case.[11]

The core chapters of this book focus on the years 1965 through

1990: the whole of the Brezhnev period, ending with data for 1985, and the first five years of Gorbachev's stewardship.[12] Despite the disparity in the length of periods covered (twenty years under Brezhnev, five under Gorbachev), the greater policy activism and openness of the Gorbachev years provide sufficient material for comparison. In a critical sense the study ends in early 1990, when the Communist party formally ceded its claim to a monopoly of political power in the Soviet Union.[13] The party's declaration ended the social contract as it has been defined, because Soviet society would no longer be subjected to the Communist party's authoritarianism, which denied it political rights and voice. In addition, legislative bodies elected with a degree of genuine competition and popular participation (the All-Union Supreme Soviet and the republics' Supreme Soviets) were beginning to affect policy outcomes, as were newly independent trade unions and grass-roots worker activists.

By early 1990 the conditions specified for the contract had significantly broken down: the regime no longer demanded or received political passivity and compliance from its society, and no longer monopolized control of policy and allocational outcomes. The last two chapters in this volume follow the development of labor politics through the Soviet collapse and the first twelve months of Boris Yeltsin's Russian government, focusing on the political, organizational, and structural legacies of the social contract in the postcommunist era.

Empirical Requirements and Evidence

The social contract thesis has three main empirical requirements:

1. that the Soviet regime consistently deliver to workers economic security and social welfare;
2. that the regime deliver these policy goods because it is constrained by its perception of workers' expectations or its fear of labor discontent if it fails to deliver them;
3. that workers give in exchange political compliance and quiescence.

Various types of evidence will allow us to judge how well the Soviet polity met these requirements.

The first requirement, that the regime deliver economic security and social welfare, leads to an examination of Soviet labor and social spending policies in three areas: employment, wages and prices, and social services. I want to see whether the regime maintained full employment and job security, equality of income distribution, price stability and subsidies, and socialized human services. Consistent delivery requires that per capita spending on social services must be stable or increasing over time, and that wage policies must maintain or lessen disparities. Soviet sources and statistics on all these policy areas must, of course, be used carefully and critically.

For this first part of the study, I will assess the record of the Brezhnev regime in each of the three policy areas, using statistical indexes for each five-year period (1965 through 1985) as well as other sources. To assess full and secure employment, I will look at rates of labor force growth and participation, as well as information about legal and de facto protections of workers' job security; for an assessment of wages, I will examine rates and disparities; for prices, official and alternative consumer price indexes and other indicators; for social services, per capita expenditures for total social consumption funds, education, and health care. These data will indicate whether the Brezhnev leadership increased, or at least sustained, its delivery of social contract outputs in each policy area, and to what extent the contract was a casualty of the late-Brezhnev period of stringency.[14]

To support the thesis of a tacit contract or exchange, it must also be shown that the leadership was *constrained* in making social policy and allocational decisions. In looking for evidence of constraint, it should prove useful to consider two questions. First, did the Brezhnev leadership sustain delivery of social contract outputs even in the face of rising costs, declining resources, and strong pressures to make different policy and allocational decisions? Second, did the leadership explicitly cite concerns about popular expectations, or fears about unrest, in defending social contract policies to critics or competing claimants?

These questions will be approached through case studies of *pressured decision points,* that is, points at which the leadership faced clear-cut decisions to commit a greater proportion of resources, or to abandon other policies at significant cost, in order to maintain the social contract. These case studies examine (as far as possible with the evidence available) the politics and debates surrounding each pressured decision. I will try to determine what drove these policy decisions and, in particular, whether the leadership's concerns about popular expectations and reactions significantly motivated it to maintain social contract outputs.[15]

I have chosen one set of pressured decision points in each of the three policy areas—employment, prices, and social services. The first is a case of political intervention to ensure full employment: the 1966 youth *bronia,* when the Brezhnev leadership pressed managers into hiring unwanted young employees, in the face of its own previous commitment to increase managers' autonomy in hiring and staffing decisions. For price policy, the pressured situation is provided by a series of decisions to raise agricultural procurement prices while retaining retail food prices at more-or-less stable levels. In this case the Brezhnev leadership repeatedly decided to absorb (and cover with new subsidies) wholesale food price increases, rather than pass them on to consumers. A third set of pressured decision points came with the allocation of spending cuts during the late-Brezhnev period of stringency. In Chapter 2, data will show how social services fared in the competition for resources, by focusing on spending for health and education.

I must also determine whether workers' compliance and quiescence were given in exchange for social contract policy outputs—the third requirement in the contract thesis. Two types of evidence bear on this question. First, the thesis implies that periods of labor quiescence should correlate with delivery of social contract outputs, periods of unrest with deterioration or failures in delivery; I will see whether this correlation holds for the Brezhnev period. Second, I will assess the value Soviet workers placed on economic security and social welfare, as revealed in available data on attitudes and in the grievances and demands actually raised during periods of labor unrest.[16]

The second half of the book presents a parallel study of the Gorbachev period. As I have noted, Gorbachev's reform program threatened to erode central provisions of the hypothesized social contract, but it stopped short of making deep cuts in social welfare. I will examine the reformers' critique of Brezhnev's welfare state and their debates about social justice; look at the explicit goals and official policies of the Gorbachev regime in the areas of employment security, prices, and socialized services, and contrast them with Brezhnev-era goals and policies; and look at actual policy and spending outcomes in these areas during the years 1985 through 1990 and compare them with outcomes during the Brezhnev period.

To examine the issue of constraint under Gorbachev, I have chosen another set of case studies (paralleling those for the Brezhnev period) focused on pressured decision points—points at which the Gorbachev leadership faced decisions to cut social contract benefits in order to pursue its declared reform strategy. I will review a case in which the leadership reversed a reform policy (specifically, its hasty retreat from extensive privatization of medical care); a case in which it delayed a decision long characterized as necessary (retail price reform); and a case in which the harsher consequences of an enacted reform policy were averted (the continued subsidies and bailouts provided to enterprises that were rendered legally insolvent by the Law on the State Enterprise). I will examine closely the politics of each decision and try to specify the pressures inhibiting reform in each policy area, in order to determine whether the hypothesized social contract was a significant constraint on the Gorbachev regime's social and allocational policy decisions.

Finally, I will look at the rise of labor activism under Gorbachev and check for a correlation between working-class unrest and declining delivery on the social contract.[17] An analysis of the record created by this activism—the demands of strikers, and the programs and popularity of the new, independent workers' organizations—will provide information on workers' attitudes toward social contract issues. It should be especially useful to see whether or not Soviet workers used their new rights in substantial measure to protest erosion of the social contract under Gorbachev and to demand revival of the old policies of state control and provision.

Competing Explanations for Social Policy Outcomes

While many of the most highly regarded Soviet specialists subscribe to the social contract thesis, it is by no means universally accepted. The literature contains a number of explanations for social policy outcomes that, explicitly or implicitly, challenge the thesis. Their proponents reject the claim that Soviet policy was significantly constrained by mass societal pressures or expectations, and present the regime either as autonomous of society or as influenced only by institutional or societal elites.

Some specialists assert that welfare-oriented social policies were a consequence of the Soviet leadership's ideological commitments or paternalistic inclinations, rather than a response to popular expectations.[18] They argue that egalitarianism and social welfare are classic socialist principles that informed policy-making because the leadership believed in them. Most recognize that state provision of welfare and security constituted a powerful source of post-Stalin regime legitimation, but they see workers as still-powerless dependents of an authoritarian state rendered somewhat more acceptable by its paternalism. For the purposes of this study, the critical claim is that the elite provided working-class welfare because of its own values and commitments, *not* because its decisions were constrained or its power contingent. As one proponent of this view stated the case: "ideology influence[d] . . . policy and the approach to the labor process. The Soviet ideology of labor provide[d] constraints on the political leadership . . . the ideological environment contribute[d] to the provision of employment."[19] The thesis of elite paternalism or ideologically based commitment to workers' welfare challenges the social contract thesis, because it provides a competing explanation for policies protective of employment and social security.

A second competing explanation for full and secure employment is proposed by economists, many of whom argue that full employment was a consequence of the operation of Soviet planning and economic mechanisms. According to the well-known analysis of Janos Kornai, for example, the Soviet system of financing industry produced "soft budget constraints" that gave managers few incentives to economize on production inputs.[20] Soft budget constraints, in combination with other features of the Soviet planning system and labor market, motivated managers to inflate labor forces and hoard workers, producing systemwide overdemand for industrial labor and, in turn, full employment accompanied by chronic shortage and competition for labor.[21] In contrast to the social contract thesis, then, the soft budget constraints argument explains full employment as a spin-off of the economic system and managerial incentives, not as a response to the interests, expectations, or potential power of workers.

Still other Soviet specialists, mainly political scientists, claim that the interests and interplay of bureaucratic actors were the chief determinants of Soviet policy and allocational outcomes, including those in the sphere of labor and social policy.[22] The most important of the bureaucratic politics approaches, and the one that has been most explicitly applied to social policy outcomes, is Jerry Hough's "institutional pluralism."[23] According to this view, in the Brezhnev period Soviet party leaders functioned as brokers among bureaucratic or institutional claimants who competed for political goods and allocations. The claimants included bureaucracies responsible for welfare, labor, and wage policies. Hough proposes a policy-making process in which the trade unions, the State Committee for Labor and Social Issues, and other specialized bureaucracies participated seriously, influenced outcomes, and genuinely represented and defended some workers' interests. He asserts: "The trade unions frequently [spoke] out in defense of the immediate interests of the urban poor and industrial workers . . . Policy [was] an outcome of puzzling, bargaining, and brokering among interests, probably somewhat responsive to popular opinion."[24] According to the institutional pluralism model, then, workers got policy goods because they were clients of powerful institutional claimants in a bureaucratized polity, not because of a tacit social contract between the political elite and the mass of workers.

A bureaucratic politics approach is also commonly used to account for policy outcomes in the Gorbachev period. Most analysts seeking to explain the limits and failures of reform policies, especially in the first three or four years of perestroika, pointed to bureaucratic resistance as the central problem. In many accounts, the reformist political elite was thwarted by ubiquitous bureaucratic obstacles—ministries unwilling to give up control over industry, conservative local bureaucrats blocking the cooperative movement, entrenched central-state bureaucracies resisting all forms of marketization.[25] Little attention was paid to the question of societal response to reform policies, though some analysts did consider the leadership's possible ambivalence about policies that threatened the economic and social security so often cited as a major source of regime legitimacy and stability.[26]

These three conceptually distinct explanations for Soviet social policy—leadership paternalism or ideological commitment; the planning mechanism and managerial incentives; and bureaucratic bargaining—have coexisted in the literature with the social contract thesis. Each poses a challenge to the thesis, because each identifies a different central source of social policy outcomes.

Competing Explanations for Workers' Political Quiescence

The social contract thesis holds that Soviet workers were politically compliant because they consented to the regime in exchange for beneficial labor and social policies. Some prominent political sociologists have challenged the claim that workers' compliance resulted from consent.[27] They argue instead that the absence of solidarity and collective action among Soviet workers resulted from the credible threat of repression and from social and political mechanisms that intentionally atomized and depoliticized the working class. They agree that workers valued the welfare and security provided by the state, but disagree that these were given in tacit exchange for compliance. Rather, in their view, the state manipulated benefits to promote segmentation and to enforce dependence of workers.

Victor Zaslavsky, for example, argues that social peace in the Soviet period was largely a consequence of atomization and bureaucratic manipulation of workers. According to his analysis, the Soviet state relied on three central mechanisms to control workers: it purposely constructed artificial barriers to segment the working class into multiple political and economic-status groups; it monopolized the direction of organized activity; and it threatened and used repression. In addition, both social mobility and lateral labor mobility (that is, high job turnover) provided workers with individual solutions to work and status-related problems, atomizing their discontent and giving them alternatives to collective action. Zaslavsky argues that the combination of these factors undercuts the potential for solidarity and collective action: "It is difficult to expect workers to resort to collective initiatives when individual action proves at least partially effective, the repressive apparatus is strong, the inertia of fear is still strong, and there is improving personal consumption."[28]

Andrew Walder also argues that control rather than consent accounts for labor quiescence in communist states (including the Soviet Union). He stresses the importance of the extreme and multiple personal dependencies of workers—dependence on political authorities and on factory managers—for provision of many welfare benefits distributed through the workplace. Walder also emphasizes the system's granting of preference to pro-regime activists as a practice that divided workers and class loyalties. He concludes that workers looked after their interests largely through particularistic relationships with patrons and authorities, and that such pervasive patterns of "organized dependence" in factories militated effectively against the development of working-class solidarity.[29]

Each of these authors poses a challenge to the claims of the social contract thesis. The challenge is somewhat less direct in Walder's case, because his study focuses on authority relations in factories rather than in society in general. Nevertheless, his central thesis contradicts the social contract in its stress on state-bureaucratic manipulation of differential access to benefits as a means of dividing workers. The social contract, by contrast, holds that the state pacifies workers with collective goods distributed on egalitarian principles.

The Soviet Social Contract and Western Corporatism

Present discussion of the Soviet social contract thesis resonates with much of the recent corporatist writing on politics in the industrial democracies.[30] The corporatist literature commonly focuses on state-sponsored or state-mediated bargaining between representative organizations from industry and labor over wage, employment, labor market, and social policies. Successful bargaining results in exchanges of political and economic goods (among the state, industry, and labor) that stabilize industrial relations, assuring continued economic production and political stability.[31]

Corporatist agreements, or contracts, generally require organized labor to accept constraints on its demands and tactics (typically, wage restraints, no-strike pledges, promises of no nonnegotiable demands) in return for concessions from employers. The most comprehensive packages, often called social compacts, involve constraints on state fiscal policy as well (for example, pledges on taxes and transfer payments). Trade union leaders must deliver the cooperation and compliance of their rank and file, while industrialists and governments must deliver promised benefits to labor, or the pact will not hold.[32] Some scholars see corporatist mediation as detrimental to labor, because it allows the state and capitalists to depoliticize class conflict, to co-opt organized labor's leadership, and to deny authentic participation to rank-and-file workers.[33] Others argue that corporatist bargaining has the potential to maximize both public and individual workers' goods.[34]

Several similarities between corporatist agreements and the Soviet social contract should be apparent: both involve a deal between political-economic elites and societal actors that constrains policy options and mass-organizational behavior; both conceive of labor as a powerful interest because of its strategic position and critical function in the economy (not as just one societal interest among many, as in the pluralist conception); both conceive of the state as an organization that seeks stability as a major goal and actively structures the policy process to secure labor peace.

There have, in fact, been one or two attempts by political scientists to apply corporatist concepts or models to the Soviet polity (though at different levels of analysis and for different purposes than in this study).[35] The most far-reaching attempt, by Bunce and Echols, concluded that the Soviet regime under Brezhnev was a type of corporatist polity, because it was dominated by an activist state that incorporated major interests into the policy process, engaged in pragmatic bargaining, expanded the welfare state, and sought consensus and stability.[36]

It seems, however, that corporatist models developed in studies of the industrial democracies do not fit the Soviet polity very well, because the overall structures of state-socialist and democratic-capitalist political economies are too dissimilar. In the Soviet system (before 1988) there was no legal market or distinct economic elite. The party-state had concentrated responsibility for economic planning (coordination), productivity, and sociopolitical stability, functions that are significantly dispersed among the market, financial and industrial elites, and political elites in Western systems. Trade unions that represented and bargained for workers' interests were strongly penetrated and controlled by the party. The Soviet political economy was closed to both economic and political competitors.

Thus, while Western states may (as corporatist writers claim) influence the definition and organization of societal interest groups, the Soviet state did so much more directly and completely.[37] While Western corporatist arrangements may limit trade union officials' responsibility and responsiveness to their rank and file, the balance shifted very far to the state side in the Soviet case.[38] Challengers from outside or within officially sanctioned organizations, who are disadvantaged in Western corporatist systems,[39] were systematically excluded and repressed in the Soviet system. The entire Soviet economy, including workers, managers, and administrators, was largely insulated from the pressures of international and domestic competition that Western corporatist arrangements were designed and developed to manage.

The issue here is not formal definitions or typologies; it is the practical utility of corporatism as a framework for analysis of the Soviet polity. Corporatist studies analyze the political process in systems that are significantly more open, flexible, and competitive than the Soviet system. While such studies criticize and correct for the pluralist concept of a completely open, unstructured policy arena, they generally describe a more structured competition in which labor has some options in terms of bargaining tactics, negotiating strategies, and political alliances. Much of the stuff of corporatist studies—the formation and collapse of governing coalitions, the crafting of organized labor's responses to market threats, rank and file discontent, and militant challenges to union leaderships—are absent or irrelevant in the Soviet context. Further, Western "concertation" often produces explicit agreements or compacts, and scholars can trace the political and organizational forces that sustain or jettison those compacts.[40]

By contrast, in the Soviet case the political arena was narrow, and there was little open, visible competition. Officially sanctioned trade unions did articulate workers' interests and grievances. However, the party denied the possibility of basic conflicts of interest between workers and the state. As a result, in Blair Ruble's apt phrase, "the arena for labor-management discord [became] severely constricted."[41] Soviet workers had much more limited options than their Western counterparts for pressing their case; they could channel grievances through official unions and courts, withhold labor (through poor discipline, absenteeism, and low productivity), or use the blunt and extreme instrument of strikes. So, in spite of the similarities between our hypothesized Soviet social contract and some Western corporatist social compacts, the corporatist framework provides very limited help for most of this study.

The situation changed, however, when the Soviet system began to democratize. By 1990, the Soviet polity featured activist labor movements, independent trade unions, political competition, empowered legislatures, and emergent organizations of industrialists and entrepreneurs. Moreover, government and labor leaders looked to Western corporatism as a model for structuring the state-labor relationship. In chapters 7 and 8 I will return to the discussion of corporatism, focusing on the contradictions and dysfunctions of its Soviet/Russian variant.

Conclusion

In spite of the closed nature of the Soviet political process (especially in the Brezhnev period), a strong case can be made for the social contract thesis by specifying patterns of social policy outcomes, correlating workers' compliance and noncompliance, and studying closely selected pressured decision points. Accordingly, I will begin by looking at employment and wage patterns, retail price levels, and social service expenditures for the Brezhnev years. The evidence will support the state-provision requirement of the thesis to the extent that employment was full and secure, retail prices were stable, and per capita social service expenditures were stable or increasing. The evidence will support the requirement of an exchange of policy outputs for labor quiescence if workers remained compliant during periods of delivery, were activist during periods of slackening delivery, and cited inadequate social contract outputs as a central source of their discontent. The evidence will support the constrained-political-elite requirement if, at pressured decision points, leaders maintained social contract outputs at the expense of competing policy goals, and cited concern about workers' expectations or dissatisfaction as an important motive for the decision.

For the Gorbachev period, I will look briefly at policies in the same three areas, including major policy initiatives and enacted measures in each area. The Gorbachev leadership tried, with very limited success, to implement a reform program that would have undercut workers' social and economic security. The important question is whether the social contract constituted a significant obstacle to reform. The case studies of pressured decision points should provide information about why and how specific reform policies were abandoned or moderated. The social contract thesis will be supported to the extent that social contract outputs were maintained at pre-Gorbachev (1985) levels and reform policies were abandoned or moderated because of concern about workers' expectations or reactions. There was a rise of working-class unrest during the reform period. The social contract thesis will be supported to the extent that evidence shows worker discontent to have been motivated by deteriorating delivery of social contract outputs.[42]

I must also take account of the major competing explanations for Soviet social policy outcomes and workers' quiescence. How can we deal with claims that these social and labor policies, even if they seemed to respond to the interests of workers, actually resulted from leadership paternalism, the planning mechanism, or bureaucratic bargaining? First, it is important to recognize the influence of these factors: the Brezhnev leadership did hold some paternalistic values, the economic planning mechanism did support high demand for labor, and powerful bureaucracies did play a role in Soviet policy-making. I wish to determine whether the social contract thesis provides a cogent and compelling explanation for a linked set or pattern of outcomes across policy areas and regimes. Certainly the social contract would have coexisted with other influences on policy outcomes.

This said, I would like to indicate how and where the evidence may refute, or indicate some limitations of, the competing explanations. First, taking the claims for economic-system causes, full employment might well have resulted from the planning mechanism and managerial incentives. However, if there are cases where system-generated demand was inadequate to maintain full employment in local labor markets, or cases where the party intervened to increase staffing levels of some groups of workers above those desired by managers, this will constitute evidence that political decisions (separate from systemic demand or managerial preferences) contributed significantly to the maintenance of full employment. Similarly, employment security might have resulted solely from managers' incentives to hoard labor, but if security was buttressed by legal protections and informal norms that constrained managers to keep workers they didn't want, then there is evidence of political intent to maintain job security.

Second, there is the argument that powerful institutions dominated policy-making through bargaining, competition, or resistance. I have chosen for case studies two policy areas—retail food price subsidies and health care allocations—that would tend to be relatively insulated from the interests of the most powerful bureaucratic actors because policy benefits in these areas go first and foremost to amorphous societal groups.[43] In fact, increasing subsidies on agricultural goods benefited collective farmers and urban consumers (including those with lower incomes), presumably at the expense of powerful bureaucratic claimants for state funds. The maintenance of health care allocations during the late-Brezhnev period of stringency would have benefited society rather than powerful bureaucratic actors in the system (for example, industrial ministries and the military). To the extent that allocational decisions frequently maintained benefits for workers at the expense of powerful institutional claimants, the case can be made that bureaucratic actors did not dominate decision making, that there was either societal constraint or leadership paternalism.

Leadership paternalism or ideological commitment is the most difficult of the alternative explanations to counter, because it can account very well for social policy outcomes protective of workers. Moreover, the Brezhnev leadership claimed it was paternalistic. However, if there is evidence that Brezhnev was more consistent in his delivery of social contract outputs to worker strata that posed a potential threat to political order (for example, because of their age or concentration), this will support the case that paternalism was secondary to fear of discontent. Further, if leadership values and attitudes were the primary determinants of social policy in the Soviet system, as the paternalism argument assumes, then different leadership values should produce different policy outcomes. The Gorbachev leadership clearly repudiated the paternalism of its predecessors, but it was not so clearly able to break with the old leadership's social policies.[44] The social contract thesis is supported to the extent that societal constraints can be shown to influence policy in the absence of paternalism.

Finally, there is the matter of the competing explanations for workers' quiescence, the claims of Walder, Zaslavsky, and others, that Soviet workers were compliant because of threatened repression, manipulation, and dependence. These are powerful arguments, and they present a serious challenge to the social contract's basic claim that workers had the potential power to enforce a contract or exchange with the regime. Three types of evidence seem relevant here. First, Walder and Zaslavsky stress the centrality of bureaucratic domination and manipulation in segmenting and dividing workers, but major trends in labor policy during the Brezhnev years were in the direction of extending universal legal and normative protections that should have limited managers' discretionary and discriminatory powers. Second, the repressive controls on workers' expression and organization were more or less consistent throughout the Brezhnev period, and so cannot account for variation in levels of open discontent. Third, the repressive controls were lifted in 1988 and 1989, providing us with some direct evidence of workers' discontents, and indirect evidence of the degree of their satisfaction with past social policies.

TWO

Brezhnev's Welfare State:
Delivering on the Social Contract

The Soviet social contract was, as I have noted, not a contract in the strict sense of the term, but an implicit agreement dictated by the state and accepted by the workers. Nevertheless the state's side of this agreement was substantially codified in major programmatic statements, resolutions, and other official documents during the 1960s and 1970s. In fact, we can identify the 22nd Congress of the Communist Party of the Soviet Union (CPSU), in November 1961, as the point at which the leadership declared improvements of social welfare and increases in distributive equality to be central goals of party policy. The 22nd Congress promulgated the new Third Party Program, replacing the Second Party Program (which had been formally in effect since 1919) and promising Soviet society large, long-term increases in levels of income and social security.[1]

The Third Party Program

The Third Party Program set out a general plan for building the material and technical base of communism in the Soviet Union by 1980. It made grandiose promises about assuring abundance, exceeding U.S. rates of industrial production, increasing the national income by a factor of four, and raising the population's living standard above that of any capitalist country.[2] It projected the equalization of conditions of work and distribution in Soviet society between city and countryside, between those engaged in mental and manual labor, and among workers at different income levels. It included plans for rapid extension of state-subsidized social services that would, by the end of the period, have become freely available according to need. Many Western analysts dismissed the Third Party Program as an empty exercise in radical rhetoric and utopianism—in Robert Tucker's words, "one more set of grandiose promises destined to go unfulfilled"—and in reference to its broadest and grandest claims, this was surely right.[3] However, beneath such rhetoric the program also set forth a list of specific policy directions and concrete goals that had real significance for Soviet society.[4]

First, the program made a number of more or less realistic commitments to improvements in social welfare. It is important to remember that, in 1961, much of the Soviet population had only a primary education, infectious diseases were common, incomes remained low, and housing was extremely overcrowded—in sum, the welfare state was very poorly developed.[5] Much of what the Third Party Program promised was an expansion of state-funded social services and benefits:

in education, the achievement of universal compulsory secondary schooling for youth, and the transfer of all schools to single-shift schedules;

in housing, the provision of an apartment for every family and newly married couple;

in health care, measures to eliminate mass contagious diseases and to increase longevity;

in child care, extension of the network of children's institutions with the goal of fully meeting the need for preschools, and extension of maternity leave;

in social security, the extension of maintenance payments to all citizens incapacitated through old age or disability.[6]

The program also guaranteed full employment of the able-bodied population (with planned training and transfer for those displaced through mechanization), systematic price reductions, and pay increases.

Second, the Third Party Program promised substantial increases in distributive equality within Soviet society during the coming two decades. Along with wage increases, it called for steady reduction of disparities in levels of pay between those with high and "comparatively low" incomes: while incomes of all workers and employees were to double over the coming ten years, they were to triple in low-paid categories. And while payment according to work (wage income) would remain the primary source of income, the proportion of distribution through social consumption funds (social services provided at minimal cost and transfer payments distributed partly according to need) would increase. The program specified that "personal needs [would] be increasingly met out of social consumption funds, whose rate of growth [would] exceed the rate of growth of individual payment for labor."[7] By 1980, social consumption funds were to comprise approximately half of income and would make possible the provision, at public expense (that is, completely free of direct charge to the user), of a long list of basic necessities and social services, including education, child care, medical care, housing, public utilities, public transport, stipends, disability payments, and lunch programs. The Soviet Union would thus be progressing toward the realization of the communist principle of distribution according to need.

The Third Party Program set clear directions and concrete goals for the guidance of long-term Soviet social and income policies. In fact, Nikita Khrushchev had already adopted and begun implementing policies directed toward some of these goals, including priority expansion of secondary education, lowering wage disparities, and increasing pensions and maternity benefits.[8] But the program went well beyond such individual policy measures, making fairly explicit commitments about future patterns of income distribution and levels of social spending, and thus implying rather severe constraints on future allocational decisions and options. (Though it is important to note here that the program was premised on rising levels of overall national income, and did not commit a growing proportion of national income to social spending or even clearly to consumption.[9]) With the program's promulgation, the Soviet Communist party committed itself to deliver to the working people steadily rising real incomes, improving social welfare, and increasing equality.[10]

Even when the Third Party Program is taken seriously as a set of policy commitments and guidelines, however, there remains a problem with presenting it as the codification of the Brezhnev-era social contract: it was, first of all, Khrushchev's program, formulated and written predominantly under his influence, showing clearly his style and his overoptimism about potential Soviet economic progress. Moreover, Khrushchev himself soon reneged on some of its major commitments. In 1962, disappointed with labor productivity gains, he canceled wage increases and raised retail prices on some foods (precipitating serious labor unrest, which will be discussed further).[11] And, of course, the Brezhnev leadership abandoned or repudiated major elements of Khrushchev's domestic and foreign policy approaches after his ouster in the fall of 1964, including his penchant for utopianism and grand schemes.

Despite its sponsorship by the ousted Khrushchev, however, the Third Party Program remained the touchstone for social and distributive policy through much of the Brezhnev period. The Program was explicitly and repeatedly cited as the basis for policies in these areas at Brezhnev-era party congresses. At the 23rd Congress in March 1966, for example, Brezhnev stated in his concluding remarks that "the activity of the Party . . . was aimed at fulfilling the CPSU Program"; at the 24th Congress in March-April 1971, Aleksei Kosygin declared in his plan report, "The distribution of the national income is carried out in accordance with the principles of socialism written into our party's Program."[12] Additionally, the program's language, watchwords, and conceptions of future goals remained constants in the political dialogue of the Brezhnev years. The post-Khrushchev leadership clearly reaffirmed the central substantive commitments of the program; Brezhnev, for example, stated in his opening address to the 23rd Congress, "The material well-being of *each working person* rises *in proportion* to the growth of public wealth."[13]

Brezhnev-Era Social Policies and Principles

The social and distributive policies announced by the Brezhnev leadership followed the program's guidelines and were regularly justified in terms of its principles of comprehensive state provision of benefits and egalitarianism. This will be evident from a brief review of Brezhnev's major policy commitments in the areas of employment, wages, prices, and social consumption spending, along with their central justifications in ideology or principle.

The promise of full employment under Soviet socialism predated the 1961 party program by thirty years, and the Brezhnev leadership simply ensured its continuation, asserting that workers would be spared capitalism's "unemployment . . . and the degradation of individual economic regions."[14] The leadership promised a decrease in manual and physically arduous labor, retraining and reassignment for workers displaced by planned automation, and, late in its tenure, improvements in labor safety. The major gain for workers was to come in the area of wages, especially for low-paid groups. Every Brezhnev-era Five-Year Plan provided for substantial wage increases (averaging more than 20 percent for the plan period), invariably including increases in the minimum wage and in the wage and salary rates of middle-income workers in some branches (Table 2.1). The stated goal of these policies was to raise incomes while decreasing income disparities, thus lessening differentiation in living and cultural conditions between workers in different sectors (for example, mental and manual labor, rural and urban workers).

Every Brezhnev-era party congress report and Five-Year Plan also guaranteed retail price stability and, indeed, planned price reductions for some products (children's goods, medicines). They also typically promised improved supplies of goods and services, and regularly announced substantial increases in the volume of retail trade turnover *with* stable prices. While not explicitly recognizing inflationary pressures, both Brezhnev and Kosygin, at the 24th Congress (March–April 1971), inveighed against attempts to circumvent state prices and called for intensified price controls. In the mid-1970s, there was a subtle but significant change in their stated policy, from the blanket guarantee of stable retail prices to the somewhat more qualified one of stable prices for basic foodstuffs and manufactured goods (along with the promise of an expanded assortment of new and fashionable, but presumably more expensive, goods). Despite this qualification, the party's guarantee of stable prices for food and other necessities remained in force, and, as Kosygin pointed out at the 25th Congress, only the maintenance of stable prices could guarantee real income security.[15]

The Brezhnev-era Five-Year Plans provided for regular and substantial increases in the level of social consumption funds, ranging from 20 percent to 40 percent for each of the Five-Year Plans (see Table 2.1). These funds were directed primarily to the uses earmarked by the party program, specifically, increases in pensions, preschool child care, housing, and public health. During the 1970s, the Brezhnev leadership added a program of income supplements to low-income families (typically those with many children), extended paid

Table 2.1 Planned increases in national income, average wages, social consumption funds, and per capita real income, 1965–1985 (percent increases over previous Five-Year Plan [FYP])

Five-Year Plan	National income	Average monthly wage, production and office workers	Social consumption funds	Per capita real income
8th FYP[a] (1966–1970)	38–41%	≥ 20%	40%	30%
9th FYP[b] (1971–1975)	37–40	20–22	40	30
10th FYP[c] (1976–1980)	24–28	16–18	28–30	20–22
11th FYP[d] (1981–1985)	18–20	13–16	20	16–18

a. *Current Soviet Policies V, 23rd Congress of CPSU,* pp. 95, 105–106 (from Kosygin's report; figures based on draft plan). Wage and real income figures are approximate.

b. *Current Soviet Policies VI, 24th Congress of CPSU,* pp. 119, 121, 131–132 (from Kosygin's report; figures based on draft directives). Real income figure is approximate.

c. *Current Soviet Policies VII, 25th Congress of the CPSU,* pp. 74–75 (Kosygin's report on the FYP; figures based on draft directives). Figures for real income are from *25th Congress of the CPSU: Documents and Resolutions* (Moscow: Novosti Press Agency Publishing House, 1976), pp. 60–61.

d. *Current Soviet Policies VIII, 26th Congress of the CPSU,* pp. 16–19, 110–113 (from Brezhnev's report; figures based on draft directives).

maternity leaves, and introduced cash allowances for children. Student stipends and other categories of spending on education were also increased.[16]

There were some significant changes in official social policies toward the end of the Brezhnev years, as the leadership began to recognize and react to (however inadequately) serious performance problems in the economy. The goals of increasing efficiency and quality were raised to a level equal with that of raising living standards. More attention was paid to the incentive role of wages, and excessive leveling was criticized. After two decades of apparently equalizing policies, the Brezhnev leadership turned its attention to the still poorly developed social and cultural infrastructure in the eastern and northern regions of the country, and declared the need to "even out social distinctions on the territorial level."[17] While the commitment to full employment remained in place, the leadership recognized the presence of surplus manpower in Central Asia and the Caucasus and the need to develop new training and industry-siting policies in these regions. The quality of the social services bought with the ever-increasing social consumption funds was also called into question.

The final Brezhnev-era party congress in February 1981 repeated the guarantee of further growth of the Soviet people's well-being, but this time with a list of necessary preconditions: stable, progressive development of the national economy; acceleration of scientific and technical progress; changeover of the economy to an intensive path of development; more efficient use of the country's production potential; every possible saving of all types of resources; improvement of work quality.[18]

Why did the Brezhnev leadership adopt and, more important, maintain these policies? There are two credible explanations. Perhaps the leaders acted from paternalistic motives, their collective commitment to a socialist system that protected workers from market forces and promoted equality and welfare. Alternatively, perhaps these policies were delivered as an anticipatory or preemptive response to workers' presumed demands. Full employment, job security, and income guarantees certainly were major goals of organized labor in the West during this period. It is reasonable to suggest that Soviet leaders assumed they could keep labor peace by ensuring these conditions even while prohibiting independent workers' organizations. A case can be made for either explanation, and we will sort out the evidence later. First, it will be useful to examine the Brezhnev leadership's record of actual delivery of social-contract-policy goods.

State Provision of Full and Secure Employment

The Soviet state defined work as both a right and a duty of its citizens, and claimed to provide full employment. Western experts on Soviet labor broadly accept the claim of full employment (defined as a full-time job provided for all able-bodied, working-age job seekers), with a few minor qualifications.[19] David Granick, in an authoritative study, characterized the Soviet labor market from the mid-1960s to the mid-1980s as one of "overfull" employment, meaning that, with rare exceptions, "within each small locality of the country—defined in terms of the practicality of commuting to work from an individual's current residence—the probability is minimal that an unemployed individual will remain unemployed for longer than a month."[20]

There is, moreover, broad agreement that the vast majority of Soviet workers and employees enjoyed a high degree of job security, including protection against downgrading of their job and wages, during the Brezhnev period. A worker's right to his or her existing job was protected by labor legislation that sharply restricted managers' ability to fire or transfer workers, placed multiple procedural barriers to dismissal even for incompetence or disciplinary violations, and extended strong guarantees to marginal workers (including youth and women with young children). Workers released because of technological change had the de facto right to be placed in a new job by the dismissing enterprise, and in the vast majority of cases they were simply reassigned within that enterprise.[21] The strengthening and reinforcement of workers' claims to job security led Blair Ruble to conclude in a 1977 study, "Over the past two decades, the focus of legislation and policies . . . [has] shifted from guaranteeing a citizen's right to work toward guaranteeing a citizen's right to continue to work at his or her current job."[22]

The consensus on full employment is supported by data on amounts of manpower used in the Soviet economy—in particular the size of the labor force, its rate of growth, and labor force participation rates. First the data show that, through the mid-1980s, "except [during WWII] state employment in the USSR [grew] in every year since 1922, without cyclical or periodic downturns."[23] Table 2.2 provides figures on annual average employment during the Brezhnev years, including total state sector employment, industrial and construction, for the USSR, the Russian Soviet Federated Socialist Republic (RSFSR), and the Ukrainian Soviet Socialist Republic (UkSSR). Total state sector employment grew from 62 million in 1960 to more than 115 million in 1982, with growth averaging approximately 2 percent annually and industrial employment increasing at a faster rate than that of the state sector overall. For the RSFSR and Ukraine, which had the vast bulk of Slavic workers and of industrial workers overall (including some three-fourths of all state sector employment and 80 percent of industrial employment), growth was even more rapid. Moreover, these numbers reflect extremely high labor participation rates for the working-age population, defined as men age 16 through 59 and women age 16 through 54. These rates exceeded 90 percent

Table 2.2 Annual average state sector employment for the USSR, RSFSR, and UkSSR: Total, industrial, and construction, 1965–1982 (millions)

Sector	1960[a]	1965[a]	1970[a]	1975[a]	1980[b]	1982[b]
USSR						
Total	62.0	76.9	90.2	102.2	112.5	115.2
Industrial	22.6	27.4	31.6	34.1	—	—
Construction	6.3	7.3	9.1	10.6	—	—
RSFSR						
Total	39.5	47.5	54.4	60.7	—	—
Industrial	15.3	18.1	20.2	21.4	—	—
Construction	3.9	4.3	5.2	6.3	—	—
UkSSR						
Total	10.7	13.4	16.2	18.4	—	—
Industrial	4.1	5.0	6.0	6.6	—	—
Construction	1.1	1.3	1.7	1.9	—	—

a. Data from Stephen Rapawy, "Regional Employment Trends in the U.S.S.R.: 1950 to 1975," in *The Soviet Economy in a Time of Change* (JEC, 1979), pp. 603–605.

b. Data from David Lane, *Soviet Labour and the Ethic of Communism: Full Employment and the Labour Process in the USSR* (Boulder, Colo.: Westview, 1987), p. 31.

for both men and women in the prime of their working lives. An average of 88 percent of the able-bodied population was in the labor force during most of the Brezhnev period, a figure that is extremely high by comparative standards and that, according to Murray Feshback and Stephen Rapawy, left "no significant untapped labour resources."[24]

The available labor force was virtually fully employed during the Brezhnev years; in fact, through much of its tenure the Brezhnev leadership faced a labor shortage. In 1967, after years of growth that substantially exceeded plan projections, industrial-production personnel for the first time fell short of plan requirements. Beginning in 1970, largely because of demographic factors (specifically, a decline in the supply of new entrants to the labor force, combined with a high level of retirements and some increase in middle-aged male mortality), growth in overall and especially industrial employment declined precipitously. From an average annual rate of 3.7 percent for 1950 through 1970, the increase in industrial employment declined to 1.3 percent for 1971 through 1975, and to less than 1 percent (planned) for 1976 through 1980.[25] The resulting labor scarcity was particularly severe in the industrially developed regions of the RSFSR and Ukraine. The RSFSR alone had one million unfilled jobs in 1970, mainly in Siberia and the Far East, where many enterprises could not go into full production because of the shortage of workers.[26] The problem worsened in Slavic regions throughout the 1970s and early 1980s, with a net decrease in able-bodied age cohorts in the RSFSR and Ukraine beginning in 1980. From the mid-1970s the Brezhnev leadership regarded the labor shortage as a problem of some urgency and responded, inter alia, with measures to further increase labor force participation, particularly of pensioners and women.[27]

Sufficient demand and even overdemand for labor does not necessarily translate into a job for every job seeker, however; the structure of demand must also match the structure of supply, and this match inevitably remains less than perfect. The Soviets did not publish unemployment statistics (and, again, we know from labor force participation rates that overall employment was comparatively quite high), but there is evidence of low levels of frictional, structural, and technological unemployment in the Soviet economy. Labor specialists generally consider some level of each inevitable in any economy.

Frictional unemployment is that of a job changer who has left one position and is seeking another; it is estimated at 1.5 to 3 percent for the Brezhnev-era economy. Most job seekers found a new position within 20 to 30 days, though this is an average and studies show that some individuals remained involuntarily jobless for longer periods.[28] There was also structural unemployment in the Soviet economy, though mainly in non-Slavic regions (Central Asia, the Caucasus). In the Slavic regions, with which we are concerned, lack of employment opportunities primarily affected inhabitants of small- and medium-size cities and towns. It was most common among women in single-industry areas or settlements (for example, mining regions) that employed predominantly male labor. There are no data to indicate how many of these women sought jobs and how many remained unemployed voluntarily, but there were clearly population pockets where the available labor force exceeded the supply of jobs. Young people might also have experienced a prolonged period of unemployment in the transition from school to job; again, it remains uncertain to what extent they did so voluntarily.[29] A small percentage of workers displaced by technological change also remained unemployed for extended periods. Finally, during the Brezhnev period jobs were often denied to the politically nonconformist, to those seeking to emigrate, and to whistle-blowers.[30] Though significant for enforcing political conformity, these individual cases of discrimination did not affect aggregate employment levels. Authoritative estimates place the rate of unemployment from all these causes at under 2 percent in the mid-1980s, and we can safely assume that the figure was somewhat lower for Slavic regions.[31]

Many nevertheless argue against characterizing the Soviet Union as a full-employment economy, because of its poor and inefficient use of labor. They point to pervasive overstaffing of production facilities and consequent underemployment of workers as endemic features of the Soviet economy, and argue that there was much hidden unemployment in the factories.[32] Indeed Soviet factories were chronically and heavily overmanned, because multiple systemic pressures and incentives induced managers to overstate their need for workers and to hoard labor. Estimates commonly placed overstaffing at 20 percent of the labor force.[33] Many workers were also underemployed: that is, underutilized in terms of work time, educational qualifications, or both. But pervasive underemployment does not contradict the state's claim to provide full employment, as long as every job seeker finds full-time work with a wage income and social consumption benefits. To assess the validity of the social contract, I am concerned only with the status and welfare functions of employment, not its efficiency functions. (Of course, inefficient use of labor contributes to poor labor productivity, low wages, and shortages of consumer goods, all of which militate against fulfillment of other social contract provisions.)

With the few qualifications noted, the Soviet state during the Brezhnev period met the social contract's requirement for provision of full employment to Slavic workers. But it also matters, for the argument, *how* this goal was attained, what mechanisms within the economic and political systems ensured full employment. The social contract thesis requires that the political leadership purposely design its policies to guarantee this outcome, as part of the trade-off for labor's political quiescence. We might imagine that a leadership committed to full employment would have developed a comprehensive system and administrative apparatus for the assessment and allocation of labor resources. Research by Peter Hauslohner and others has shown conclusively that the Brezhnev leadership had no such system, that its few efforts to establish an administrative apparatus for labor allocation accomplished little, and that the Soviet labor market remained largely unplanned and unregulated.[34] More than 70 percent of all hires were carried out by and at the initiative of the employing enterprise, as was most retraining, with the state playing no direct role.[35] How, then, was full employment maintained?

Some economists hold that full employment in Soviet-type economies results directly from the economic mechanism. They argue that soft budget constraints (associated with Kornai's analysis) produce inflated managerial demand for all inputs into the production process, including labor; inflated demand and competition for labor throughout the industrial sector in turn produces a full-employment, chronically labor-short economy.[36] In this view, leaders and their policies are irrelevant to the maintenance of full employment (except, of course, to the extent that they keep the basic mechanisms of the centrally planned economy in place). According to Philip Hanson, for example, "The typical Soviet enterprise's insatiable demand for additional labor [was] sufficient to ensure both a general regime of job security and aggregate full employment. The central planners' erroneous labor balance and the law's . . . provisions [for job security were] not crucial functioning parts of the mechanism that produced these results."[37] So long as the Soviet economy continued to expand on the basis of a centrally financed, extensive development pattern, Hanson and others argued, it would continue to absorb all available labor.

The economic mechanisms pointed to by Hanson and others certainly do account for high labor demand in the Soviet economy, and they constituted a critical structural support for full and secure employment. They were not sufficient to ensure these outcomes, however, for a number of reasons. First, empirical studies of the Soviet labor market show that, in spite of inflated demand and a shortage of labor, some groups of workers (specifically youth, women with young children, older displaced workers) were viewed as relatively unproductive, and were not readily absorbed into the economy. At numerous points, the Brezhnev leadership relied on political and legislative interventions to press managers into hiring or retaining these least-valued categories of workers. It required managers to offer to a worker displaced by plant modernization any other available job within the enterprise, or to find him a new placement. It protected women (when pregnant or with very young children) against dismissal except in cases when their employing enterprise was liquidated, and then only with mandatory job placement.[38] In 1966, faced with an oversupply of students graduating from secondary schools, it increased the quota of openings *(bronia)* that enterprises were required to hold for the employment and training of youth.[39]

Each of these cases demonstrates both the Brezhnev leadership's commitment to full employment, and the need for political intervention to ensure jobs for some groups of workers. They further demonstrate that Brezhnev-era employment policies incorporated, and imposed on managers, numerous restrictions that were clearly designed to serve social and welfare goals extraneous to production (that is, to assure jobs and wages even for the least-productive workers). Moreover, these measures were adopted and enforced despite strong pressures from economists and labor experts to give managers more control over the selection and composition of their labor force, to increase productivity and efficiency. The first case study in chapter 3 will look more closely at one of these decisions to ensure employment for unwanted workers: the 1966 decision to increase the youth *bronia,* the quota of young workers that enterprises were required to hire and train. I will seek to establish what motivated this and related decisions, whether paternalism, fear of disaffection among those who would otherwise remain unemployed, or other factors.

Political and legislative interventions during the Brezhnev period also played a major role in ensuring job security for all workers and employees. Under the labor codes promulgated during the 1970s, management's right to terminate a worker's contract without cause (that is, except in cases of disciplinary violations) was subject to numerous restrictions and requirements. Both the trade unions and the courts had responsibilities for monitoring managerial compliance with protective labor legislation and for ruling on workers' grievances and challenges to dismissals. Workers who claimed they had been dismissed in violation of legislative provisions could appeal the decision, first to the factory trade union committee, then through higher levels of the trade union bureaucracy or in civil court. Available evidence indicates that in most cases the unions and courts strongly defended these procedural guarantees. Rates of reinstatement of workers who challenged dismissal in the courts were consistently high—50 percent to 60 percent for the years 1960 through 1980 for the USSR as a whole—and decisions and guidelines from the higher courts during the Brezhnev period generally extended workers' rights.[40] Overall, the thrust of labor legislation was to extend universal protections to workers while restricting managerial arbitrariness and abuses as well as managerial control and flexibility in staffing and personnel decisions.

Some scholars have nevertheless questioned the Brezhnev regime's effective provision of job security. Nick Lampert, for example, challenges the claim that Soviet workers were effectively protected from arbitrary dismissal. He argues that workers who violated informal norms of behavior (particularly whistle-blowers and others perceived by management as being troublemakers) were commonly dismissed, and that legislative and procedural guarantees were generally not enforced against powerful managers even when they engaged in blatantly illegal actions. It is clear from other sources as well that illegal dismissals of workers took place in Soviet industry, that trade unions sometimes did little or nothing to prevent them, and that the politically powerful sometimes dictated court decisions.[41] Moreover, as noted earlier, workers could clearly be dismissed for political nonconformity. Nevertheless, the scale of such dismissals was quite limited, affecting 1 percent to 2 percent of the industrial labor force annually; the courts did often reinstate workers who had been dismissed illegally; and overall such cases seem to be exceptions that do not seriously qualify the state's claim to strong protection of job security.[42]

In sum, Brezhnev-era labor policy was characterized by a strong and effective commitment to employment security for its population, and thus conformed quite well to the requirements of the social contract. However, the leadership accomplished this goal by relying on the economy's general overdemand for labor, and by intervening (with particularistic measures) in behalf of those groups still threatened with exclusion from the work force. It did not have a comprehensive policy for guidance of the labor market. And though Brezhnev and Kosygin recognized and insisted on the need for technological modernization, their regime failed to develop capacities for managing the necessary restructuring and redistribution of the labor force.[43]

As a consequence, the structure of the labor force remained remarkably stagnant, with extremely high levels of manual labor, much of it used to perform loading and unloading, transport, and construction tasks long since mechanized or automated in other industrial economies. Even at the end of the Brezhnev period, almost one-half of industrial labor and more than one-half of labor in construction was occupied with unmechanized physical work.[44] The leadership did take some well-known steps to spur modernization and improve utilization of labor, including the 1965 economic reform and the Shchekino experiment, but these had little long-term effect.[45] While the Brezhnev leadership kept virtually everyone employed, it did not deliver on its promise to decrease manual and physically arduous labor, nor did it develop the capacity for retraining and reassignment that would raise workers' qualifications and ease them through the planned modernization of industry to less arduous, and more productive, labor.

Brezhnev-Era Wage Policies

The social contract calls for egalitarian wage policies: specifically, policies that result in declining wage disparities in Soviet society, especially in its industrial sector. Throughout its tenure, the Brezhnev leadership committed itself to the steady reduction of disparities in levels of pay between those with high and comparatively low incomes. Brezhnev and Kosygin also promised steady and substantial increases in average wage levels (though the rate of planned increases did decline over time, from some 20 percent in the Eighth Five-Year Plan to 13 percent to 16 percent in the Eleventh; see Table 2.1). An examination of actual Soviet wage levels over the years 1965 through 1985 will reveal how well they conformed with the leadership's announced policies. Keep in mind that this is a discussion of money (or nominal) wages; the real value of wages depends on what they can buy. I will discuss real wages and incomes later in this chapter, after considering the critical matters of prices and supplies.

The Brezhnev leadership continued the practice (begun by Khrushchev) of centrally directed, active reform of the Soviet wage system. Its reform efforts extended over time to all sectors of the labor force, raising the wages of agricultural workers, clerical workers, and white-collar service personnel (including doctors, teachers, and others). Those at the bottom of the income scale—collective farmers and minimum-wage workers—gained the most. But the central beneficiaries of the changes in wage distribution were industrial workers, who gained in relation to both managerial and technical personnel and clerical workers. A review of data on minimum wages, average wages, and pay differentials reveals that Brezhnev-era wage policies promoted distributive equality throughout the state sector, while at the same time favoring the interests of the predominantly Slavic, blue-collar industrial workers.

Increases in Minimum and Average Wages

During its tenure the Brezhnev leadership doubled the minimum wage in the Soviet economy, increasing it from 40 to 45 rubles per month in 1964 to 60 rubles in 1968, 70 rubles in 1971, and 80 rubles in 1980.[46] The first increase, which raised minimum wages nearly 50 percent, was announced in January 1968 and went into effect immediately for all state employees. Its impact was dramatic, both in raising the lowest incomes and in reducing intra- and interindustry differentials. It produced a sharp contraction in the wage scale, including a temporary elimination of some wage grades.[47] The second increase, to 70 rubles, was included in the Ninth Five-Year Plan and was introduced gradually, as part of a reorganization of wages and salaries in all sectors of the economy that was completed (a year behind schedule) in 1976.[48] The final increase, to 80 rubles, was announced at the 26th Party Congress and introduced during a period when the regime was already operating under conditions of economic stringency.[49] These increases primarily benefited clerical and service personnel, especially women. The vast majority of industrial workers earned above the minimum wage, and only a small percentage—the least skilled and youngest—gained.[50]

Average wages also grew steadily and rapidly throughout the Brezhnev period, increasing from 96.5 rubles per month in 1965 to 190.1 rubles per month in 1985 (see Table 2.3). The percentage increase in average wages per month did, in fact, meet the leadership's commitment for each of the Five-Year Plan periods (as we see by comparing column two of Table 2.1, which gives planned increases of 20 percent for 1966–1970, 20 percent for 1971–1975, 16 percent for 1976—1980, and 13 percent for 1981–1985, with column two of

Table 2.3 Average nominal wages of all Soviet nonagricultural workers and employees, and of industrial workers, 1960–1985 (rubles per worker per month)

Year	All workers and employees[a]	Including social consumption funds[b]	Industrial workers[d]
1960	80.6	107.7	89.9
1965	96.5	129.2	101.7
1970	122.0	164.5	130.6
1975	145.8	—	160.2
1980	168.9	—	185.4
1985	190.1	268[c]	211.7

a. Data for 1960–1970 are from *Narodnoe Khoziaistvo (Narkhoz) SSSR 1922–1972 gg.* (Moskva: Statistika, 1972), p. 350; for 1975 and 1980, from *Narkhoz SSSR v. 1980 g.* (Moskva: Financy i statistika, 1981), p. 364; for 1985, from *Narkhoz SSSR v. 1985 g.* (Moskva: Financy i statistika, 1986), p. 397. The percentage increase for all wages was 26% for 1970 and 20% for 1975; see Gregory Grossman, "An Economy at Middle Age," *Problems of Communism,* vol. 25, Mar.-Apr. 1976, p. 22.

b. *Narkhoz SSSR 1922–1972 gg.,* p. 350.

c. *Narkhoz SSSR v. 1985 g.,* p. 397.

d. Janet C. Chapman, "Recent Trends in the Soviet Industrial Wage Structure," in Arcadius Kahan and Blair Ruble, eds., *Industrial Labor in the USSR* (New York: Pergamon, 1979), p. 168, for 1960 to 1975 data; data for 1980 and 1985 from the respective *Narkhoz SSSR.* Chapman reports the average annual rate of growth for industrial wages as follows: for 1960–1965, 2.49%; for 1965–1970, 5.12%; for 1970–1975, 4.26%.

Table 2.3, which shows the actual increases for each five-year period). When contributions from social consumption funds are added to wages the increase becomes even steeper, from 129 rubles per month in 1965 to 268 in 1985. Besides raises for whole categories of workers and employees, higher increments for work in the far north and Siberia (regional premiums), as well as for especially hard or dangerous work (special conditions), contributed to the increase.

In keeping with the general pattern, industrial workers fared considerably better than average during this period (see Table 2.3). Their average wages grew at a rate of 5.12 percent per year during 1965 to 1970 and 4.26 percent per year during 1970 to 1975, increasing by more than 50 percent over this ten-year period, and they continued to grow.[51] Overall (even allowing for some deflation of these figures) the Brezhnev leadership delivered impressive increases in the population's income during an extended period.[52]

Decreases in Wage Disparities

Wage policies in the Brezhnev era also brought a substantial (though apparently not consistent) decline in wage differentials throughout the Soviet economy. The policy of successive increases in the minimum wage was combined with one of more moderate increases for those in intermediate wage and salary scales and a virtual freeze on upper-level salaries.[53] The result was a marked reduction in inequality throughout the economy. The intraindustry spread between minimum and maximum wage was substantially reduced. In practical terms, the gap between the wages of the lowest-paid employee and the boss narrowed, from a ratio of 11 to 1 in 1960 to 6.5 to 1 in 1975.[54] The differentials in basic wage rates for different levels of skill also narrowed substantially, as did those between industrial branches and sectors of the economy.[55]

The major indicator of interpersonal income differentials for all workers and employees, the decile ratio (by the Soviet definition, the ratio of average earnings of the bottom of the highest-paid 10 percent to the top of the lowest-paid 10 percent) declined from 3.69 percent in 1964 to 3.26 percent in 1966 and a low of 2.83 percent in 1968 (with the latter decline caused in part by the large increase in the minimum wage in that year).[56] The decile ratio increased again after this point—for reasons which have been a matter of some dispute among experts—to 3.10 percent in 1972 to 3.35 percent in 1976.[57] Thus, the degree of overall interpersonal income equality did not continue to increase throughout the Brezhnev period. Nevertheless, the Brezhnev leadership did fulfill its commitment to reduce disparities in levels of pay between those with high and comparatively low incomes. Brezhnev-era policies produced a substantial decline in wage disparities and maintained the level of disparity below that of the early 1960s.

Production workers benefited from the new wage distributions of the 1960s and 1970s, relative to other groups in the industrial labor force. Table 2.4 shows the wage ratios of managerial/technical, production, and office workers in Soviet industry for 1950 through 1984.

Table 2.4 Wage ratios of production, managerial/technical, and office
workers in Soviet industry, 1950–1984

Type of worker	1950	1960	1970	1975	1981	1984
Production	100	100	100	100	100	100
Managerial/technical	175	148	136	124	112.7	111.1
Office	93	82	85	82	77.9	77.3

Source: Data from David Lane, *Soviet Labour and the Ethic of Communism: Full
Employment and the Labour Process in the USSR* (Boulder, Colo.: Westview, 1987), p. 178
(Table 7.1), calculated from *Narkhoz,* 1922–1982 and relevant years. See also Gertrude
E. Schroeder, "Consumption," in Abram Bergson and Herbert S. Levine, eds., *The Soviet
Economy: Toward the Year 2000* (Boston: Allen and Unwin, 1983), p. 337 (Table 10.9).

The wages of both managerial/technical and office staffs fell in relation to those of production workers. The steady reduction in the relative wage advantage of managerial/technical staff over production
workers is particularly significant: the differential in industry declined from 48 percent in 1960 to just over 11 percent in 1984. The
decline was even more precipitous in construction, from a
managerial/technical wage advantage of almost 56 percent in 1960
to 4 percent in 1979.[58] The average wage of workers in the most
highly paid industrial sectors (particularly coal, steel, and oil) exceeded those of managerial/technical personnel in less-favored sectors; the average wages of coal miners, an especially favored group
(in part because of regional premiums) exceeded those of man-
agerial/technical workers in most industries.[59] The wages of clerical
workers, which equalled 82 percent of workers' wages in 1960, declined less sharply, to 77.3 percent in 1984. These changing wage
patterns tended to increase the attractiveness of blue-collar jobs at
the expense of white-collar ones. They also tended to produce a very
narrow differential between the wages of skilled blue-collar workers
and their managerial and technical supervisors, which had obvious
implications for status and authority in the enterprise.

Wage Security and Stability

The Soviet state in the 1960s and 1970s both determined basic wage
rates and guaranteed payment of wages. The State Committee for

Labor (Goskomtrud), in collaboration with the State Planning Agency (Gosplan), set basic wage rates for the entire economy, with the goals of rationalizing and simplifying rates and more-or-less equalizing pay for similar jobs and skill levels throughout industry.[60] The state also provided management with its wage fund, and basic wages were paid virtually irrespective of the employing enterprise's performance. Direct state subsidies, lax credit, and ministerial reallocation of funds kept factories in operation, even if they were long-term loss-makers; bankruptcies were unknown and factory closures extremely rare. This safety net for enterprises, combined with job security, provided workers with a high degree of financial stability.[61] Those at any given skill level could expect substantial uniformity of pay, while all enjoyed secure wages.

But did the various economic reforms of the 1960s influence wage distribution and affect the overall trend toward equality and blue-collar advantage? The Kosygin and Shchekino reforms were both designed to spark greater economic efficiency, in part by giving managers more direct control over wage and bonus distribution in the enterprise and encouraging them to reward productivity increases. Shchekino in fact encouraged managers to release unneeded workers and divide the excess wages among a smaller, presumably more productive, work force. Implementation of these reforms could have created some counterpressure to the equalizing thrust of central wage policies, but cumulative statistics on wage distribution suggest that they had little effect. The available direct evidence also indicates that the reforms had limited impact on wage levels, in the short term because central authorities intervened to curtail the effects when management did deviate from the prescribed wage patterns, in the longer term because implementation of the reforms was abortive.[62]

Explaining Brezhnev's Wage Policies

What motivated the Brezhnev leadership to pursue a policy of successive increases in the minimum wage, steady increases in average wages, and a marked reduction in wage inequality? A number of explanations have been proposed, including policy-makers' concerns for equity and welfare, their desire to influence the size and distribution of the labor force, and "labor market" conditions.

Some analysts have suggested that the Brezhnev leadership increased wages, especially minimum wages, because it realized that a substantial part of the Soviet labor force was living at or below the newly defined official poverty level in 1965. McAuley, for example, argues that the 1968 increase in the minimum wage was a response to new information that the minimal cost of living for a household exceeded 50 rubles per month.[63] Similarly, other increases in average and minimum wages may be seen as efforts by a leadership increasingly conscious of its international status to raise the consumption standards of the lower and middle levels of a comparatively very poor population. Alternatively, the decision to increase wages at the bottom of the wage scale may be seen as an effort to draw more women (who constituted the bulk of those at the bottom) into the labor force, by increasing the attractiveness of work and the opportunity cost of leisure.[64] Keep in mind that there was a worsening labor shortage through much of the Brezhnev period, and that the first big increase in the minimum wage did coincide with the first measurable shortfall in the labor force. Improving popular welfare on the one hand, and drawing more women into the labor force on the other, are different, though not mutually exclusive, motivations. The first is primarily paternalistic, the second primarily instrumental.

Still other explanations have been proposed to account for the increasing average wages and the growing wage advantage of blue-collar workers. McAuley argues that some wage growth during this period was inevitable because of developments intrinsic to the labor market, especially the increasing qualifications and education level of workers.[65] Others point to the stiffening competition for labor throughout the 1970s and early 1980s as a factor driving up wages.[66] As to the growing wage advantage of blue-collar production workers, some suggest that relatively high wages had become necessary to attract better-educated youth to blue-collar jobs which disappointed their status aspirations, while white-collar jobs could be filled even at lower pay. Finally, it may be that powerful industrial ministries were able to claim a disproportionate share of the wage bill for their workers, that is, that the bureaucratic politics of the Brezhnev period accounts for the blue-collar advantage.

All of these explanations are credible and some—particularly the leadership's desire to increase labor force participation and the tight, competitive labor market—must have influenced wage policies. But each suggests a motivation for only one piece of what seems to be a consistent long-term policy of promoting wage equality and favoring industrial workers.[67] Moreover (as can be seen from the pre-Brezhnev data in Tables 2.3 and 2.4), these policies followed a pattern which was set in the Khrushchev period, before the economy was labor-short and while industrial ministries were dissolved into weaker regional economic councils.[68] It makes more sense, then, to try to explain these policies mainly in terms of broader post-Stalin changes in labor's position: when Khrushchev de-Stalinized the system and removed controls on workers' mobility, he also set in train measures to improve their welfare and living standards. By the time of the Third Party Program he had codified these into policy commitments couched in a great deal of excessive rhetoric; the Brezhnev-Kosygin leadership adopted most of them, absent the rhetoric.

It is difficult to determine whether these leaders were acting out of paternalism—that is to say, out of a conception of the socialist state as one that should provide welfare and security—or in "anticipatory response" to the presumed interests and aspirations of workers, who were now freer to dispose of their own labor.[69] Either explanation is consistent with the information reviewed to this point: leaders' pursuit of popular welfare, egalitarianism, and favored treatment for blue-collar workers could certainly have been driven by ideological socialist commitments. On the other hand Soviet leaders might well have been responding to what they assumed workers wanted. David Granick, in his study of Soviet job rights, proposes these two possible explanations, and cautions against trying to choose between them; indeed, he suggests that the Soviet leaders themselves may not have known which drove their decisions.[70] I will nevertheless try to judge which of these explanations holds up better by examining pressured decision points in employment and income policy in chapter 3.

Retail Prices and Real Incomes

The social contract promised a stable and protected cost of living for Soviet workers, and Brezhnev repeatedly committed his regime to maintaining retail price stability. Indeed, the Brezhnev leadership used its control over price setting to keep the costs of mass consumption goods, especially food, very low; throughout the 1970s, despite rapidly rising wages, bread continued to be sold at its 1954 price level, meat at its 1962 level.[71] Prices for essentials were frequently set below their cost of production and below market-clearing levels. These policies were partly intended to further equalize distribution of income (to make the distribution of real income less unequal than the distribution of money income) by setting lower prices for the basic goods which predominated in the budgets of lower-income groups, and higher prices for luxuries and other goods bought mainly by higher-income groups.[72] Even in the late 1970s, when some retail prices were officially raised, the regime continued to assure the population that prices for basic food and nonfood goods would not increase.

Price Levels: Official and Alternative Indexes

According to the official Soviet consumer price index, price stability was very nearly maintained throughout the Brezhnev years (Table 2.5). Officially reported overall price increases for goods and services in legal retail trade were negligible during 1965 through 1975, and averaged only about 1 percent per year in the late 1970s.[73] State Pricing Committee chairman N. N. Glushkov claimed in 1978 that state retail prices on 99 percent of foodstuffs and 90 percent of nonfood goods had not been changed in the past ten years.[74] Proposals to raise prices in the understaffed and underpaid service sector had been rejected. Only in 1981–82 was a substantial increase of some 4 to 5 percent in the price index recorded.

There is, however, evidence that Brezhnev-era prices increased somewhat more rapidly than official figures indicate. A number of factors contributed to the increases. First, production of some of the most inexpensive consumer goods simply ceased, raising the average price of the assortment actually available (though, apparently, not the index). Second, temporary price increases were permitted for new and improved goods, and by the early 1980s such increases were being applied to 25 percent of the total light-industry output.[75] Third, beginning in 1977 official prices for a number of consumer goods were raised, with sharp increases for luxuries and durables that were in high demand.[76]

Western economists argue that the Soviet index does not take adequate account of the upward pressure exerted on prices by these and other factors, and have constructed an alternative index (see Table

Table 2.5 Official and alternative consumer price indexes, 1950–1985

Year	Official[a]	Alternative[b]
	(1950 = 100)	
1950	100.0	100.0
1960	75.1	87.2
1965	75.8	93.4
1970	75.4	99.6
1975	75.8	108.0
1978	—	114.1
	Official[c]	Alternative[d]
	(1980 = 100)	
1980	100	100
1981	101	103–104
1982	105	109–111
1983	105	112–115
1984	104	113–117
1985	105	116–121

a. Data from Gertrude E. Schroeder and Barbara S. Severin, "Soviet Consumption and Income Policies in Perspective" in *Soviet Economy in a New Perspective* (JEC, 1976), p. 631; *Narkhoz SSSR, 1922–1972 gg.,* p. 409.

b. Schroeder and Severin "Soviet Consumption," (JEC, 1976), p. 631. Explanations for the construction of this alternative price index are on pp. 630–632 as well as in indexes A and B, pp. 646–660. The alternative index, while believed to be more accurate than the official index, is also assumed to underestimate real price increases. This index does not take into account price increases resulting from the disappearance of low-priced goods. See M. Elizabeth Denton, "Consumer Price Policy: Trends and Prospects," in *Soviet Economy in a Time of Change* (JEC, 1979), p. 766. Denton's alternative ("implicit retail price") index differs very slightly from Schroeder and Severin's.

c. Data from *Narkhoz SSSR v. 1985 g.,* p. 478.

d. Calculated from *PlanEcon Report,* vol. 6, nos. 27–28, July 13, 1990, p. 5, statistics on official and realistic retail price index; numbers are approximate.

2.5), which is broadly considered more realistic. The alternative index shows an increase of 15 percent from 1965 to 1975, then increases of an additional 6 percent from 1975 to 1978. A different set of calculations produces an additional increase of approximately 10 percent for 1980 to 1982. Even taking account of these alternative figures, though, it remains true that the Brezhnev leadership delivered a remarkable level of price stability for basic foods and other essentials.

State Price Subsidies: Levels and Costs

While prices for foods and many essentials remained fairly stable during the Brezhnev period, agricultural procurement and other production prices rose substantially. Most of these increases were covered by subsidies from the state budget, which skyrocketed during these years. The cost of subsidies for government purchases of agricultural products, by far the largest category, increased from 3.5 billion rubles (R3.5 billion) in 1965 to R14.3 billion in 1970, R28.8 billion in 1981, and R48.7 billion in 1985.[77] Most food subsidies were paid for meat and dairy products, and by the end of the Brezhnev period subsidies covered a substantial part of the cost of these products; in 1983, the retail price covered only 37 percent of the state's cost for beef, 57 percent for milk, and 41 percent for butter.[78] Subsidies also became a significant drain on the state budget, constituting 11 percent of total budget expenditures in 1979, and more than 13.3 percent in 1985.[79] Prices of books, medicines, children's clothing, and selected other goods were also subsidized, though at much lower levels.[80] The allocation of such large subsidy payments from the state budget constitutes the strongest evidence of the Brezhnev leadership's commitment to a policy of price stability for mass consumption goods.

The key to the stability of retail food prices was the regime's decision (really a series of decisions) not to pass along to consumers most of the increases in agricultural procurement prices. In each of the years 1965, 1970, and 1982, the Brezhnev leadership radically increased procurement prices in an effort to improve agricultural incentives and productivity, and covered the increase with massive new subsidies, while keeping retail prices in state stores virtually stable. Each of these years thus presents a pressured decision point: a point at which the leadership faced a decision on whether to pay substantially increased costs to maintain the social contract. The leadership could have passed some or all of the procurement price increases directly on to Soviet consumers, increasing retail prices rather than subsidies. Instead it repeatedly and consistently decided to absorb virtually all of the increase into the state budget. The second case study in chapter 3 will examine the factors and pressures that drove those decisions.

Repressed Inflation: Shortages, Savings, and the Second Economy

Economists broadly agree that the economy under Brezhnev was characterized by rising levels of "repressed" and "hidden" inflation, which was not acknowledged in official data sources. Repressed inflation occurs when the pressure of excess demand is present in an economy, but administrative price controls prevent this pressure from pushing up official prices.[81] The rapid growth of wages during the late 1960s and 1970s was a major factor contributing to the development of repressed inflation, as the continuing increase in the population's money income outstripped growth in the supply of goods and services available for purchase. Hidden inflation occurs when inexpensive product lines disappear and more expensive, often cosmetically improved goods are substituted. One study estimated that the true rate of inflation in the Soviet economy averaged 2.3 to 4 percent per year in the late 1960s, and accelerated through the 1970s to 2.8 to 5.8 percent per year in 1980.[82] The results of repressed inflation included persistent shortages of consumer goods, steady increases in the ratio of collective farm market (CFM) prices over state retail prices for comparable goods, rapid increases in the population's savings, the proliferation of gray and black markets and corruption, and, eventually, formal and informal rationing.

Shortages were present in the Soviet economy from the beginning of the Brezhnev period, but in the early years they tended to be specific, affecting some goods and services while others were available in surplus. Over time, as money incomes grew and state prices in retail trade remained fairly stable, the prices fell well below market-clearing levels, especially for meat and other quality foodstuffs which the state subsidized heavily. As a consequence, consumers increasingly confronted inadequate supplies, queues, and the temporary disappearance of particular goods from local markets. When a succession of poor harvests in the late 1970s exacerbated food supply problems, the Brezhnev leadership responded by increasing procurement prices and subsidies as well as grain imports, while keeping state retail prices low and stable and, thus, demand high.

By the end of the 1970s local food shortages and lengthening queues had become widespread, and in 1981 formal rationing was instituted for some goods.[83] Closed distribution networks, which provided foodstuffs at state retail prices through an employing enterprise or organization, also proliferated. Workers were somewhat insulated from shortages by the establishment of these special distribution systems for meat and other deficit items, usually set up at the initiative of local governments, trade union authorities, and management.[84] However, the diversion of available supplies into closed distribution systems (as well as black markets) further intensified shortages for workers and others who lacked special access and had to rely on the open retail trade network.

Private CFMs operated legally in Soviet cities throughout the Brezhnev period, selling agricultural produce at prices which were, with some exceptions, determined by supply and demand. While these markets accounted for only a small percent of total retail sales, they were significant suppliers of some types of foods, especially in major cities. In 1964, CFMs had 12 percent of the market share of selected food groups and 20 percent to 40 percent of major food products in some large cities; by 1984, they supplied 25 percent of food and 50 percent to 75 percent of fruits and vegetables in some major cities.[85] Prices in the CFMs rose throughout the Brezhnev period, and the differential between CFM prices and state retail prices for comparable goods (which were held stable by administrative price controls) constitutes a valuable indicator of the extent of repressed inflation. Available data show that the ratio of CFM prices to state retail prices increased throughout the Brezhnev years, growing from 1.35 in 1960 to 1.47 in 1965, 1.61 in 1970, and 2.00 in 1979.[86] They rose even more steeply in the largest cities, more than doubling in Moscow during the 1970s.[87] The increase in this ratio provides one of the best (though still flawed) measures of the state's failure to "drain off" excess purchasing power.[88]

The increase in personal savings among the Soviet population during the Brezhnev years constitutes another indicator of repressed inflation. Over the ten years from 1965 to 1975, per capita savings deposits increased at more than twice the rate of disposable money income and outlays for goods and services; in 1975 they amounted to 357 rubles, equalling more than two-fifths of per capita annual disposable income.[89] Deposits continued to increase through the late 1970s (though they declined after 1979).[90] The rapid build-up of deposits has frequently been interpreted as a form of forced savings: monies held because there were no available goods and services which people wanted to purchase. This interpretation remains controversial, however. Some economists argue that an indeterminate part of these savings was held voluntarily for the purchase of expensive consumer durables in an economy which lacked a system of consumer credit.

Finally, chronic shortages and unsatisfied consumer demand provided fertile soil for the growth of a "second economy" during the Brezhnev years. While information about the second economy is fragmentary and impressionistic, a wide range of sources agree that it expanded steadily during the 1970s into a system of privately, illegally sold goods and services which paralleled much of the legal state economy.[91] Gray and black market activities commonly included: the theft and resale for private profit of state-produced goods; the production of consumer goods for profitable sale, often with components stolen from state supplies; the performance of maintenance, construction, and other services for private fees, often using materials and equipment for state enterprises; the provision of educational instruction, medical consultations, and similar services for a fee, without registration or payment of taxes.[92] Needless to say, diversion of substantial quantities of goods into parallel markets multiplied and intensified shortages in the state retail sector.

Illegal economic activity is, in Gregory Grossman's terms, "inextricably hooked up with the corruption of officials."[93] Black market trade and production commonly required bribing officials to overlook the theft, transport, and illegal sale of goods. Those directly engaged in black market activity, and those they bribed, became recipients of unofficial, unrecorded income. While we have no reliable estimate of the scale of this second economy, authorities conclude that by the late 1970s black market activity and the corruption it generated was having a measurable impact on personal income and distribution patterns in Soviet society.[94]

Real Income

The cumulative impact of hidden and repressed inflation, poor harvests, growing shortages, black markets, and corruption was at once to weaken and to distort the intended effects of Brezhnev's wage and income policies. The growth of money (or nominal) wages of Soviet workers was impressive during the Brezhnev period, and according to the official Soviet price index, the growth of real wages nearly equalled that of nominal wages. However, if we deflate the nominal wages of industrial workers using the alternative, more realistic price index presented in Table 2.5, we find that real wages increased at a substantial rate, but quite a bit less than did nominal wages (and officially reported real wages).[95] Average annual rates of real wage growth were, obviously, also significantly lower than those planned and reported.

Overall real per capita disposable income likewise shows slower growth than was officially planned or reported during the 1970s, when the alternative consumer price index is used: from an agreed per capita income of R220 in 1950, official figures show an increase to R650 in 1965, R909 in 1970, R1,150 in 1975, and steady growth through the early 1980s. By contrast, the alternative index shows more modest increases to R528 in 1965, R688 in 1970, and R807 in 1975, and a virtual cessation of growth by the early 1980s.[96] The rate of growth of per capita consumption also slowed during the 1970s, dropping to less than 2 percent in 1981 and less than 1 percent in 1982, as the Brezhnev era drew to a close. All of this amounts to what Gertrude Schroeder has characterized as a "marked across-the-board slow down in the improvement of living standards . . . in the 1970s," approaching stagnation at the beginning of the 1980s.[97]

We are left with a picture of steady progress in the level and equality of industrial wages and income during the Brezhnev years, but progress at a lower rate than officially planned, promised, or claimed, and at a declining rate. Brezhnev's wage and price policies also substantially increased equality of income distribution. Wage increases at the bottom and middle of the salary scale, combined with relative stability at upper levels, resulted in significant narrowing of differentials. At the same time, pricing policies were designed to make the distribution of real income more equal than the distribution of wage/

money income by setting low, heavily subsidized prices for mass consumption goods which predominated in the budgets of lower-income groups, and high prices for consumer durables and luxuries which comprised a larger part of the budgets of higher-income groups. However, the egalitarian thrust of these policies was somewhat blunted after the mid-1970s by the growth of corruption, the proliferation of special distribution networks to which elites generally had better access than mass groups, and stagnation in the growth of food consumption, the largest and most heavily subsidized budget item for low-income groups.

Social Consumption Expenditures under Brezhnev

The social contract promised state provision of social services: education, health care, child care, housing, and municipal services were to be subsidized by the state and made available free, or at nominal cost, to users. The Brezhnev leadership made commitments to increasing expenditures and expanding services in each of these areas. In education, it promised the achievement of universal secondary schooling for youth as well as increases in student stipends and other categories of spending. In the area of child care, the leadership proposed to extend the network of children's institutions with the goal of fully meeting the need for preschools, and to increase maternity leaves and benefits as well as child allowances. Improvements in health care sufficient to eliminate outbreaks of contagious diseases and increase longevity were promised, as was steady progress toward the provision of a separate apartment for every family and married couple.

Brezhnev-era Five-Year Plans also made specific and substantial commitments to increases in the level of social consumption funds, a budgetary category which includes spending for social services as well as direct transfer payments (including pensions, stipends, sickness and disability benefits, and others). As is shown in Table 2.1, social consumption funds were slated to increase by 40 percent during each of the Eighth and Ninth Five-Year Plans, almost 30 percent during the Tenth plan period, and 20 percent during the Eleventh.

Indeed, social consumption funds were to be the fastest growing component of income throughout the Brezhnev period; they were to grow at twice the rate of average wages for most of the period, and considerably faster than per capita real income (see Table 2.1). The increase in the proportion of distribution through social consumption funds (versus wage income) would, in theory, move the system toward the communist idea of distribution according to need.[98]

How well did the Brezhnev leadership deliver on these commitments? Overall, the record seems impressive; total social consumption expenditures increased from R27.3 billion in 1960 to R116.5 billion in 1980, and to planned expenditures of R139 billion in 1985. Reported annual per capita expenditures increased from R128 in 1960 to R438 in 1980.[99] Per capita expenditures in every area, including transfer payments, education, medical care, social security, and housing subsidies, grew throughout most of the period, as did the main physical indicators of the level of service. These figures indicate a substantial increase in the scale of state provision.

The Brezhnev leadership used these increases, inter alia, to increase pensions, extend paid maternity leaves, add a program of income supplements for low-income families (typically families with several children) and cash allowances for children, and extend the system of social security to the collective farm peasantry.[100] Benefit levels in most cases remained quite low—at best raising poor families above the state's minimal poverty level—and eligibility was often tied to a person's employment record, but improvements were marked. The state also extended its heavy subsidization of social services: at the beginning of the 1980s users paid approximately 5 percent of the cost of education, 6 percent of the cost of health care, 20 to 25 percent of the cost of preschool child care (this figure is for 1970), and 37 percent of the cost of housing (with the result that an average urban family spent 3 to 5 percent of its income for rent).[101]

Official Soviet statistics on social consumption spending are, however, considered by most Western economists to be somewhat inflated (as I noted with the official statistics on wages and real income). Alastair McAuley has calculated the annual average rates of growth of real per capita social consumption expenditures as follows (using the Schroeder and Severin index to deflate the official statistics):[102]

	Nominal	Real
1950–1960	5.8%	7.2%
1960–1970	7.5%	6.1%
1970–1980	5.2%	3.6%

Both sets of figures show a declining rate of growth in social consumption funds from the 1960s to the 1970s, but that decline appears somewhat more precipitous after deflation. The structure of social consumption expenditures also changed over this period, with growing proportions going to pensions, social security, and other transfer payments (as well as to housing subsidies), and declining proportions to education and medical care. As pension and social security levels were tied to the level of earnings during working years, their effects on overall income distribution tended to be regressive. However, state sector workers living in urban areas generally benefited from both increased transfer payments and spending on state services (though this was much less the case for those living in small cities and workers' settlements served by the rural health subsystem).[103] Ofer and Vinokur estimate that, in 1980, the total value of social consumption funds to families of state employees equalled almost 70 percent of the net wage fund.[104]

The spending patterns for critical categories of services bear closer examination. Table 2.6 provides summary data on the average annual rates of growth of per capita gross national product (GNP) for overall consumption, education, and health for the period 1966 through 1981. There is a fairly consistent pattern for each of the three areas: growth rates peaked in the late 1960s, then declined significantly in

Table 2.6 Average annual rates of growth in per capita consumption, USSR: Total consumption, education, and health, 1966–1981

Consumption	1966–1970	1971–1975	1976–1980	1979	1980	1981
Total	5.1%	2.8%	2.4%	2.3%	2.9%	1.9%
Education	2.9	1.4	1.6	1.2	1.7	0.6
Health	3.2	1.4	1.1	0.7	0.3	−0.1

Source: Adapted from Gertrude E. Schroeder, "Soviet Living Standards: Achievements and Prospects," in *Soviet Economy in the 1980's: Problems and Prospects, Part 2* (JEC, 1983), p. 370 (Table 1).

1971 through 1975 and (except in education) continued to decline in 1976 through 1980. Annual data show, further, that per capita GNP spent in each of these areas increased every year from 1966 through 1980 (though at a sharply declining rate toward the end of this period).[105] The first absolute decrease came in per capita spending on health care in 1981, while growth in spending for education fell to less than 1 percent per capita in that year (see Table 2.6).

Changes in levels of physical services tended to parallel changes in funding patterns, with impressive growth in availability through the mid-1970s, then a leveling off relative to demand. In the area of preschool child care, for example, the state system of nurseries and kindergartens provided places for 13 percent of all children under age seven in 1960, 32 percent in 1970, and 37 percent in 1975; actual numbers of children in preschools increased from 4.4 million in 1960 to 9.3 million in 1970 and 11.2 million in 1975.[106] In 1970, the number served included some 50 percent of urban children and 30 percent of rural children aged three to seven.[107] In spite of these impressive advances, however, the system remained inadequate and uneven in coverage. In large cities the majority of children over age three were generally accommodated, but child care shortages remained serious in smaller cities, and shortages were universal for the under-three group. In 1972, 1 million children remained on waiting lists, and in 1979, millions continued to be cared for by sometimes-reluctant *babushki* while their parents were at work.[108] Complaints about the quality of care were also becoming common, as educated urban parents were dissatisfied with their children's often poorly trained (and badly remunerated) care givers. (Indeed, the state eventually gave up its intent to provide care for most children under three, and instead offered extended, partially paid work leaves to their mothers.)

In the area of education, as well, impressive achievements gave way to stagnation in the level of service, declines in quality, and frustration for users. The number of secondary school graduates increased dramatically during the Brezhnev years, from 1 million in 1960 to 2.6 million in 1970 and approximately 4 million in 1980.[109] By the mid-1970s the goal of universal (ten-year) secondary education was virtually achieved, with 95 percent and more of eighth-grade graduates transferring to an institution which would provide a "complete" secondary education.[110] On the other hand, through the 1960s and 1970s the number of secondary school graduates increased much more rapidly than college enrollments, leading to frustrated aspirations for many young people. Failure to attain college admission was a problem especially for children of blue-collar workers, who found themselves at a disadvantage in the toughening competition with offspring of the more affluent, and better-connected, urban intelligentsia.[111] The quality of secondary education, and of recreational and other services for youth, were also subjected to growing criticism.

The pattern of stagnation and decline was repeated, once more, in the area of health care. After a period of long-term improvements, expenditures dropped to a negative per capita growth rate in the early 1980s, while health conditions in Soviet society demonstrably worsened.

In sum, the data show that although the rate of growth of per capita spending on social services declined in the 1970s, absolute levels of per capita spending for overall consumption, health, and education increased through 1980, and growth continued in both nominal and real terms. The Brezhnev leadership did fulfill the social contract in this area—though at a declining level of performance—until 1981. At that point, per capita spending on critical social services actually began to decline, a clear indicator that the regime was no longer willing or able to hold up its end of the bargain.

The Brezhnev leadership delivered much (though never all) of what it promised in terms of full and secure employment, egalitarian wage policies, price stability, and social service subsidies. With the general downturn of the Soviet economy from the mid-1970s, however, Brezhnev's welfare state began to deteriorate. Workers remained fully employed, but the stagnant labor force structure doomed large numbers to a lifetime of arduous, inefficient manual labor. Wage policies were progressive and egalitarian, but the disparity between the rise in nominal wages and the rise in real wages and incomes grew. Food prices were held stable, but shortages of basic foodstuffs grew, and by 1981 had led to formal rationing, closed distribution, large increases in collective farm market prices, and growing black market activity. Official price indexes masked significant hidden inflation, and wage increases accumulated in savings accounts. Social consumption expenditures continued to grow, but at steadily declining rates. The housing stock and child care facilities remained inadequate for the population's needs, and the education system was unable to fulfill students' aspirations. In 1981 per capita expenditures for health care actually fell, while health conditions in Soviet society worsened.

At the same time, growing political and economic corruption militated against the egalitarian ethic of Brezhnev's policies. Privilege, connections, and bribery often determined who got access to decent social services and subsidized goods; often doctors, housing administrators, and store clerks were on the take, and many necessary and desirable goods could be acquired only through payoffs or in the black market. We lack the data to estimate the scale of corruption in the late Brezhnev period, but experts conclude that it was sufficient to have a significant, corrosive effect on the equality of income distribution.[112] Industrial workers (particularly those in large urban areas) were generally better insulated from shortages and hardships than the mass of the population, but the regime's delivery on its part of the social contract was faltering.

THREE

Full Employment, Price Stability, and Labor Quiescence under Brezhnev

Pressured decision points—points at which the Brezhnev leadership faced clear-cut decisions to commit a greater proportion of resources, or to abandon other policies at significant cost, to maintain the social contract—offer a valuable opportunity for assessing the government's commitment to the contract. The two case studies presented in this chapter consider, as far as is possible with the evidence available, the politics and debate surrounding each pressured point, to determine what drove the policy decisions.

The second part of the chapter examines working-class attitudes and behavior during the Brezhnev period. I will look for evidence, both in available data on attitudes and in the grievances and demands actually raised during incidents of labor unrest, of whether Soviet workers highly valued social contract policy output. I will also examine patterns of labor quiescence and unrest during the Brezhnev years to see whether they correlate with the state's delivery on the social contract, and I will consider the regime's responses to workers' activism.

Political Intervention to Ensure Full Employment: The 1966 Youth *Bronia*

Some economists claim that full employment in Soviet-type economies results directly from the economic system's overdemand for labor, but in fact empirical evidence reveals that in the Soviet Union some groups, especially youth, women with young children, older workers, and the disabled, were not readily absorbed into the labor force. The Brezhnev leadership regularly adopted political and legislative measures requiring managers to hire or retain these least-valued categories of workers. I wish to focus on the decision to adopt one such measure: the February 1966 resolution which substantially increased the quota *(bronia)* of openings that enterprises were required to reserve for the training and employment of youth.

In 1965 and 1966, shortly after its accession to power, the Brezhnev leadership confronted the problem of insufficient job openings for youth, especially fifteen- to eighteen-year-olds who sought work upon leaving general education schools. Both previous policy decisions and demographic trends contributed to the scale of the problem. First, new labor legislation required that workers under the age of eighteen be exempted from overtime or night work, be paid for a full (eight-hour) work day while working only six hours, and be given paid leave for part-time study.[1] This legislation, while obviously designed to protect adolescent workers, at the same time made them comparatively expensive and inconvenient employees, and exacerbated managers' general predisposition against hiring inexperienced youth. Second, the post–World War II Soviet baby boomers were finishing school in the mid-1960s, producing a large bulge in the cohort entering the labor force.[2] Third, the Brezhnev leadership's decision to revert to a ten-year system of secondary education in 1964 (abandoning Khrushchev's eleven-year production-education school experiment) produced a double graduating class in June 1966: a tenth grade and a final eleventh grade, each with approximately 1.3 million members.[3] As a consequence of the baby boom combined with the double graduation, some 2 million graduates entered the labor force in 1966, twice the number in 1965.[4] There had been difficulties with assimilation of youth into the labor force in many areas, including the central Slavic industrial regions, since the late 1950s.[5] In 1966, the magnitude of the youth employment problem pressed for a leadership response.

At the same time, the Brezhnev leadership had recently introduced economic reform measures which promised to reduce central control over manpower utilization. The 1965 Economic Reforms, which were designed to increase productivity and efficiency in the Soviet economy, broadened managers' control over the size, composition, and wages of their labor force. They also created strong incentives for managers to economize on labor, in part by reducing and releasing unnecessary personnel.[6] These measures were strongly supported by economists and labor experts, who saw overstaffing and inflexible labor force structures as serious obstacles to economic efficiency.[7] Administrative intervention at this point to force hiring of youth would contravene the intent of the Economic Reforms, both by introducing new central controls over the composition of enterprise labor forces and by requiring managers to hire additional unwanted and unneeded workers. Thus the Brezhnev leadership faced a pressured decision point: whether to mandate full employment of youth, and thus maintain the social contract at the expense of economic reform, or to adhere to reform principles and allow a significant level of youth unemployment, abrogating the contract.

Faced with the flood of students scheduled to graduate in the spring of 1966, the leadership chose to maintain full employment by increasing the *bronia* of youth that factories and other institutions were required to hire. The February 1966 joint resolution by the Central Committee and the Council of Ministers, "On Measures for Expanding the Instruction of and Employing in the National Economy Young People Who Will Graduate from General Education Schools in 1966," reserved for minors "a quota of jobs equal to 0.5% to 10% of the total number of workers and employees of enterprises and organizations."[8] This resolution effectively doubled the maximum youth quota which had been in effect up to this point, and further, it permitted the various republic Councils of Ministers to require hiring of young people in excess of the quotas in 1966 "on the basis of hiring plans sufficient to cover all school leavers."[9] It assigned responsibility for job placement of youth to a combination of governmental, party, and Komsomol organizations, all of which would help pressure local enterprises into hiring up to and above their established quotas. It also mandated that enterprises put into place training programs for youth, and that for any worker under eighteen who was released for any reason, a new job must be found by the releasing enterprise in cooperation with responsible local authorities.[10] Subsequent reports on the resolution's implementation showed that, through a combination of planning, coordinating, badgering of factory officials, and pressure tactics including "inspection raids" and the "storming" of enterprises by youth employment commissions, political (especially Komsomol) authorities managed to place most students in jobs.[11]

The Brezhnev leadership's labor market intervention in this case was only one of many intended to ensure employment for unwanted workers. Other Brezhnev-era legislation established hiring quotas for disabled workers, protected women (when pregnant or with very young children) against dismissal, and required managers to offer a worker displaced by plant modernization any other available job within the enterprise, or to find him a new placement.[12] However, the youth *bronia* makes an especially good case study for the social contract thesis. First, the timing excludes potentially complicating motivations and assures a case in which the leadership's overriding policy goal was to maintain full employment. The youth *bronia* took place while labor was still in excess in the Soviet economy. After the beginning of the generalized labor shortage in the 1970s, by contrast, all policy interventions in the labor market were complicated by the leadership's desire to increase overall labor force participation.[13] Similarly, much of the later employment legislation protecting women was complicated by pronatalist motives.[14] Second, the 1966 intervention in youth employment affected core working class strata, including a large contingent of male Slavs, whose incorporation is central to the social contract thesis. Most other interventions affected strata which were less critical both economically and politically.

The decision on the 1966 youth *bronia* provides evidence that the Soviet economy did not spontaneously generate full employment, and that the Brezhnev leadership did in fact intervene to deliver on this provision of the social contract. Moreover, it continued to deliver even in the face of competing policy commitments and strong political pressures to act otherwise. The leadership pressed managers into hiring more youth despite its own previous commitment to extend managers' autonomy and flexibility in structuring their labor forces. It did so against the weight of expert opinion, which at this point held that labor forces were inflated and that enterprise managements required greater control over the selection and use of labor to improve industrial performance. The initiation of the 1965 Economic Reforms indicates that the political leadership generally shared this view.[15] However, faced with a direct choice between measures to improve economic efficiency and measures to maintain full employment, the Brezhnev leadership unequivocally chose the latter, overrode managerial autonomy, and forced hiring.

Was this choice a product of paternalism or constraint? Did the Brezhnev leadership give priority to youth employment because it was committed to a conception of socialism which included job rights, or because it feared the destabilizing potential of thousands of jobless youth? There is no explicit evidence on this point. It seems relevant, however, that this regime accepted some level of open unemployment in small- and medium-size towns, where it was scattered and affected predominantly women. Later, in the 1970s, the Brezhnev leadership also failed to take effective measures against rising levels of unemployment among Central Asian youth.[16] Both situations indicate that the leadership was willing to tolerate some joblessness among politically and regionally peripheral strata, and thus argue against a paternalistic commitment to full employment as its sole and sufficient motivation.

The possible social and political ramifications of collective joblessness among young males concentrated in Slavic regions and large cities were obviously great. The leadership's timely and effective measures to assure them jobs show that this cohort and these regions were given different, high-priority treatment. A strongly suggestive case can thus be made that fear of disaffection and protest among jobless youth constrained the leadership's decision. At the very least, Brezhnev was willing to forgo major competing policy commitments and pressures to maintain the social contract with the younger generation in the Slavic heartland.

Agricultural Subsidies and Retail Price Stability

The Brezhnev leadership backed its promise of price stability with large food subsidies. Between 1964 and 1983, prices paid to farmers were raised several times without a corresponding increase in retail prices, and state revenues were allocated to cover the growing disparity. Virtually all agricultural products were subsidized, though the rates varied greatly among products and over time. Table 3.1 shows the magnitude of these subsidies, overall and for selected products, for the years 1965 through 1985. They increased dramatically, from 3.5 billion rubles when first introduced in 1965 to almost 60 billion rubles in 1985—an enormous sum, which Alec Nove characterized (even in 1981) as "the highest food-and-agriculture subsidy known in human history."[17] In 1980, these subsidies equalled approximately 54 percent of total national income generated in agriculture, almost

Table 3.1 Estimated state procurement price subsidies, 1965–1985: Total for selected products (billions of rubles)

Product	1965	1970	1975[a]	1981	1982	1983	1985
Meat	2.8	8.7	11.9	15.2	15.3	21.4	22.1
Milk	—	3.1	4.1	8.3	9.0	13.8	15.2
Grain[b]	0.3	0.7	0	1.4	2.0	3.7	3.6
Potatoes and vegetables	—	0.2	0.5	1.1	1.7	2.2	2.4
Price surcharges for weak farms[c]	—	—	—	—	—	9.3	10.0
Total subsidies	3.5	14.3	17.2	28.8	29.9	54.6	58.8

Source: Morris Bornstein, "Soviet Price Policy in the 1970s," in *Soviet Economy in a New Perspective* (JEC, 1976), p. 49, for the years 1969, 1970, 1975; Morris Bornstein, "Soviet Price Policies," *Soviet Economy,* vol. 3, no. 2, Apr.-June 1987, p. 116. Some figures in the above table are rounded.
a. Data for 1975 are according to Five-Year Plan.
b. Figures for grain include oilseeds for 1965 and 1981–1985.
c. Price surcharges for weak farms were added in 1983.

25 percent of gross agricultural output, and more than 11 percent of total state budget expenditures.[18] Brezhnev's 1982 Food Program brought further increases.

Why did the Brezhnev leadership burden itself with such a huge subsidy bill? Its motivations for raising agricultural procurement prices are clear enough: higher prices were intended to increase incentives and production in agriculture by increasing collective farmers' profitability and income. Increased agricultural production was necessary, in turn, to raise living standards and absorb growing urban incomes. Having increased procurement prices, the leadership had two choices: it could pass the increases on to consumers through higher state retail prices, in violation of the tacit social contract, or it could absorb the new costs into the state budget and maintain stable retail prices. The Brezhnev leadership dramatically raised agricultural procurement prices at three points: the March 1965 Central Committee Plenum, the March 1970 Central Committee Plenum, and the May 1982 Central Committee Plenum. At each of these plenums, the leadership faced a critical decision point—a point at which it had to either violate the social contract or allocate substantially greater budgetary resources to maintain it.

The decision in each case was, obviously, to absorb most costs into the state budget. It is important to note, however, that while they had a common outcome, these three decisions differed in a number of respects. First, they were made under very different sets of fiscal constraints: the allocation of a few billion rubles annually in the comparatively robust economy of the mid-1960s did not entail large political costs. But the considerably larger subsidy provided in 1970 was more costly, while the enormous 1983 increase, coming at a time of severe budgetary stringency, meant real losses for competing claimants. Second, the optimistic expectations of 1965 that the subsidies would be temporary and would trigger a large, sustained increase in farm productivity, were discredited by 1983; policy-makers must have known by then that they were buying less for more. Third, the political environment and pressures in each case were distinct and contributed to different levels of concern among elites about popular expectations and discontent. I will examine in sequence the complex sets of factors and pressures which drove each of these decisions, keeping in mind the requisites and trade-offs of the social contract.

1965: Increased Procurement Prices with Stable Retail Prices

When the Brezhnev-Kosygin leadership came to power in the fall of 1964, it faced a situation of rising consumer demand for food and nearly stagnant farm output. Khrushchev's policies had increased incomes, especially for those at the bottom of the income scale (minimum wage workers and pensioners), thereby pushing up demand for higher-quality food products. At the same time his agricultural policies, while initially successful, had resulted in declining rates of productivity growth after 1958.[19] The single biggest obstacle to growth of farm production was the lack (or inadequacy) of incentives. Production of livestock, in particular, remained generally unprofitable; for most farms, the cost of raising and feeding animals simply exceeded the state purchase price.[20] The Brezhnev leadership was committed to continued wage increases and improved living standards, and both would require better food supplies. Brezhnev himself championed agricultural interests, and with the support of Agriculture Secretary Polyansky and his ministry (much buffeted about under Khrushchev) and party officials from agricultural regions, he initiated a major new agricultural development program at the March 1965 Central Committee Plenum.[21]

The plenum directed its resolutions to "raising the material interest of kolkhozes and sovkhozes [collective and state farms] in increasing the production and sale to the state" of all major categories of agricultural products.[22] It adopted three concrete sets of measures designed to enhance profitability and procurement. It increased state purchase prices for a broad range of products. For wheat, rye, and other grain products, the increase averaged 12 to 19 percent (with regional variations). For cattle, pigs, sheep, and goats the increments were on average much higher, ranging from 10 percent to 100 percent.[23] It also established modest, realistic procurement plans, and guaranteed that these would remain stable through 1970. Finally, it set substantial premiums (up to 100 percent and more) for sale to the state of above-plan production.[24] The March plenum also passed resolutions on numerous issues relating to agricultural development and rural incomes, including taxation, pensions, land reclamation, subsidized sale of machinery, and other forms of financial assistance which would entail additional state spending for agriculture.[25]

Official spokesmen, beginning with Brezhnev (in his speech to the March Central Committee Plenum), repeatedly stressed that the costs of price increases for agricultural produce would not be passed on to consumers.[26] As far as can be determined from the available record, increases in retail food prices to cover some or all of the new costs were neither considered by the leadership nor advocated by any official. A number of factors would seem to bear on the explanation. First, the new leadership was clearly on record as having assured price stability, and it would at least have lost credibility by reneging at this early stage. Second, the costs of the subsidy program were quite manageable, it was introduced as a temporary measure which would be phased out once agricultural productivity had begun to rise, and there was apparently broad leadership support for the policy.[27] Third, Khrushchev's decision to raise meat prices (some 35 percent) in 1962 had triggered serious strikes in at least one or two industrial regions.[28] There was no explicit reference to the 1962 experience in the published discussions surrounding the 1965 decisions, so I can only speculate that it contributed to the seemingly unquestioned consensus that the state should absorb all costs and maintain price stability.

1970: Further Increases

The measures initiated in 1965 did lead to substantial increases in agricultural production, and per capita consumption, of all major food groups (Table 3.2). For a number of reasons, however, these results were not sustained. First, after an initial period of impressive success (including a record harvest in 1966) the leadership made major cutbacks in its original plans for allocations to agriculture in 1967 through 1969, so that overall spending for the Five-Year Plan period was well below the level promised.[29] Second, profitability in many areas, especially livestock production, remained uncertain. Third, incomes continued to rise and, given stable retail food prices, pushed up demand for food products. Soviets had relatively few outlets for

Table 3.2 Changes in consumption of basic types of foodstuffs, 1965–1980 (kilograms per capita per year)

Food group	Recommended consumption	Actual consumption			
		1965	1970	1975	1980
Meat and meat products	82	41	48	57	57
Milk and dairy products	405	251	307	316	314
Eggs[a]	292	124	159	216	238
Vegetables and melons	146	72	82	89	93
Fruits	113	28	35	37	34
Fish and fish products	18.2	12.6	15.4	16.8	17.0
Grain products	110	156	149	141	139
Potatoes	97	142	130	120	112

Source: V. P. Mozhin and E. N. Krylatykh, "Why Is the Food Program Necessary?" *Ekonomika i organizatsia promyshlennovo proizvodstva,* no. 6, June 1982, pp. 5–18, trans. in *Current Digest of the Soviet Press,* Sept. 1, 1982, p. 4. Recommended levels are taken from *The Living Standard of the USSR's Population (Uroven zhizni naselenia SSSR)* (Moscow: Mysl, 1977), p. 102.

a. Number of eggs per year.

spending their steadily rising incomes, since most services were heavily subsidized, most housing was state owned, and most desirable consumer durables were in deficit; as a result, rising incomes translated disproportionately into a shift in the structure of demand toward high-quality foods (mainly meat, dairy products, vegetables, and fruits).[30] As the pace of improvements in diet decreased in the late 1960s, with per capita availability of meat leveling off in 1968 and 1969, dissatisfaction grew.[31] In 1970 the agricultural lobby, newly mobilized and with Brezhnev again at its head, spoke of a "meat crisis" in Soviet cities and stressed the urgency of new initiatives in agriculture.[32]

The procurement price increases adopted by the March 1970 Central Committee Plenum were more selective than those of the 1965 farm program and focused on meat products, fruits, and vegetables. Delivery prices for milk and cream were increased 20 percent, and base prices for meat were raised in some regions. Beyond this, increments were designed to improve the quality of meat delivered to the state; for example, premiums would be paid only for well-conditioned animals and those over specified weights.[33] To improve incentives for production of potatoes, fruits, and vegetables, the plenum decrees guaranteed farmers a profit of 15 to 25 percent on produce.[34] Like its 1965 counterpart, the 1970 program promised stable procurement targets for the duration of the Five-Year Plan (1971 through 1975) and offered substantial premia for sales to the state above plan levels. It also provided investment funds to improve the "material and technical base of agriculture," including expansion and improvement of feed-grain supplies (the weak link in livestock production) and development of storage and processing facilities for fruits and vegetables.[35] Overall, capital investment in agriculture for the 1971 through 1975 plan was to increase 70 percent over the previous plan period.[36]

Despite the similarity in the policies adopted by the 1965 and 1970 agricultural plenums, there were important differences in the politics of decision making. The 1970 decision involved a much more intense struggle over resource allocations, as well as serious dissension among agricultural officials over the value of price increases as an effective means for raising agricultural productivity.[37] In addition, the leadership's claims of concern about popular expectations and dissatisfaction, especially with inadequate meat supplies, were explicit—indeed, prominent—in the debate this time. Brezhnev, for example, speaking on agricultural policy in mid-April 1970, said, "Once we took the course of raising the welfare of workers, [we had to achieve a] corresponding expansion of production of consumer goods, including livestock products."[38] At the July plenum he said, "We must direct our main attention to how the growing demands of the population . . . are being met."[39] Finally, the subsidies were voted as a more-or-less permanent allocation this time. While a small part of the price increase for potatoes and vegetables was passed on to consumers in 1970, most procurement price increases were covered by new subsidies; as a result the annual subsidy bill nearly doubled, from 7.8 billion rubles in 1969 to 14.3 billion rubles in 1970 (see Table 3.1).

1982: The Food Program

Again higher state spending contributed to increases in agricultural production and per capita consumption, and again the increases were not sustained. Annual per capita consumption of meat and meat products, for example, increased from 48 kilograms in 1970 to 57 kilograms in 1975, and remained at this level in 1980 (see Table 3.2). Consumption of dairy products increased between 1970 and 1975, then declined slightly by 1980; consumption levels for most other food groups declined or improved only slightly from 1975 to 1980. Why was the food problem still unresolved?

The massive investments and subsidies poured into agriculture had improved both production and rural living standards, but the problems of the countryside ran deep and often frustrated attempts at development. Larger crops, for example, meant bigger storage and transport problems. Efforts at mechanization were continually undermined by the unwillingness of technically qualified personnel to remain in the countryside. Subsidies designed to ensure a profit kept marginal farms in production. Overall expenditures per worker increased more rapidly than productivity during the 1970s, so production costs rose; by 1980, one-half of all kolkhozes and sovkhozes were unprofitable and were surviving on state subsidies.[40] And the Soviet agricultural sector seemed incapable of feeding and fattening livestock, in part because of poor-quality feed grains and in part because of very variable harvests. After livestock herds were developed in the early 1970s, for example, the extremely poor 1975 harvest forced farmers into distress slaughtering of cattle (in spite of substantial grain imports), and the difficulty and expense of herd recovery combined with successive poor harvests in the late 1970s to keep meat production depressed despite state subsidies.[41]

Through the latter half of the 1970s, incomes continued to increase (albeit at a declining rate) while food supplies stagnated and prices remained stable. Indeed, retail food prices had remained nearly stable since 1962, while average money wages had increased 70 percent.[42] As a result excess demand, shortages, queues, and hoarding of food became common, and collective farm market prices rose substantially (see chapter 2). Meanwhile the Brezhnev leadership, which had repeatedly committed itself to raising living standards and improving food supplies, seemed able to respond to the situation only with more procurement price increases.[43] By the early 1980s, its public statements evinced an acute consciousness that frustrated expectations and frustrated demand pervaded Soviet urban society. Developments in Poland also influenced events at this point: the emergence and legalization of Solidarity in the summer of 1980 moved the Soviet leadership (at least temporarily) to a greater responsiveness toward workers' concerns and aspirations.[44] In 1981, closed distribution of deficit food goods was extended beyond the traditional elite recipients to some industrial workers, and formal rationing was introduced on a limited scale.[45]

In the spring of 1982 Brezhnev introduced his last major domestic policy initiative, the Food Program. Billed as a comprehensive, decade-long program for resolving the Soviet Union's food problem, it included resolutions on agricultural management, retention of personnel, improvement of housing and communal facilities, and technical and economic systems, as well as production incentives.[46] Its goal—to provide a stable supply of all types of food and improve the structure of the Soviet diet—was designated by Brezhnev as "the most important programmatic requirement of our party . . . a paramount economic as well as urgent social and political task."[47] In spite of the fanfare, though, the basic approach of the Food Program was familiar: it further raised procurement prices for virtually all major crops and products. It also provided additional supplements to low-profit and loss-making farms in poorly endowed regions, compounding the problem of costly marginal producers.[48] The additional cost to the state for procurement subsidies was (accurately) estimated at 16 billion rubles per year, plus several billion in new surcharges for weak farms (see Table 3.1). The overall agricultural subsidy rose dramatically, to 54.6 billion rubles in 1983, while state retail food prices remained essentially stable.

As this case study reveals, the Brezhnev leadership chose to pay increased state subsidies at each critical decision point, to maintain retail price stability. Those stable food prices, set well below market-clearing levels, exacerbated the food supply problem by keeping demand high. The leadership might have reduced both subsidies and demand by raising retail prices to cover most of the costs of food production. Yet while there is clear evidence of leadership conflict over the general pattern of allocations (that is, allocations to agriculture versus consumer goods, heavy industry, and defense) and over the efficacy of Brezhnev's agricultural policies, as well as evidence of rising concern over the size of the subsidy bill, there is no evidence that direct advocacy of retail price increases entered the political debate. The leadership took its promise of retail price stability quite seriously, judging by its demonstrated willingness to commit increasing resources, which were thus denied to competing claimants. It acted as if bound by a social contract.

Was the Brezhnev leadership so bound by its chosen commitment to a paternalistic ethic, or by fear that food price increases would spark popular unrest? Several pieces of evidence seem relevant here. First, when Brezhnev spoke (as he did repeatedly and at length) about the food problem, he spoke in terms of the regime's imperative task to satisfy the population's needs, raise living standards, and satisfy the consumer demands which had resulted from increased income. Admittedly his speeches were often intended as advocacy for particular policies, and he may have cynically manipulated claims of popular demand to strengthen his case. It is nevertheless striking that Brezhnev consistently represented his regime as significantly constrained by previous commitments and the popular expectations these had generated. It is my judgment that the 1970 and, especially, 1982 decisions were driven primarily by those commitments and perceived expectations.

Second, food price increases had sparked discontent among otherwise quiescent Soviet workers in 1962 and among more restive Polish workers in 1970 and 1976. Food shortages were a major issue in the modest Soviet strike wave of 1980 and 1981. Moreover, dissatisfaction growing in significant part from economic deterioration had produced the Solidarity movement, a potentially destabilizing external influence from the summer of 1980 through 1981. Elizabeth Teague, in her study of Solidarity's impact on Soviet domestic politics, finds a connection between Polish events and Brezhnev's attention to consumer priorities in 1980 and 1981. She notes, in the context of Polish events, "the spate of decrees on agriculture [parts of which] suggested how concerned Soviet leaders were about the possibility of consumer discontent."[49] It is surely credible that Solidarity would have produced heightened concern about worker discontent among Soviet leaders (though they never cited it as a factor in published discussion), especially in light of the simultaneous, modest increase in domestic labor unrest. It is fair to argue that such a compelling pressure would have been necessary to motivate the Soviet leadership to commit 50 billion rubles annually for agricultural subsidies in a time of stringency,[50] and therefore a reasonably supported case can be made for constraint. But given the limits of published policy debate under Brezhnev, the evidence is not conclusive.

Workers' Attitudes and Behavior

The social contract thesis makes two central claims about Soviet workers' political attitudes and behavior: that workers valued highly social contract policy outputs, and that workers' compliance and consent were contingent on the regime's consistent delivery of these outputs. If the state failed or ceased to deliver, workers would presumably have withdrawn their consent and turned to political challenge and unrest. In other words, labor's quiescence should correlate with delivery on the social contract, while a rise in unrest should correlate with deterioration or failures in delivery. The thesis also assumes that the Soviet regime needed workers' political compliance, that it was willing to pay a substantial price in terms of constraints on policies and allocations to secure popular consent.

Two types of evidence are available on workers' political attitudes and values in the Brezhnev period: surveys of émigrés, and reported grievances and demands actually raised by Soviet workers. A considerable amount of information is also available on workers' behavior, including collective protest, strikes and unrest, and organizing activities. It is important to note at the outset that all the evidence on these points is somewhat flawed from a scholarly perspective. Émigré surveys are necessarily limited as indicators of societal attitudes because their respondents are neither randomly selected nor representative of the Soviet population. Available evidence on workers' grievances, protests, and strikes comes to us mainly through the Western press and samizdat sources. As a result, it is very likely to be both incomplete and overrepresentative of workers in proximity to large cities or in communication with dissidents. Most important, such partial information may skew our interpretations and conclusions. This is, nevertheless, the only relevant evidence that reached us through Brezhnev-era information controls.[51]

The Brezhnev regime's response to working-class protest and unrest is also important. It will be useful to examine how the leadership reacted both to specific instances and to general increases in unrest. Did it, for example, typically make concessions to strikers' demands? Did it reallocate resources in response to workers' protests? Did Brezhnev adjust internal labor policies in reaction to the rise of labor unrest and the Solidarity trade union in Poland? The answers will reveal more about how willing the regime was to deliver policy and allocations to secure Soviet workers' quiescence and compliance. Moreover the problems of evidence are fewer here, as the regime did provide a fairly complete record of its own behavior.

Workers' Attitudes toward Social Contract Policy Outputs

The best available data on Soviets' attitudes toward politics comes from surveys of émigrés.[52] The conclusions of these surveys across time and across samples indicate consistently and unambiguously that a high percentage of Soviet citizens from all social strata valued state provision of social services and welfare, and that this was the most positively evaluated feature of the system.

The Harvard Interview Project of the early 1950s found that even post–World War II refugees from the Soviet Union, who were generally hostile to the Stalinist regime, strongly supported the system of universal public education and socialized health services. The refugees also gave virtually universal approval "in principle" (that is, in an ideal state) to a cradle-to-grave welfare program and government guarantee of full employment.[53] These attitudes were held even by the most disaffected respondents, and were stronger among younger than older refugees. While respondents favored a paternalistic state, however, they found the Stalinist state both deficient in its provision of social welfare and far too authoritarian. The authors of the survey extrapolated from their sample to Soviet society "a deep-rooted expectation . . . that their government and society will provide extensive social welfare benefits" and concluded, "it must be recognized that if the regime is able to deliver such welfare benefits as the people expect they will tap a strong reservoir of favorable popular sentiment."[54]

The WWII refugees, who were mainly Russians and Ukrainians, left the Soviet Union in the 1940s; a survey of Soviet Jewish émigrés in Israel almost thirty years later produced some remarkably similar responses.[55] While the vast majority of these later émigrés did not see the Soviet government as "acting generally on behalf of the people," many did express approval for its social and welfare policies. One-half of the respondents favored broad governmental activism, and of those who thought Israel could learn something from the USSR, the largest number (more than one-fourth) listed welfare and other services first.[56] The study's author noted the "striking continuity with [the WWII refugee study] . . . especially in regard to the positively regarded aspects of Soviet life, . . . welfare services."[57]

The Soviet Interview Project surveys, conducted among predominantly Jewish Soviet émigrés in the United States during the 1980s, both confirm the earlier survey results and suggest some interesting implications for the social contract. One researcher, Brian Silver, looked specifically at patterns of popular support for regime norms and practices. He found that the strongest support for any established practice was given for the provision of free public medical care, with 52 percent of respondents giving the strongest possible support to this feature of the system, while more than 50 percent cited either education or health care as aspects of the Soviet system that should be kept (the third most frequent response here was to "keep nothing"). Silver also found that respondents' level of education was negatively related to regime support, implying that blue-collar workers (most of whom had, at best, a secondary education) were more supportive than the sample overall. Finally, his results showed deterioration in the assessment of public medical care during the last years of the Brezhnev period.[58] Silver concluded, "This study provides empirical evidence for an interpretation of government-society relations in the Soviet Union based on an exchange: from the government to the society, a supply of material goods to satisfy people's wants; from the society to the government, a store of political capital in the form of support for the established political order. These are not the only items in the exchange, but they are important ones."[59]

Finally, the Gorbachev leadership, and Gorbachev himself, referred frequently (and critically) to a set of broadly shared attitudes toward welfare, distributive justice, and state responsibility that became entrenched in Soviet society during the Brezhnev period. Gorbachev charged that "all kinds of negative phenomena have spread throughout society: dependence and wage-leveling . . . our understanding of social justice is deformed."[60] The reformist economist Otto Latsis spoke of "the notion of an omnipotent, omniscient, and omnibenevolent state . . . [which] penetrates our society deeply."[61] These themes were common in the speeches and writings of the Gorbachev leadership during its early years.

Despite their flaws, the survey results are both highly consistent and highly supportive of the social contract thesis. Assuming that the attitudes of émigrés are not entirely anomalous, these data constitute strong evidence that provision of social benefits was highly valued and was a critical source of popular acceptance for the Brezhnev regime. Silver's study also suggests some erosion of the contract by the end of the Brezhnev period: rising educational levels were undermining popular support for contract norms, while respondents reportedly perceived a deterioration in the state's delivery of services.

Workers' Collective Political Behavior

The first reports of labor unrest in the post-Stalin period reached the West in the late 1950s and told of individual, brief work stoppages over norms, pay, or housing and living conditions. The early 1960s brought a brief upsurge in strike activity, triggered by a sharp increase in prices of meat and butter in early 1962.[62] In the most serious incident of this period, several thousand workers in Novocherkassk struck because of simultaneous price and production norm increases; they occupied local party headquarters and were removed by troops, with significant loss of life. Similar disturbances were reported in other areas.[63] The strikes of the early 1960s form a backdrop to

Brezhnev-era labor policy. While there is no direct evidence that they influenced the new leadership's decisions to maintain social contract policy, such a linkage is at least quite plausible, as the following quotes from works on the late Brezhnev period suggest: "As far as is known, no riots on a scale comparable [to those in Novocherkassk in 1962] have occurred anywhere in the USSR since then. The Brezhnev leadership . . . took care to be more generous to the workers on the matter of wages than Khrushchev had been."[64] "Since 1963, sudden and large price increases in foodstuffs have been avoided."[65]

GRIEVANCES AND STRIKES

During the first fifteen years of the Brezhnev period Soviet workers remained (so far as can be determined from available data) largely quiescent. To be sure, some labor unrest continued throughout this period, but it was limited to sporadic, isolated, poorly organized strikes and protests. During the years 1964 through 1978, strikes typically took the form of walkouts or work stoppages lasting a few hours, or at most a day or two. Participants usually engaged in little advance planning or coordination, chose temporary spokesmen, and improvised tactics. Grievances were limited and localized; goals were specific and, in most cases, economic or material. Strikes were reported in many sectors of the economy, including machine building, oil refining, and transportation, but with greatest frequency in construction and mining. They took place in various regions of the USSR, including outlying areas and republic capitals. Reports indicate that worker unrest was most common in the Ukraine, where it sometimes carried nationalist overtones (as was also the case in the Baltics), though one must be especially conscious of sample bias problems here.[66]

Causes of reported strikes may be divided into two categories: working conditions (including work norms, pay, and management conduct), and social conditions (including food prices and supply, and housing and living conditions). Information on the causes of some thirty strikes by Soviet workers during the years 1965 through 1978 is presented in Table 3.3.[67] During these years the grievances which precipitated strikes were divided fairly evenly between factory-specific issues and living conditions. In the first category, grievances commonly concerned increases in work norms, conflicts over bonuses, and managerial abuses. For example, in September 1978 truck

Table 3.3 Soviet labor strikes and their causes, 1960–1979

	Number of strikes			
Cause	1960–1964	1965–1968	1969–1973	1974–1979[a]
Change in work norms; pay grievance	4	2	7	4
Management abuse or incompetence	1	—	1	1
Food prices or supply	10	1	3	1
Housing or living conditions	4	—	2	1
Unspecified	9	—	7	1

Source: Adapted from Alex Pravda, "Spontaneous Workers' Activities in the Soviet Union," in Arcadius Kahan and Blair Ruble, eds., *Industrial Labor in the USSR* (New York: Pergamon, 1979), p. 349, (Table 14.2).

a. Figures for reported strikes during 1974–1979 are from the sources listed below. (I have incorporated all strike reports found, including those in non-Slavic areas, to parallel Pravda's data.) *Radio Liberty Research* 139/75, Apr. 4, 1975 (Donbass Mines; protest over forced overtime); *RL* 427/75 Oct. 7, 1975 (Baikal-Amur Railroad strike over living and working conditions); *RL* 484/76 Nov. 29, 1976 (Riga dockworkers' strike over meat/food shortages); *RL* 148/78 July 5, 1978 (Kaunas rubber-goods factory strike over wage reductions); *RL* 194/78 Sept. 4, 1978 (Stavropol truck drivers' strike over bonus payments). Ludmilla Alexeyeva, *Soviet Dissent: Contemporary Movements for National, Religious, and Human Rights* (Middletown, Conn.: Wesleyan University Press, 1985), p. 403 (Shauliai bus drivers' strike, cause unknown, and Kirov plant strike in Leningrad over administration's actions). Betsy Gidwitz, "Labor Unrest in the Soviet Union," *Problems of Communism*, vol. 31, Nov.-Dec. 1982, p. 33 (Togliatti bus drivers' strike over pay and working conditions).

drivers from Stavropol struck after they failed to receive promised bonuses for harvest work.[68] In the second category, food shortages most often sparked unrest, while poor housing conditions were sometimes a cause or a contributing factor.[69] Analysts of labor discontent during this period agree that workers turned to open protest as a last resort, and that strikes were typically preceded by an accumulation of grievances combined with managerial indifference or intransigence and then a triggering incident. Workers apparently turned to riot or violence only in those rare instances when they were confronted with armed force.[70]

In the last years of Brezhnev's rule, strikes became larger and more frequent. In 1980 and 1981, a wave of strikes affected the major Soviet automotive plants at Togliatti, Gorky, and Cheliabinsk, idling tens of thousands of workers. A steady stream of strike reports came from other sectors and regions as well.[71] Moreover, there is evidence of some planning and coordination of strikes in this period; one strike sometimes precipitated others, with similar grievances and demands, in a local area. Repeated, organized, collective protest developed in a few large factories, implying the emergence of an informal leadership with some authority among the workers. At Togliatti, the belated arrest of leaders of a 1979 strike reportedly sparked a more serious one in 1980, while Kiev experienced a succession of strikes during 1981.[72] It may be that the rise of the Solidarity trade union in Poland during this period spurred labor unrest, or the deteriorating economic conditions in the Soviet Union could constitute the whole explanation.[73]

Local food shortages and supply problems emerged as a particularly prominent strike issue in 1980 and 1981; at Togliatti and Gorky, at the showpiece Kama River Truck Plant, and at Pripat' in Kiev Oblast, workers struck over shortages of foodstuffs (especially meat and dairy products) in local stores. Other grievances included increases in work norms and other changes that effectively reduced wages, poor housing and living conditions, and poor management.[74] Significantly, despite the example of Solidarity and their own rising level of activism, Soviet workers confined their demands to "bread and butter" issues—economic and material goods. As this was precisely the category of goods the Brezhnev leadership was prepared to deliver, the increased level of labor unrest remained manageable.

INDEPENDENT WORKERS' ORGANIZATION

There were a few efforts to establish independent trade unions in the Soviet Union during Brezhnev's last years.[75] In January 1978 Vladimir Klebanov, a mining foreman from the Donetsk, founded the short-lived Association of Free Trade Unions (AFTU) for the defense of workers' rights.[76] Klebanov and his associates, while maintaining their loyalty to the Soviet system, protested against their own unfair dismissals, poor working conditions, low pay, high industrial injury rates, and inflated production norms which resulted in waste and low-quality production. The AFTU claimed a membership of 200 and sought International Labor Organization (ILO) recognition. It achieved a measure of visibility and support in the West, mainly from European labor organizations, and some domestic publicity through Voice of America radio broadcasts. The AFTU never attained significance as an organization within the Soviet Union, but it stood as the "most coordinated and articulate expression of purely worker-related grievances."[77] Its founding was followed in early 1978 by the formation of the Working Group for the Defense of Labor, Economic, and Social Rights in the USSR. Established by Vsevolod Kuvakin, a specialist in labor law, the Working Group prepared and published (mainly in the samizdat journal *Poiski*) reports on Soviet labor abuses.[78] It did not function as a labor union but sought to prepare the base for worker organization.

In October 1978 the (by then defunct) AFTU was succeeded by the Free Interprofessional Association of Workers (generally known by its Russian acronym, SMOT). SMOT initially claimed a membership of more than 100 who were organized into several autonomous groups, each supposed to elect a representative to a Central Coordinating Committee which met irregularly.[79] The groups were to remain secret and fairly independent, providing aid and support to their members as each saw fit. By 1981 the organization claimed as many as 300 members, organized into fifteen to twenty autonomous groups.[80] Thus, SMOT remained very limited in scope, with a small number of activists and little apparent continuity of leadership. It did, however, manage to sustain publication of the samizdat *SMOT Information Bulletin*. The *Bulletin* published expressions of support for Solidarity, as well as a list of the Twenty-One Demands accepted by the Polish Communist state in the August 1980 negotiations which legalized the trade union.[81] Articles also appeared documenting corruption, elite privilege, police abuses, food shortages and rationing, and violations of workers' rights in the Soviet Union, and proposing that the Soviet system should be conceived of as "state capitalist." More than thirty-five issues of the *Bulletin* appeared.[82]

All of these reports no doubt underestimate the extent of working-class unrest and organizing initiatives during the Brezhnev period. It is difficult to assess the significance of these activities, both for workers and for the regime. At most a few score workers seem to have been involved in the independent trade unions, which generally included a significant number of intelligentsia and supervisory personnel as members and especially as leaders.[83] The limited appeal of these organizations to workers, combined with their successful repression, suggest that they posed little threat to the regime. On the other hand, the possibility for linkages with either the domestic dissident movement or Solidarity increased the potential threat.

More concretely, at least a few SMOT members were connected to centers of embryonic labor activism, including Togliatti and the Donbass.[84] There is, moreover, retrospective evidence that there was significant silent sympathy and support for such activists, as several rose to positions of informal and elective leadership in workers' districts during perestroika (see chapter 6).

The Brezhnev Regime's Response to Activism and Unrest

The Brezhnev regime's responses to labor unrest and organizing initiatives were quite consistent over time: with few exceptions, mass protests and strikes brought rapid concessions to workers' demands, while attempts to form independent organizations brought harsh repression. In its last years, the leadership also had to manage the potential challenge (or spillover) from events in Poland; it reacted with a media campaign to discredit Solidarity and a temporary shift in the posture of its own trade union organizations toward stronger defense and protection of workers' interests.

Though official doctrine claimed that Soviet workers could have no reason to strike against the socialist state, the leadership took a conciliatory approach to incidents of actual unrest. Ranking party and state officials were typically dispatched to settle strikes. These officials were clearly deputized to make deals on a broad range of labor and social issues and, apparently, to replace managers who had become targets of workers' grievances.[85] For example, three strikes were reported in Kiev during March and April 1981, and each was settled by officials' concessions to the strikers' demands. In the first, workers protested increased production norms and gained reinstatement of the old norms; in the second, the main grievance was local unavailability of water, and officials responded with immediate completion of long-delayed repairs to the water supply system; in the third, the factory's director was fired and its party and trade union leaderships changed in response to the strike.[86] Strikes over food shortages brought well-stocked shelves in local stores and very likely contributed to the decision to extend closed distribution of deficit foodstuffs to major enterprises in the early 1980s.[87]

While it usually avoided the use of mass repression and other measures which might escalate a conflict with striking workers, the regime did, however, eventually punish strike leaders in many cases.

Well after tensions had subsided, those workers identified as trouble-makers often were arrested on false, unrelated charges, or were accused of violating labor discipline and fired or transferred.[88] The security forces, which usually had played no overt role during the strike, often were involved in these measures. The obvious intent of such delayed repression was to remove from the factories emerging grass-roots leaders and to intimidate others.

The response to attempts at organizing independent trade unions was, by contrast, rapid and ruthless repression. Virtually all identifiable leaders or members of these organizations were tried and sentenced to prison or labor camps on various charges, were involuntarily committed to psychiatric hospitals, or were forced into emigration. The Brezhnev regime unleashed the full range of its punitive measures against these miniscule organizations from their inception. Klebanov's AFTU was effectively neutralized within a matter of weeks by the harassment, arrest, and detention in psychiatric hospitals of all those associated with the movement.[89] Members of SMOT were regularly detained and charged with anti-Soviet slander, hooliganism, parasitism, or (usually falsely) common offenses such as theft.[90] Such persistent persecution made it impossible for SMOT to sustain any continuity of leadership, either at its center or in its autonomous groups. Indeed it was a major achievement, under such conditions, to maintain a focus on labor issues and publication of the *Bulletin*. In spite of extensive negative publicity in the West and embarrassing criticism in international labor organizations, however, the Brezhnev regime remained unrelenting in its persecution of those (workers and others) who challenged the party-state's organizational monopoly.

In its last years, the Brezhnev leadership also faced a potential challenge to domestic labor peace from neighboring Poland: the independent trade union Solidarity was legalized in August 1980 and existed in a state of uneasily shared power and rising tension with Poland's Communist government for the next fifteen months, until it was suppressed under Jaruzelski's martial-law regime in December 1982. While the Soviet regime had a much stronger base of stability and legitimacy than its Polish counterpart, the presence of a free trade union with a genuine working-class base, challenging a Communist government in a bordering state, must have posed some threat of demonstration or spillover effects. In any case, the Brezhnev leadership had to take a position on the unprecedented political events in Poland during these months.

Soviet media from the outset defined Solidarity as a politically subversive organization, and sought to discredit its claims to represent the interests of Polish workers. While obscuring information about the Gierek government's concessions to Solidarity in the fall of 1980, Soviet sources focused on the role of "anti-socialist," "extremist," and "politically adventurist" elements in the union's leadership.[91] When Solidarity continued to use the strike weapon to press its demands, Soviet party and government sources accused it of aggravating political and economic difficulties to promote counterrevolutionary goals, opposing efforts to normalize the situation, and setting itself up as a political opposition to the party. Charges of collaboration with Western intelligence services and "reactionary Polish émigrés" became common, while the specter of West German revanchism and other threats to the security of socialist states were raised.[92] *Pravda* and *Trud* enlisted Soviet work collectives to appeal to their Polish brethren for socialist solidarity, and issued dire warnings.[93] Finally, in the weeks before the crackdown, *Pravda* moved to a total condemnation of Solidarity, declaring, "Adventurist and extremist tendencies . . . have become the official program of the whole organization."[94]

Available data indicate that a hardening of Soviet public opinion paralleled the intensifying hostility of official sources: some 44 percent of the Soviets surveyed expressed negative attitudes toward Solidarity in the fall of 1980, and that number increased to 64 percent by the following spring, and to 71 percent after December 1981 (Table 3.4). While the numbers in the table are drawn from a highly unrepresentative population of Soviets traveling in Western Europe, they are generally confirmed by an unofficial poll taken by Soviet sociologists in and around Moscow in the fall of 1980.[95] In addition, the approximately 25 percent of respondents who expressed support for Solidarity were disproportionately well educated, suggesting that support among blue-collar workers was quite weak, while Slavs were most negative in their attitudes.[96] While we cannot be certain how many Soviets were influenced by the campaign of vilification, and how many were simply mouthing the official line, there is some evidence that the Brezhnev leadership succeeded in turning opinion against Solidarity. Elizabeth Teague, who took part in the cited surveys, concluded: "The opinion samples . . . suggest that the attempts

Table 3.4 Evolution of Soviet attitudes toward the crisis in Poland, September 1980–May 1982

Attitude	Sept. 1980–Feb. 1981 (N = 398)	Mar.–May 1981 (N = 188)	June–Aug. 1981 (N = 260)	Sept.–Nov. 1981 (N = 366)	Dec. 1981–May 1982 (N = 505)
Support liberalization	24%	25%	22%	23%	15%
No opinion	32	24	14	14	13
Oppose liberalization	44	51	64	63	71

Source: Elizabeth Teague, "Workers' Protests in the Soviet Union," *Radio Liberty Research* 474/82, Nov. 29, 1982, p. 15. The data were collected from interviews with Soviet citizens traveling to the West during this period, as part of Radio Free Europe/Radio Liberty Soviet Area Audience and Opinion Research. The sample is neither random nor representative of the Soviet population; it overrepresents urban, educated males and Communist party members. However, the findings were largely confirmed by an unofficial poll conducted by Soviet sociologists in and around Moscow during September 1980 (see Teague, p. 14). Besides the steady increase in negative attitudes, the intensity of Soviet respondents' opposition also increased over time.

made by the Soviet authorities to discredit Poland's free trade union movement were successful in playing on Soviet citizens' inherent distrust of disorder . . . latent anti-Polish sentiments, and simple human envy of the Poles . . . Apprehension comes across strongly in the replies."[97]

Beginning in autumn 1980, the Brezhnev leadership also pressed its own trade unions toward greater activism in behalf of Soviet workers. At the 26th Party Congress in February 1981, Brezhnev criticized Soviet trade unions for taking insufficient initiatives in defense of workers' rights, and called for broadening their activities; his remarks became a standard component of official statements on the trade unions' tasks.[98] The Ukrainian Communist party also showed heightened concern for worker-related issues, holding meetings with the republic's trade union council on problems of improving working conditions, organizing food supplies, enforcing labor legislation, and improving health services for workers in industrial centers. Ukrainian trade unions were criticized for neglecting "people's work, life, and everyday circumstances."[99] The press reported more often on both the positive effects and the problems of trade union work, and encouraged the holding of forums in which officials were required to respond to workers' complaints ("open letter days").[100] No substantive reforms of the trade unions were introduced, but on balance the unions' work was tilted away from the production function toward the defensive function. The Brezhnev leadership certainly did not acknowledge that any of these measures were taken in response to events in Poland, but the timing and the focus of attention on regions bordering Poland strongly suggest the connection to Solidarity. Scholars who have studied this question agree; in his work on Soviet labor relations during this period, for example, Blair Ruble concludes, "A variety of mass/elite linkages [became] the object of renewed interest in the Soviet Union to a degree which can be explained at least in part by concern over the rise of Solidarity."[101]

The patterns of working-class unrest and regime response during the Brezhnev period fit the requirements of the social contract thesis: workers were generally quiescent from the mid-1960s to the late 1970s, when the regime was delivering consistently on the contract; the rise of open discontent in the early 1980s paralleled the deterioration in delivery at the end of the Brezhnev period. Moreover, social

contract issues were the major (though not the only) source of workers' discontent: grievances over food, housing, and living conditions
caused approximately half of documented strikes during the period
of relative quiescence (1965 through 1979), while food prices and
supplies were the central issues in the strike waves of the early 1960s
and early 1980's. Most strikes throughout the Brezhnev period were
staged to protest erosion in workers' living standards, rather than to
demand improvements or political rights. The focus was on basic
issues of maintaining material standards, and when those issues were
addressed workers generally returned to quiescence. Walter Connor
aptly summarizes the argument: "There is good evidence that
Brezhnev-era strikers saw themselves as standing up against violations of a just social contract."[102]

The Brezhnev regime, for its part, consistently responded to
strikes by accommodating (and thereby legitimating) workers' material demands, while moving to repress any potential grass-roots leadership. It was also unrelenting in its repression of unauthorized organizations which sought to recruit and represent workers, and in its
escalating campaign of vilification against Solidarity. The regime, in
other words, acted as if it were willing to pay in material terms for
workers' compliance but determined to prevent the emergence of a
political challenge.

The Social Contract Thesis: Implications for the Soviet Political Economy

The idea that there was a state-society trade-off of socioeconomic
security for political quiescence fits the evidence of social policy and
popular behavior for the Brezhnev period. Although the welfare state
began to deteriorate in the late 1970s, it did so in the context of a
general economic decline, during which the leadership nevertheless
maintained and even increased some categories of social contract
spending (particularly food price subsidies). And, at the pressured
decision points examined, the leadership paid increased costs and
sacrificed competing policy goals to maintain the contract.

The social contract thesis has critical implications for the relationship between politics and economics in the Soviet state. It ties Soviet
political stability to the capacity of the centralized command economy

to control distributive outcomes and socialize loss and risk, thereby insulating workers from many of the effects of market competition, enterprise failure, and technological innovation. The centralization of the system in turn focuses all responsibility for economic decisions and allocational outcomes on the political regime. As David Lane explained in his recent study of Soviet labor and employment policies:

> The organization of political and economic institutions in the USSR has important effects on policies . . . In any society, the costs of economic efficiency in political terms may be measured in the weakening of public loyalty and social solidarity. But the accepted division in capitalist society between politics and economics diverts responsibility for unemployment away from the formal arena of politics . . . In the USSR the greater fusion of politics and economics and the responsibility the state assumes for public welfare make it impossible for the government to ignore the social and political costs of economic change.[103]

The strength of the authoritarian welfare state is that it concentrates control over all allocational decisions at the political center; its potential weakness is that it makes acceptance of that control (that is, legitimacy) contingent on state provision.

FOUR

Gorbachev's Reforms: The Critique of Brezhnev's Welfare State and Erosion of the Social Contract

The reformist leadership under Gorbachev quickly launched a broad ideological assault on Brezhnev's social contract. Gorbachev cited existing social and labor policies as sources of the system's "stagnation," and contended that under Brezhnev, "contradictions in the sphere of labor and distributive relations [accumulated] . . . the basic socialist principle . . . 'to each according to his work' was frequently sacrificed in practice to an oversimplified understanding of equality."[1] The most prominent and influential of Gorbachev's chosen early advisers, including the sociologist Tatyana Zaslavskaya and the economists Abel Aganbegyan and Leonid Abalkin, set forth a critique of those policies which was broadly publicized in academic and party journals, in the economic and popular press, and in interviews. Gorbachev and other high officials echoed these critics in speeches and policy statements, and their arguments influenced and informed the new leadership's social policy.[2]

The critics charged that Brezhnev's welfare state had become economically dysfunctional, morally debilitating, and frequently unfair, arbitrary, or corrupt in its actual distribution patterns. They argued that excessive social guarantees and security undermined productivity by providing benefits without relationship to work performance, while a too-egalitarian system of wages and incomes failed either to reward and encourage talent and education or to recognize individuals' different contributions to the economy. They made the case that distribution of subsidized goods and services had come to depend more on an individual's access than on either need or merit, and that a plethora of special and privileged means of access blocked the creation of an economically rational and fair distribution system. The reformers claimed, furthermore, that the authoritarian and paternalistic welfare state no longer corresponded to the level of development of Soviet society, that it fostered a psychology of dependence which stifled initiative and frustrated growing aspirations in society for independence and participation. I wish to look more closely at this critique as it was applied to each of the main policy areas—employment and wages, pricing and subsidies, and socialized services—before turning to the reformers' actual policy program.

The Reformist Critique

Wage Leveling and Job Security

Brezhnev's egalitarian wage policies, and the resultant wage leveling in the industrial sector, were a central object of reformist attack. Economists and officials argued that the tendency (beginning in the late 1960s) to reduce differentials between blue-collar and engineering-technical staffs and to increase pay disproportionately at the lower end of the salary scale had, by the mid-1980s, produced a wage scale which was characterized by excessive leveling. They saw such leveling as detrimental to scientific and technical progress, because it lowered the prestige and material reward for engineering and technical work which forms the basis for economic development. Critics claimed that the low pay differentials between workers and engineering staff made it difficult to recruit, train, and retain good engineers, and to stimulate and reward the talented, creative, and inventive who could contribute most to economic success.[3] Moreover, wage leveling tended to undermine the incentive role of pay throughout the labor force, since workers in similar skill grades generally earned similar wages whether they worked well or badly.[4]

In the view of his critics, Brezhnev's wage policies had not only hampered progress but had also violated the fundamental principle of just distribution under socialism, "to each according to his work." They insisted that pay should depend on performance, that the more productive, efficient, and creative deserved greater material rewards, and that near-equality of pay was unfair and demoralizing for conscientious, disciplined workers and promoted "loafing and free-loading attitudes."[5] In the reformers' view, both social justice and economic efficiency would be much better served by substantially increasing income differentials between the educated, talented, and productive on the one hand, and the less-skilled, often manual blue-collar workers favored by Brezhnev's wage policies on the other. According to Tatyana Zaslavskaya, "In the course of several Five-Year Plans preceding the 27th Congress, a number of elements of unfairness accumulated in various spheres of our social life. Socialist justice means, first of all, encouraging and comprehensively supporting those groups which make the greatest contribution to social progress."[6]

The reformers applied the principle of "reward according to performance" equally to industrial enterprises, arguing that all must become self-financing and profitable. Reformist economists saw the Brezhnev-era practice of ministerial cross-subsidization as wasteful, and detrimental to economic performance and development. Leonid Abalkin condemned "the [widespread] harmful practice of redistributing income from profitable enterprises, ministries and regions to unprofitable ones, in order to cover the latter's losses . . . [which] conditions people to expect endless handouts from Moscow."[7] Central Committee secretary N. N. Slyunkov argued that massive subsidies and lax credit encouraged inefficient management of resources and labor, and that economic acceleration demanded the creation of, "a direct linkage between the lowering of outlays, the efficiency of economic management, and the material remuneration of labor collectives."[8] Gorbachev's economic advisers agreed that enterprises must be subject to financial discipline, and that some of the least productive and efficient should face bankruptcy. They regarded the attendant displacement of workers as a necessary and acceptable cost of reform.[9]

The Brezhnev-era policy of employment security was also to become a casualty of technological acceleration. Job stability was premised on a nearly stagnant labor force structure heavy with manual and manufacturing workers. Economic reform would entail major changes in the job structure, including automation of much unskilled manual work. Most reformists saw staff cuts and layoffs as a policy which would have both costs and benefits for workers, at once eliminating many of the most dull and dirty jobs and thereby "satisfy[ing] the . . . need [of younger, better-educated cohorts] for more skilled and interesting work," but also displacing many people. Some argued that a little insecurity would enhance labor discipline and "the social value" of jobs in public production.[10] The most strident of the reform-ist economists, Nikolai Shmelev (who went well beyond Gorbachev and the official policy line), defended labor displacement and even potential unemployment as both economic and moral goods, writing in a well-known piece in *Novyi Mir,* "Let's not close our eyes to the harm caused by parasitic confidence in guaranteed jobs . . . The real danger of losing a job . . . is a good cure for laziness, drunkenness, and irresponsibility."[11]

The reformist intellectuals' arguments about social justice, produc-tivity, and accountability seemed simple and elegant on paper, con-vincing both logically and morally. But such principles were not eas-ily applied to the complex reality of the Soviet industrial sector, where irrational and distorted prices rendered economic accountability meaningless for many production branches, poor supplies and equip-ment often undermined the efforts of even the most conscientious and disciplined workers, and the shop-floor consensus generally as-signed greater value to physical labor than to the work of technical specialists, not to mention administrators.

Prices and Subsidies

On March 4, 1985, a week before Gorbachev's accession, then-chairman of the USSR State Pricing Committee Nikolai Glushkov re-cited the familiar laudatory claims for the Soviet record in providing a stable and protected cost of living:

> Prices of basic foods have remained unchanged for thirty years now, of meat and dairy produce—for more than twenty years, . . . housing rent for over half a century now . . . housing rent [and] utilities equals roughly three–five percent of the average workers' pay [and covers] not even a third of the state's spending on the maintenance of housing . . . When purchasing meat and dairy produce . . . Soviet people pay only a part of what the state has to pay to keep up low prices . . . Against . . . capitalist . . . inflation, the stability of prices in the USSR is one of the most important achievements of the socialist economic management system . . . the state redistributes profits through the budget in every-body's interests.[12]

Over the following two years, reformist economists and sociologists attacked these claims as an idealization which ignored much social inequality, bureaucratic abuse, and corruption (as well as some inflation). They criticized Brezhnev's policies on prices and subsidies as economically harmful, wasteful, and often producing an arbitrary and unfair distribution of benefits within Soviet society.

The economists argued that a rational and efficient economy required prices that reflected production costs of goods, and rewarded effective use of labor and resources. Instead, the subsidized and repressed prices of Brezhnev's economy encouraged inefficient use, especially of fuel and other nonrenewable natural resources. At the June 1987 Central Committee Plenum Gorbachev castigated the current price system as "long geared to the cheapness of natural resources . . . creating the illusion of cheapness and inexhaustibility of natural resources."[13] More important, wholesale and retail prices based on production costs and market demand (rather than administrative decisions) were vital to the introduction of economic accountability and self-financing, the core of the reform program. In addition, rapid growth of subsidies from the state budget was straining finances and contributing to a deficit which would soon become a major political issue.

The reformist critique of price policy extended beyond economics into social consequences, contradicting the Brezhnevian claim that state price subsidies benefited lower-income groups by making low-cost necessities universally accessible. In a major statement of the reformist critique of Brezhnev's welfare state, published in *Kommunist* in the fall of 1986, Tatyana Zaslavskaya made the case that subsidies often (though not always) benefited population groups with access rather than those in need.[14] She recognized that administrative manipulation of prices constituted a "concealed redistribution of income by the state," which was sometimes socially justified, as in the cases of subsidized children's goods or luxury goods priced well above cost. But she argued that the most important and expensive subsidies, those on retail food prices, did not promote just distribution: "The state subsidy is distributed according to a strange principle [not according to labor or need, but] mainly to those groups of the population that purchase meat at firm state prices. Under this system, only a certain segment of the population wins, while the bulk of working people lose, especially in rural localities and small cities where the supply of meat and milk through [state] stores is much worse."[15] The system, in other words, redistributed income in favor of population strata with direct or indirect access to subsidized goods.

Zaslavskaya calculated that in fact food subsidies went disproportionately to higher-income groups who consumed more meat and milk, a claim repeated by Gorbachev in a speech to workers in Murmansk soon after the leadership had announced its intention to reform retail prices, as well as by other officials seeking to justify the planned price reforms.[16] Moreover, the coexistence of low-priced state and new higher-priced cooperative distribution networks created a segmented consumer market which made the value of workers' earned rubles unequal, and lent itself to corruption.

Socialized Services and Social Consumption Funds

Zaslavskaya and others extended the argument about unequal distribution in an effort to discredit the Brezhnev leadership's last remaining claim to just distribution: universal provision of free social services. The prolific sociologist pointed to sharp regional disparities in the spending of public funds for services and benefits (in Soviet parlance, social or public consumption funds). In a late-1986 article published in *Ekonomicheskaia Gazeta* V. Kryazhev, department head at the Labor Research Institute, confirmed her argument: "An analysis of practice in making payments from public consumption funds shows that, with respect to certain uses of these funds, the principle of social justice is realized inconsistently or is violated . . . there are still distinct differences in the level at which [these] funds are provided between urban and rural areas . . . large and small cities . . . and certain regions."[17] Gorbachev was drawing on these arguments when he pointed to serious problems with unequal regional development of social infrastructure (including housing, education, health, and other social services), particularly during his widely-publicized trips to Siberia and the Far East.[18]

The reformers had other grievances against the scope and patterns of social spending. They argued that benefits from social consumption funds helped to undermine the incentive role of pay, since benefits had grown more rapidly than wages and were distributed without regard to work performance. In addition, different industrial sectors and even individual enterprises provided widely disparate levels of benefits to their workers, depending on the size of the enterprise, levels of state funding, and other factors.

Reformist social scientists charged that the workers' receipt of benefits from the growing allocation of social consumption funds depended heavily on place of residence or employment, and produced unjustified inequality among workers in the same occupation and skill grade.[19] They claimed that, as with price subsidies, benefits were distributed according to neither merit nor need, but randomly or arbitrarily in relation to both. Zaslavskaya further asserted that sociological studies indicated distribution of benefits from social consumption funds favored higher rather than lower-income groups, and that free distribution contributed to shortages, wasteful use of services, and opportunities for speculation and unearned income. She concluded that the system suffered from "the absence of sufficiently clear and substantiated principles for distribution of free . . . benefits."[20] The economist V. Rutgaizer drew the logical reformist conclusion: "Distribution according to labor . . . means that obtaining benefits on a *paid* basis must predominate over free distribution."[21]

The reformist critics added to their arguments a recitation of the more familiar deficiencies and abuses of Brezhnev's welfare state: the poor quality of services, long waits, and common reliance on bribery by benefit users and extortion of payments by service providers. The system of medical care came in for especially harsh criticism, with Gorbachev's minister of health, E. Chazov, detailing in the press the wretched state of many hospitals, "grave condition" of rural public health care, deficient diagnostic equipment, and outdated research of the Soviet health care system.[22] Experts and policy-makers questioned both the quality and advisability of public day care for young children. The existence of genuine poverty and hardship in Soviet society (particularly among pensioners and large families) was acknowledged, as was the penury of many types of state transfer payments, including pensions, disability benefits, and income supplements for children. Reporting and discussion on all these topics was fully in the spirit of glasnost, but also carried the underlying message that Brezhnev's state had never really delivered adequate social services, and that the problems could not be fully resolved within the existing socioeconomic framework.

The Reformist Prescription for Social Justice

The reformers held that a just socialist system should distribute predominantly according to work; the state should provide a guaranteed minimum of provision for all, with people paying for benefits over and above that minimum in each area (for example, housing, health care). On the basis of this principle, they developed a number of proposals for reform of pricing, the social service sector, and state spending patterns. These included creation of fee-charging and for-profit social services to supplement state services, differentiation of rents according to the quality and amenities of the housing, and dras-tic reductions in retail price subsidies. As Zaslavskaya explained, the "tens of billions of rubles" that the state would collect in rents, or save from retail price increases and expansion of paid social services, would provide a reserve for radical improvements in the wage system (including greatly increased differentiation according to rank and performance).[23] The reformers' arguments at once constituted a repu-diation of Brezhnev's welfare state and provided both practical and theoretical justifications for a more meritocratic and competitive eco-nomic reward system with more highly stratified patterns of distribu-tion.

In retrospect, it is impressive how few voices among intellectuals or policy-makers were raised at this stage in principled defense of Brezhnev's welfare state and social contract. To be sure, there was some elite opposition to particular proposals: a few ideologues ob-jected to any increase of private property or earnings as being a re-treat from communism; the trade union leadership opposed privatiza-tion of social services; Ligachev, the most prominent critic of reform, spoke in defense of "socialist morality" and against creation of a "capi-talist labor market."[24] But very few defended with any conviction the principles of universal social protection and egalitarian distribution which had been so central to the old leadership's self-justification and legitimacy formula, or called for a program which would better realize these principles rather than abandon them.

As a case in point, a much-discussed series of articles on social justice, published in the journal *Kommunist* at this time, included only one cogent defense of egalitarianism and the comprehensive welfare state. It was written by two economists, A. Bim and A. Shok-hin (later minister of labor and deputy minister in Yeltsin's govern-ment), who disputed reformists' claims that the present system was "overburdened with social guarantees" and that privatization and in-creased income differentiation would create a more just society. Ad-dressing the issue of for-fee medical services, they argued that intro-ducing payments would mean "encouraging wide disparities in satisfaction of priority social needs," and that free and equal access for all members of society was preferable to paid and unequal access. Though not wholly opposed to price reform, they pointed out that food price increases would inevitably hurt low- and fixed-income individuals most, and that these groups should continue to be protected by limited rationing and price controls.[25] But such views had little support from the social scientists who dominated the debate. Anders Aslund concludes (from his exhaustive research on the early stages of reform) that among intellectuals, defense of the old system was largely confined to provincial academics.[26]

How can the broad rejection of Brezhnev-era ideology and social policy among Soviet intellectuals be explained? The critique of Brezhnev's welfare state had been developing among social scientists and other specialists for more than a decade. According to Peter Hauslohner:

> Since approximately the mid-1970s, every element of the social contract [had] been subjected to increasingly pointed criticism . . . Wage egalitarianism [was] probably the most popular target. Perhaps more significant [were] the multiplying attacks on full employment and job security, which [were] openly blamed for encouraging sloth, indiscipline, and excessive labor turnover. While there was relatively little substantive change in social policy before Brezhnev's death, there is reason to think that whatever elite consensus once existed in support of the social contract had, by that point, largely disintegrated.[27]

Hauslohner proceeds to argue that large segments of the Soviet public shared the elite's disaffection with the old social contract, but here the evidence seems to be much more mixed. Several sources, including opinion surveys and letters to the editor of various publications, indicate that much of the Soviet public remained deeply attached to social security, egalitarianism, and state provision. This can be seen, for example, in the results of surveys conducted by the Moscow All-Union Center for the Study of Public Opinion in the spring of 1990 on the critical issues of job and wage security (Table 4.1).[28] In the spring of 1990, the majority of Soviets (and a slightly larger majority in the RSFSR) judged the emergence of unemployment in their country as "intolerable," while nearly 90 percent held the state responsible for providing jobs. As to wage security, Table 4.2 indicates that a considerably larger percent (47 percent) pre-

Table 4.1 Attitudes toward full employment: USSR and RSFSR, April 1990

Question: With which of the following judgments concerning employment do you agree more?	USSR (with RSFSR)	RSFSR only
Unemployment in our country is intolerable	54.0%	56.8%
Unemployment is quite bearable	9.4	7.0
Unemployment on a small scale may be useful	15.3	17.1
Unemployment is in general necessary for effectively running the economy	8.1	6.4
Difficult to answer	13.4	12.8

Source: Obshchestvennoye Mneniye v Tsifrakh, vyp. 12(19) (Moscow: VTsIOM, April 1990), p. 13. This survey was conducted by the All-Union Center for the Study of Public Opinion and involved interviews with 2,705 people throughout the USSR, including 1,288 in the RSFSR. The report, titled "Problems of Full Employment of the Population," was written by V. L. Kosmarsky. It is confirmed by the results of a second poll, reported to me in an interview with the Center's project director, Dr. Nikolai Popov (May 4, 1991), which speaks more directly to the question of the state's responsibility for job provision. In answer to the question, "What should be the role of government in job provision?" respondents answered as follows: the state should provide everyone with a job according to his profession/occupation and education (56%); the state should provide some job to those who lose their job (32%); the state has no necessary role in job provision (5%).

ferred guaranteed wages to higher wages without guarantees (31 percent), though this preference was much weaker among the younger and better-educated, and was reversed among those with higher education. Other survey data indicate a strong societal commitment to egalitarian norms.[29] So while there was both differentiation and ambivalence among Soviets on social contract issues, the evidence suggests a significant disparity between elite and popular attitudes, which would militate against broad acceptance of reformist social policy.

Gorbachev and the Social Contract

The Gorbachev leadership acknowledged that Brezhnev's welfare state had considerable support in Soviet society. Authoritative spokesmen, most notably Gorbachev himself, referred often to a set of general societal attitudes toward equality and state responsibility

Table 4.2 Attitudes toward employment security, by age and level of education, 1990

Question: In conditions of economic reform, terms of wages could change substantially. What would you prefer, if you could choose?	All adults	Age			Education		
		Under 25	25–55	Over 55	Some higher education	Secondary education	To nine years of school
To have even not large, but guaranteed wages	47%	39%	43%	60%	34%	43%	59%
To receive high wages, though without the guarantee of receiving them in the future	31	35	34	23	36	33	27
To have income from my own business or farm, taking risks myself	18	23	20	12	26	21	11

Source: Obshchestvennoye Mnenie v Tsifrakh, vyp. 15, (Moscow: VTsIOM, 1990), p. 25. The survey on attitudes toward conditions of labor included 2,604 respondents, of whom approximately 2,000 were from the Russian and Ukrainian republics.

which stood as obstacles to reform. Criticisms of a "leveling mentality" in Soviet society and "deformed and outdated conceptions of social justice" were a frequent theme in the general secretary's speeches. In a speech to the media in May 1988, for example, he insisted, "We must rid ourselves once and for all of notions of socialism as something that *levels* . . . as some sort of *minimum,* as a minimum of material benefits, a minimum of justice, a minimum of democracy . . . We should bring our traditional notions of socialism up to the level of present-day demands." A commentary from *Pravda's* economics department in the same period criticized "false 'welfare' notions of social protections and full employment from the period of stagnation."[30] The leadership realized that much of Soviet society expected the state to provide economic equality and security.

As we have seen, the Gorbachev leadership explicitly repudiated the paternalism of its predecessor, denying the socialist state's responsibility for comprehensive provision and universal well-being. Nevertheless Gorbachev, as well as many of his closest advisers, often seemed ambivalent about whether and how far to deconstruct Brezhnev's welfare state. In mapping out reform policies, Gorbachev repeatedly promised that costs for the working people would be limited: a comprehensive state program of retraining and placement would quickly move dismissed workers to new jobs; food price increases would be accompanied by increased transfer payments to lower-income groups; privatization of housing and medical care would be supplemented by increased spending to upgrade existing state services. Gorbachev seemed clear in his commitment to meritocratic norms, but uncertain about cutting established social protections. Indeed, each time the Gorbachev leadership confronted real, significant social costs or negative political responses to reform policies, it retreated. An examination of these retreats—from layoffs, bankruptcies, price and wage reforms, privatization of medical care—will reveal what caused them and how they contributed to the overall failure of Soviet economic reform.

Reform Policies and the Erosion of the Social Contract

From 1986 through 1988 the Gorbachev leadership initiated, or announced its intent to initiate, policies which threatened to undercut basic provisions of the social contract in all major policy areas: employment security, wage equality, price stability, and socialized services. Changes in industrial policy began to erode employment security and stability, confronting workers with heightened demands for productivity and the prospect of displacement. The new leadership introduced a wage reform which increased differentials among skill grades and between blue-collar and managerial personnel. Legalization of a limited cooperative sector began to weaken state control over consumer prices and challenged the monopolistic position of state enterprises in the consumer sector. Proposed price reforms threatened state subsidies for food and other necessities. Privatization of housing, medical care, and other social services was encouraged on a modest scale.

The following sections examine major reform initiatives in each of the four policy areas, focusing on their likely or projected adverse effects on workers' economic and social security. The Gorbachev leadership both intended and prepared for substantial erosion of that security, but in fact most actual adverse effects were quite limited, because the leadership repeatedly drew back from measures which would have imposed big costs on industrial workers.

The Threat to Employment Security

RESTRUCTURING FOR TECHNOLOGICAL MODERNIZATION

Gorbachev's original reform program called for a major and rapid transition in the structure of production and employment in the Soviet economy, a shift toward a postindustrial system characterized by high levels of production automation and a much-expanded service sector. This reform was to be imposed on a labor force which had undergone very gradual structural change in the Brezhnev decades and as a result had retained a high proportion of workers in material and manual production. The share of Soviet workers employed in material production showed a low, and declining, rate of shifting to nonproduction spheres over the years 1970 through 1985.[31] Changes in the structure of employment within sectors had likewise proceeded slowly, with the result that approximately one-third of industrial workers, one-half of construction workers, and two-thirds of agricultural workers remained engaged in manual, usually low-skilled, often physically arduous labor.[32] In a 1987 total Soviet labor force of approximately 131 million, 50 million workers were classified as manual.[33]

The *Comprehensive Program for the Social and Economic Development of the USSR to the Year 2000,* approved by the 27th Party Congress, called for dramatic cuts in the levels of manual labor throughout Soviet industry and construction. It established a goal of reductions in the use of manual labor to 15 to 20 percent from the then-current level of 30 percent—a decrease of as much as 50 percent in industry over the years 1986 to 2000. The Twelfth Five-Year Plan (1986 through 1990) stipulated that the number of manual production workers should decrease by more than 5 million (that is, by more than 10 percent of the total) by 1990, while the volume of work performed manually in construction was to be reduced by 25 percent.[34] Reductions were to be concentrated in several industrial sectors, including coal, timber, food, railroads, and machine-building, as well as construction, and within these sectors, especially among workers engaged in auxiliary functions such as lifting and transport, loading and unloading, and warehouse work.[35] The reformers further expected that technological modernization and productivity increases would produce deep cuts in levels of employment throughout the material production sector, with a corresponding shift of labor into the understaffed service sector.

State officials and their economic advisers calculated the potential effects of these policies on the Soviet working people. Goskomtrud projected that the planned economic modernization and restructuring would result in the release (from the job they held in 1985) of 3 million employees during the Twelfth Five-Year Plan, and of some 15 million by the year 2000.[36] The reformist economist Abalkin projected that up to 20 million surplus workers in agriculture and manufacturing would be moved into the service sector by the end of the century.[37] The more radical Kostakov argued that much "excess" labor should move out of the state sector into the recently legalized cooperative sector, and that some relatively marginal labor resources should be removed from the productive economy entirely.[38] Reformist leaders clearly realized that their policies would entail unprecedented displacement and dislocation for hundreds of thousands of industrial workers and would undermine the accustomed stability and security of many workers' lives.

The leadership insisted that restructuring would pose no threat to full employment, and made credible claims that large numbers of released workers could be reabsorbed into the existing economy. Gorbachev emphasized the possibilities for transfer of labor to manpower-short production sectors, pointing out that industry alone had 700,000 vacancies (in June 1986) with a predominant system of one-shift equipment use, and that a planned increase in the shift coefficient would produce some 4 million vacancies.[39] Others emphasized the great need for labor in the service sector. But at least a few of the reformist economists recognized that such large-scale displacement of workers could produce severe problems. Kostakov (obviously responding to Gorbachev's assurances) made the critical point that a "mathematical equivalence" between numbers of workers released and numbers demanded in different sectors meant little because," as a rule, the professional structures of those 'freed' and those for whom there is demand do not correspond."[40]

Indeed, one might question how many of the low-skilled manual workers who were the prime target of labor force cuts could have made the transition to new jobs, especially in the service sector (defined as culture, education, health care, and leisure), except in the most menial capacities. Nor does it seem likely that many would muster the initiative, resources, and entrepreneurial skills to enter the cooperative sector. Zaslavskaya frankly confronted the likely effects, admitting that the process of reform "does not exclude a worsening of the situation in finding jobs for honest and conscientious people, insufficiently well-educated and not ready for retraining. [Some] will need material and social assistance . . . It is difficult to imagine at the present time the entire set of social problems related to the acceleration of scientific and technical progress."[41]

THE TRANSITION TO SELF-FINANCING

A second major element of the economic reform, the transfer of all enterprises to self-financing under the June 1987 Law on the State Enterprise, also threatened Soviet workers' employment security and stability. The Law on the State Enterprise mandated a basic restructuring of the Soviet economy's operating principles.[42] Since the 1930s central ministries (and other state organizations) had controlled and distributed most enterprise-operating funds in the Soviet economy. This system of centralized financing effectively socialized risk, and kept poorly managed, unprofitable enterprises in operation through subsidies and profit redistribution. It also encouraged overstaffing, since ministries allocated wage funds according to the size of the enterprise's work force, and management had multiple incentives to maximize both.[43]

Under the reformed system Soviet enterprises were supposed to become self-supporting and economically accountable, that is, they were to cover all costs of production, including the wage bill, with their own income and profits rather than with government allocations. Income and profits were, in turn, to become increasingly dependent on private contracts between enterprises and the purchasers of their products and services, rather than on state orders.[44] Self-financing was expected to have two important effects on employment. First, it would create pressures and incentives for the release of unneeded workers from enterprises in operation. Managements would confront new requirements to pay directly for labor, along with much stronger pressures to run cost-efficient and profitable enterprises. As a consequence, it was expected they would cut presently inflated labor forces, presumably creating an unpredictable scale and pattern of redundancies throughout the Soviet economy.[45] Second, self-financing raised the prospect of a massive release of workers from unprofitable enterprises which might be subject to reorganization or dissolution. Substantial numbers of loss-making enterprises which had been maintained by ministerial cross-subsidization (together with lax industrial credit) became technically insolvent under the Law on Enterprise. The law (Article 23) made provision for bankruptcy and, in extreme cases, dissolution of chronically unprofitable production facilities.[46]

REORGANIZING RESPONSIBILITIES FOR EMPLOYMENT

With their policies for economic modernization and enterprise self-financing at least tentatively in place, the reformist leaders began to prepare the ground for the large-scale dismissals and displacement of workers which they anticipated. First they needed to revise workers' employment rights, for, as the chief of the Ministry of Light Industry's legal department stated in a discussion of job cuts (referring critically to employment guarantees for women with young children), "Labor legislation laid down in the period of the economy's extensive development is not designed to cope with massive reductions in staff going on practically simultaneously and practically everywhere."[47]

Second, as reformist economists had been arguing for some time, managers had to be relieved of responsibility for placement of released workers. (In Kostakov's terms, managers should answer only for the effectiveness of labor, and the state, for full employment).[48] Reformers called for a policy of comprehensive state planning of labor allocation, and for development of a network of labor bureaus to handle transfer and placement of released workers.

As it began full-scale implementation of the Law on the State Enterprise, the leadership adopted such a policy. In January 1988, party, government, and trade unions passed a joint resolution, "On Ensuring Effective Employment of the Population, Improving the System of Job Placement, and Strengthening Social Guarantees for the Working People." The resolution set forth plans for a national system of job placement bureaus which was intended to "resolve the tasks of predicting, planning, and regulating the population's employment . . . and organizing the systematic, prompt redistribution of manpower resources in the national economy."[49]

The resolution stressed, first, that Soviet citizens have the right to work. It retained the provision that workers released from a particular enterprise or institution would have priority in assignment to any suitable vacant position within that enterprise or in any facility under its jurisdiction. The resolution's text, along with commentary by officials from the State Committee for Labor and Social Issues and the Council of Ministers' Bureau for Social Development, indicated an expectation that many "excess" workers would be reabsorbed through introduction of additional shifts at their employing enterprise, or transferred to work in plant modernization, construction, services, or subsidiary production under the auspices of that enterprise.[50] When people were laid off, the newly established placement bureaus would work in cooperation with enterprises, labor organs of local soviets, trade unions, and ministries "to make provision in good time and on a planned basis for subsequent placing in jobs [of those released]." At one point the resolution hedged, leaving open the possibility of direct interference in dismissals by local political authorities: "In exceptional cases, with a view to better organized placing for released workers, local soviet *ispolkoms* [executive committees] may, with the consent of the labor collectives, defer schedules for releasing workers from enterprises, organizations, and institutions."[51]

The Resolution on Employment also included provisions for easing the transition of workers into new jobs or out of the labor force. It introduced or extended material and social assistance for released workers, including: maintenance of the worker's average wage for a period of up to three months after dismissal and during retraining (in effect, unemployment compensation); maintenance of a record of uninterrupted work, with attendant benefits and payments, for the same period; and maintenance after transfer of benefits accrued at a former place of work. There were also proposals for extension of a system of early retirement on partial pension, to cushion the impact of staff reductions on older and less-productive workers. Some economists went further, proposing increases in social benefits, including pensions, student stipends, and mothers' benefits, as well as expansion of the cooperative sector, to help ease marginal labor out of the state sector.

But while the provisions of the Resolution on Employment were clearly designed to cushion the impact of layoffs on workers, the central thrust of the resolution was to prepare for large-scale labor force dismissals and displacement in the coming years. Its provisions clearly stipulated that labor contracts might be broken "in connection with the implementation of measures to cut the number of workers or establishments." It instructed governmental, party, and social organizations to encourage, assist, and organize movement of released workers to labor deficit areas, including Siberia and the Far East. It provided for the organized transfer of labor resources from the generally well-paid production sector to the more poorly remunerated service sector. It called on the population to accept that the existing employment structure "inevitably leads to stagnation," that large-scale transfers of labor between sectors and regions was necessary for economic revitalization, and that the state was taking all possible measures to plan and manage the transfers to mitigate the unavoidably painful effects on workers.[52] Ultimately, though, the projected combination of curtailed employment protections, lessened demand for labor, and the increased state role in labor allocation, would mean a deterioration in the effective rights and bargaining position of Soviet workers.[53]

The Gorbachev leadership made preparations to undercut significantly the employment security of its labor force, including the mainly Slavic blue-collar workers in basic manufacturing and extraction industries. The leaders designed a reform strategy which would displace hundreds of thousands of such workers from their work collectives and enterprises, and in many cases from the industrial production sector, and laid the political and legal groundwork for unprecedented labor displacement with the Resolution on Employment.

Wage Reform and Quality Control

The Gorbachev leadership also set about reforming the wage system. In the fall of 1986, it initiated a reform which reversed the leveling tendencies of Brezhnev-era industrial wage policies by increasing pay differentials between skill levels and raising salaries of specialists and managers at higher rates than blue-collar wages. The resolution, "On Improving the Wage System in Production Branches of the National Economy," mandated an average wage increase of 20 to 25 percent for workers, 30 to 35 percent for specialists, and 35 to 40 percent for engineers (specifically, designers and technologists) directly engaged in the development of new equipment and technology. It also provided pay increments of up to 50 percent for skilled workers and engineers employed with highly productive equipment or otherwise achieving high labor results.[54] The reform would in principle raise wages for all categories of workers by the end of the Twelfth Five-Year Plan, but the authorized increases were to be financed out of enterprise resources rather than (as in the past) from the state budget. Thus enterprises would have to generate resources for the raises by improving productivity and efficiency, cutting staffs, and so on. Wage increases were also limited by the stipulation that an enterprise's productivity must grow more rapidly than its average wages. Overall, the new wage policy benefited professional and managerial employees at the expense of blue-collar workers, while at the same time singling out the most skilled and productive personnel at every level.[55]

The wage reform was clearly in keeping with the leadership's meritocratic norms, designed to tie pay more closely to performance, to provide incentives and rewards for skill and education, and to overcome "excessive egalitarianism" in the industrial wage structure. It called for self-financed wage increases, which would be differentiated according to enterprises' productivity gains, and would therefore give both workers and managers direct incentives to increase efficiency and cut costs. There were some problems with the legislation, and some inconsistencies with other more-or-less simultaneous reform measures.[56] Nevertheless, during 1987 and 1988 the Resolution on Wages did produce some of the intended effects. Its success was, however, short-lived.

The reformers' program also intensified pressures on the factory floor in 1986 and 1987 by strengthening quality controls over the notoriously poor output of civilian production. In May 1986 the Central Committee passed the resolution "On Measures to Radically Improve the Quality of Output," which created a new system for state product acceptance *(gospriemka)* in Soviet enterprises.[57] The resolution set up a monitoring body which was to be directly subordinated to Gosstandart (that is, independent of both enterprise and ministerial control), highly qualified, and paid on the basis of quality rather than plan fulfillment. Quality controllers could reject substandard output, send it back for improvement, and, in extreme cases, stop production.[58] Managers and workers were to be held directly accountable for low-quality production; the resolution stipulated that "premium pay and bonuses will not be paid for a month when defective products or lowered quality of output occur . . . and may be eliminated if problems are chronic."[59] *Gospriemka* was instituted in hundreds of Soviet enterprises over the following two years and, like the wage reform, produced some significant but short-lived effects.

Price Reform and Privatization

In June 1987 the Gorbachev leadership announced its intention to carry out a comprehensive reform of industrial wholesale, purchase, and retail prices, including actual price levels and procedures for establishing them.[60] The reform was to include higher industrial wholesale prices for fuel and raw materials, a large reduction in retail price subsidies, and some decentralization of pricing authority. Over the following months the government proceeded with preparations for the reform, instructing the State Pricing Committee (Goskomtsen) to draw up plans, and specifying that the Thirteenth Five-Year Plan must be based on the new prices.[61] Officials of the government and Goskomtsen regularly asserted that a price reform was in preparation and would be put up for nationwide discussion once a draft plan was ready (as had been done, for example, with the draft Law on the State

Enterprise), but no draft documents were published. Instead price reform was delayed, then postponed, with no significant progress on the issue for nearly four years.[62]

The Gorbachev leadership both understood and insisted that price reform was critical to the overall project of perestroika, that it was the linchpin of the reform process. In his speech to the June 1987 Central Committee Plenum (which approved the Law on the State Enterprise) Gorbachev stated, "Radical reform of price formation is the most important component of economic restructuring. Without it a complete changeover to the new economic mechanism is impossible."[63] He explained that prices must be brought into line with production costs to allow introduction of industrial self-financing, and that the present system of price formation produced distortions, irrationalities, and excessive growth of state subsidies. Reformist economists (who seemed to agree on little else) were uniformly committed to rationalization of prices and reductions of retail price subsidies.

Yet the leadership was singularly cautious in its treatment of this issue. Even in their earliest statements, leaders gave assurances that price reform would not lead to a deterioration in the working people's living standards. While insisting that state food subsidies must be reduced, for example, Gorbachev proposed a system of compensation for low- and average-income consumers, and promised that only high-income overconsumers of subsidized goods would be hurt.[64] At virtually every public mention of retail price reform, officials repeated that while "unjustified redistributive processes and subsidies" would be reduced, working people would be compensated (for example, with transfer payments and wage tax relief) and "social justice" would be enhanced. The reformers' caution on this issue, their unwillingness even to admit that price reform would impose costs on workers and others, contrasts strikingly with their open admission of new costs to be imposed in other areas, including employment security, wage equality and industrial quality control. It points to the reformers' extreme concern about popular acceptance of price reform, and perceptions of its political costs.

Finally, the reformers encouraged a modest privatization of consumer and social services for the Soviet population. A small legal private sector, including cooperative housing, tutoring, and some other activities, already existed, along with a much larger sphere of semilegal privately run consumer services. Beginning in 1986, new laws on individual labor activity and cooperatives permitted expansion of the legal private sector, which could sell goods and services at prices well above those in the state sector. The Law on Individual Labor Activity, approved in November 1986, and effective May 1, 1987, listed sectors in which individual enterprise would be allowed. They included handicrafts, consumer services, and social services such as teaching, dentistry, and medicine (with the exclusion of some specialties).[65] The more significant Law on Cooperatives, passed in May 1988, allowed the voluntary formation of self-managing, self-financing, profit-oriented cooperatives which could engage in any activity not prohibited by law, and which had substantial independent power to set prices.[66] Many restrictions continued to be applied to the private sector, both by central regulations and by often-arbitrary local officials, but it was explicitly legalized and given official support and encouragement by these measures. Reformers argued that it would complement the state sector and compensate for its severe shortages and deficiencies.

Expansion of the legal private sector held implications for several aspects of the old social contract. First, it threatened retail price stability by increasing the proportion of the consumer sector in which prices were largely unregulated by the state and could be set on the basis of supply and demand. Second, it threatened the monopoly of state enterprises and associations over rights to market entry, and thereby subjected enterprises and their labor forces to competition. Third, it threatened income egalitarianism by creating a sphere of economic activity which was profit-driven, and in which incomes were not subject to direct regulation by the state.[67] Fourth, most significantly, it threatened full state provision of social services by creating a network of for-fee services, and by allowing doctors and other service providers to establish private and collective practices. Each of these four points became a source of official debate and public protest over the private, and especially the cooperative, sector. As a consequence, privatization developed slowly and unevenly and was severely restricted or curtailed in some spheres.

The Gorbachev leadership initiated, or announced its intent to initiate, reforms which threatened the social contract in every major policy area. Employment stability and security would be sacrificed to the requirements of technological modernization and financial discipline in industry. Wage equality would give way to increased pay differentials rewarding the more productive, educated, and creative in the state sector, and the entrepreneurial in the private sector. Prices would be raised to cover production costs. Fully subsidized social services would be supplemented by privately provided, user-paid services. Moreover (with the partial exception of price reform), the leadership clearly accepted and admitted that these policies would impose real and unprecedented costs on Soviet workers: workers would face layoffs, displacement, and retraining; those with poor output quality or low productivity would lose wages; retail price subsidies would be cut; fees would be charged for some social services. The reformers calculated these costs, announced and justified them to the people, and set about making the necessary changes in laws, regulations, institutions, practices, and (they hoped) mind-sets.

At the same time, Gorbachev promised (somewhat unrealistically) that in each case the costs of these reform policies for the population would be managed and limited by the state. He gave assurances that there would be no structural unemployment and implied that the government would establish a system of compensation, counseling, and placement which could move any dismissed worker into a new job within weeks. While the wage reform widened disparities, he pointed out that it also provided for increases at all pay levels. While privatization of services such as medicine and housing were encouraged, Gorbachev promised increased state spending to improve the quality of health care and increase the supply of housing. And, as mentioned, the General Secretary insisted that retail price reform would not affect living standards—that all but the upper-income consumers would be compensated. He seemed determined to guarantee the working people that the state would not violate the old social contract too much.

There is a pattern underlying the reformers' social policies, of movement from Brezhnev's comprehensive welfare state to a more limited one which would provide specific benefit packages to needy or temporarily disadvantaged groups and individuals. This pattern can be seen clearly in the area of employment policy, where temporary wage compensation and placement assistance were to replace broad guarantees of stability and security. The pattern is evident in other policy areas as well. Threats to full state subsidization and price controls were accompanied by promises of increased transfer payments to those on fixed incomes or in particular need. In fact, while the overall thrust of reform policies was to erode broad social guarantees that extended to most of the population (and particularly benefited blue-collar workers), the reformers at the same time acknowledged the existence of the genuinely poor in Soviet society (as Brezhnev had not) and sought to alleviate their plight. A series of decrees increased benefit levels for pensioners, families with many children, and other groups with very low per capita incomes.[68] The reformers expressed full support for state provision of welfare and social security for those who could not work.

The new policy program clearly responded to the proposals made by reformist academics and officials critical of Brezhnev's welfare state. Even so, many of those intellectuals and academics who articulated the theories and justifications for perestroika, who worked out its policies and accepted responsibility for its social costs, evinced uncertainty at various points about the social justice and political wisdom of their policies. They harbored doubts about "sacrificing the achievements of socialism." The pro reform intellectual Feodor Burlatsky, commenting on the Law on the State Enterprise, wrote "that guaranteed work and social security constitute the chief gains of the socialist system. And no one in our country will agree to renounce these gains which were achieved at a high price"; and the economist Leonid Abalkin, while advocating changes in the system of price subsidies, recognized that "we have always stressed it as a merit of socialism that goods are so cheap in our country."[69] Remnants of the old paternalism contributed to these doubts, but fear of reform's social and political consequences was their dominant cause.

An explicit recognition of that fear can be found in the following comment by V. Krivosheyev, sector chief of the Academy of Sciences Institute of the Economics of the World Socialist System, made at a roundtable discussion of restructuring which was sponsored by *Literaturnaia Gazeta:* "The fear of social upheavals, of negative consequences in the social sphere, is one of the serious obstacles in the path of the new economic mechanism . . . Our hands and feet are literally fettered by fear: Suddenly we'll earn less, suddenly the enterprise will collapse, suddenly someone will find himself out of a job."[70] And Seweryn Bialer, in a trenchant analysis of the politics of reform written during 1987, emphasized the significance of these uncertainties and fears: "Today the main danger to the Soviet system may emanate from the industrial working class, which is being disrupted by the dismantling of the old social contract . . . It is the perception of these dangers, not simply personal ambition for power and privilege, that threatens the system with destabilization and drives the substantial resistance to Gorbachev's plans."[71]

Implementation and Effects of Reform Policies

The remainder of the present chapter assesses the implementation and effects of the reformist policy agenda outlined to this point. The Gorbachev leadership repeatedly drew back from its policy commitments when confronted with their real social and political costs, as will be revealed by examining the developments in each of the three broad policy areas: employment security; wages and quality control; prices and privatization. The reform did, nevertheless, erode social contract guarantees, while at the same time failing to promote either meritocracy or efficiency.

The Impact of Reform on Employment Security

DISMISSALS AND RELEASES

Releases and intersector shifts of personnel (as a consequence of reform policies) began in 1987 and intensified in 1988. According to Goskomstat (State Committee on Statistics)[72] and VTsSPS (All-Union Central Council of Trade Unions)[73] statistics, economic reform led to the release of approximately 3 million industrial workers by late 1989. The total number of personnel employed in Soviet industry began to decline for the first time in the postwar period, while numbers working in nonproduction sectors increased by several hundred thousand.[74] The cuts clearly affected the core working class (specifically, ethnic Slavs in material-goods production), as the number employed in the RSFSR production sphere was reduced by some 590,000 (from total reductions of approximately 1 million) in 1988.[75] While the scale of reported releases was in keeping with the reformers' projections for these years, the impact in displacing workers was considerably less than the numbers suggest. Most of those released fell into one of the three following categories.

1. The majority of those classified as "released" were in fact simply transferred to different jobs, sectors, or shifts within the same enterprise or production facility. Some were retrained and transferred to different work, others were released and then rehired for existing vacant positions in the same enterprise or to fill newly introduced second and third shifts.[76] The model plan for placement of 10,000 workers to be released from shops and production sections at the Chelyabinsk Tractor Plant Production Association over the course of the Five-Year Plan was indicative of the broader pattern: according to the placement plan, which was developed by the trade union committee, about 4,000 of the released workers were to be placed in new production jobs, almost 6,000 sent to nonproduction organizations of the association, and only 250 (that is, 2.5 percent of the total) were slated for actual dismissal from the association.[77] The predominance of "redistribution of the labor force basically within enterprises" meant minimal dislocation for workers, though they sometimes faced wage decreases or various hardships because of assignments to evening and night shifts.[78]

2. A substantial minority of those released, amounting to one-third of the total for 1987 and 1988, retired on pensions. There is evidence that many older workers retired early or involuntarily, and some were required to leave jobs on which they depended to supplement inadequate pensions, but all who retired were near or past the end of their normal working lives.[79]

3. A small percentage of those counted in the release figures were actually *discharged* from their enterprises and had to find new jobs or remain unemployed. Available evidence, including claims of the trade union leadership and survey data, indicate that managements tended to discharge mostly older workers, youth with little work experience, women with children, and the poorly skilled.[80] Those left unemployed for extended periods commonly lived in small towns or settlements which lacked local opportunities for reemployment, and were geographically immobile (for family or other reasons).[81]

The cost of layoffs (that is, dislocation, income loss, and job loss) during 1987 through 1989 thus fell mainly on less efficient, relatively marginal producers who had nonetheless generally been assured employment and wage income in the past. The overall effect on employment security amounted to an erosion of social contract protections, but stopped well short of seriously undercutting job security for the core of the industrial working class. The policies at the same time failed to produce most of the intended reduction and restructuring of the Soviet labor force.

EXPLAINING THE LIMITS OF EMPLOYMENT REFORM

Why was the reform's impact on employment patterns so limited? First, reform policies did not create sufficient incentives and pressures to induce managers to cut deeply into their labor force. Levels of mechanization and automation in industry remained well below those anticipated, so enterprises continued to rely heavily on manual labor. As a result, targets for reductions of manual laborers regularly went unfulfilled.[82] Second, though pressures for cost-accounting and profitability did increase, financial pressures rarely became severe enough to overcome the strong managerial propensity to hoard productive labor. Indeed, the dominant response of "redistributing workers basically within the enterprise" was a familiar subterfuge that had been used by managers in past reforms to retain labor in the face of central pressures for reductions combined with uncertainty and generalized labor scarcity.[83] Reform policies did, on the other hand, give managers both leeway and incentives to rid their enterprises of marginally productive workers. The Resolution on Employment relieved managers of responsibility for the placement of those released, while dismissals of modest numbers of the least productive qualified as a response of sorts to central demands for productivity increases and labor force reductions.

The reformist leadership was also somewhat complicit in the redistribution scheme. Gorbachev himself, always on the defensive about the prospect of unemployment, repeatedly stressed that millions of existing vacancies in Soviet industry were available to absorb released workers. The Resolution on Employment provided that those released from a particular enterprise had priority in assignment to any suitable vacant position within that enterprise, and indicated an expectation that many excess workers would be so reabsorbed. Gorbachev encouraged the increase in shift coefficients, an approach which was strongly favored by the trade unions as an alternative to layoffs.[84] So the central leadership seemed to facilitate managers' labor-hoarding behavior, at least in part because of the reformers' own ambivalence about layoffs and unemployment.

Finally, while labor officials regularly insisted that the state was preparing to manage large-scale transfers of workers, little progress was made in setting up labor bureaus or retraining and placement services. Available facilities were universally assessed as inadequate to handle even the modest levels of displacement which did occur.[85] Overall, the reformist government failed to create the conditions (especially technological conditions—automation, mechanization) for the large-scale release of workers, to enforce the policy on managers, and to create the state labor bureaus which would have been necessary to manage the anticipated scale of worker displacement and transfer. These failures amounted to an effective retreat from the ambitious plans for labor force restructuring and institution building set in 1987 and 1988. They also meant that, with few exceptions, Soviet workers remained securely employed at the end of the Twelfth Five-Year Plan.

Another major element of Gorbachev's economic reform, the transfer of enterprises to self-financing and cost accountability under the June 1987 Law on the State Enterprise, also threatened employment security by raising the prospect that workers would be released en masse from bankrupt enterprises. As I have noted, substantial numbers of unprofitable industrial enterprises had long been maintained in the Soviet economy by a combination of ministerial cross-subsidization and lax industrial credit. In the summer and fall of 1988, the Gorbachev leadership did begin serious enforcement of the bankruptcy provision. Tightened credit policies pushed scores of enterprises to the brink of collapse, while the reformers declared their intent to cut the industrial subsidies which accounted for much of the large budget deficit. However, at the fall 1988 Planning and Budget meetings the reformers retreated, renewing most subsidies and setting out new options for reorganization of loss-makers. (For a closer examination of the development of policy toward insolvent enterprises, see chapter 5).

The Impact of Reform on Wages and Quality Control

The wage reform that was broadly implemented in Soviet industry initially produced some of the intended effects on wage distribution and efficient use of labor. By May 1988, slightly more than one-half of all workers in material production had been transferred to the new wage system. Average wage increases for engineering and technical personnel were, as intended, greater than those for production workers.[86] In many enterprises the reform produced labor productivity gains, and cuts in the size of the labor force. Through 1987, overall increases in industrial productivity exceeded wage increases. Despite problems with the design of the new legislation, managerial foot-dragging, and leveling pressures on the shop floor, the early effects of the new wage policies were positive.[87] The reform was introducing greater differentiation and discipline into industrial wage structures, reversing the Brezhnev-era trends toward egalitarianism and state subsidizing of wage levels.

Like wage reform, *gospriemka* also achieved early successes. State quality controllers were placed in some 1,500 factories at the beginning of 1987 and reportedly rejected more than 15 percent of products on initial presentation.[88] In January 1988, the system was extended to more than 700 additional enterprises, including some in the construction industry.[89] Quality controllers sent substandard output back for improvement or rejected it outright, and in some cases halted production lines and construction projects because of violations in technical standards.[90] As a result plans went unfulfilled, production indicators fell, and managers and workers lost wages and bonuses. Performance pressures on the shop floor intensified at affected enterprises. The state product acceptance system was undercutting the lax labor regime and guaranteed income of the Brezhnev-era social contract.

In the course of 1988, however, the impact of reform policies on both wages and quality control markedly weakened. Wage discipline deteriorated sharply, and enterprises began to raise workers' wages well above both reform targets and productivity gains. According to Janet Chapman: "Through 1987 the increase in productivity was somewhat greater than the increase in wages in industry . . . but in 1988 wage increases [outstripped] productivity . . . Abel Aganbegyan reported: 'In 1988 we lost control over salaries. Pay increases were two times higher than planned.'"[91] By the end of the year, uncontrolled wage increases in industry had become the norm, with wages reportedly increasing faster than productivity at more than one-half of Soviet enterprises. As Table 4.3 shows, the rate of quarterly increases in average wages and salaries doubled in 1988 (from less than 4 percent on average during 1987 to almost 8 percent), and continued to rise in 1989 and 1990. Meanwhile, as Figure 4.1 shows,

Table 4.3 Growth of Soviet wages by quarter, 1988–1990

Wages	1988				1989				1990
	I	II	III	IV	I	II	III	IV	I
Average wages and salaries (rubles/month)	214	216	218	232	235	239	237	252	257
Increase over same quarter in previous year (%)	4.0	8.0	7.5	8.1	9.8	10.6	8.7	8.6	9.4

Source: PlanEcon Report, vol. 6, nos. 46–47, Nov. 23, 1990, p. 8. All statistics are *PlanEcon* reconstructions or estimates. Note that this table refers to *nominal* wages only; for statistics on real wage levels during the same period, and their comparison with nominal wages, see chapter 5.

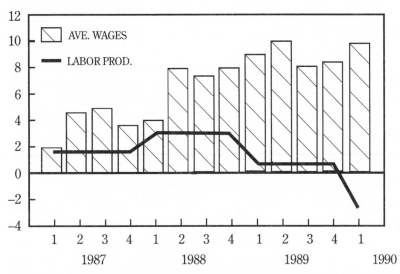

Figure 4.1 Average wages and salaries and overall labor productivity, 1987–1990. *Source:* "Soviet Economic Performance during the First Quarter of 1990," *PlanEcon Report,* vol. 6, no. 16, April 20, 1990, p. 3.

labor productivity growth remained consistently below wage increases, and from the fourth quarter of 1988, wages increased while productivity plummeted.

Enforcement and further extension of the state product-acceptance system also faltered during 1988. Summary Goskomstat statistics indicate that *gospriemka* officials were rejecting only 8 percent of output on first submission during that year, a decline of almost one-half from the previous year.[92] At the July 1988 Council of Ministers session the draft law "On Quality Control," which would have extended *gospriemka* and increased the authority of Gosstandart, met substantial opposition. Long in preparation, the draft was sent back for revision and further implementation was postponed indefinitely. That fall V. Omelianchuk, the Gosstandart official who headed *gospriemka,* stated that the system was up against many difficulties and much resistance.[93]

EXPLAINING THE LIMITS OF WAGE AND QUALITY REFORM

How can the deterioration and breakdown of reform policies on wages and quality control, after their initial period of successful implementation, be explained? One major factor was the opposition from industrial workers and managers provoked by the early effects of both policies.

In the fall of 1987, Soviet workers began striking to protest reductions in pay which had resulted from the introduction of either new wage determination schemes or *gospriemka.* The Soviet press contained detailed reports of some two dozen strikes over the following months, along with indications that there were many more—indeed, that by the summer of 1988 sporadic strike activity had become common.[94] The strikes affected various sectors. In most reported cases, pay cuts were the triggering issue and central grievance. The strikes brought a rapid response from local party and government (and sometimes higher-level) authorities, who typically negotiated with the workers or their designated representatives, agreed to meet most demands, and often replaced managers of striking plants. The partial democratization of the Soviet system at once emboldened the strikers and disoriented the authorities; workers used pro-reform slogans referring to "labor collectives' initiative and independence," and their newly conferred rights of self-management, to justify their actions.

The reformers were caught in a contradiction between democratization and industrial reform. They had called for worker (and other societal) political activism but, at least in the areas of wages and quality control, failed to convince workers to support reform goals. Instead, workers were using their new political rights to defend elements of the old social contract against reform policies. Nevertheless, the Gorbachev leadership continued a rather indiscriminate support for workers' protests against alleged bureaucrats and recalcitrant managers, thereby encouraging a pattern of managerial concessions to strikers on wages and other issues. The strikes of 1987 and 1988 were not large, long, or well organized, but most gained their goals quickly and easily. Moreover, by late 1988 industrial managers were motivated to increase wages not only by pressures from below, but also by inflation in the consumer economy and easy opportunities to increase prices for their products.[95]

In the case of *gospriemka,* worker and managerial interests largely coincided because all enterprise incomes remained tied to plan fulfillment, which strict quality control threatened. Workers struck to protest loss of wages or bonuses resulting from quality controllers' rejection of their products.[96] Managers lobbied against the system and joined forces with ministerial officials to oppose and defeat the draft law "On Quality Control" at the July 1988 Council of Ministers meeting, thus blocking further extension of *gospriemka.*[97] Managerial personnel shared with workers a clear-cut, material interest in low production standards, and in the face of their combined opposition the reformers backed off.

Cooperatives and Privatization of Services

The cooperative movement also began to develop rapidly in 1988. By the end of that year, approximately 48,000 cooperatives had been established in the Soviet Union, and they employed more than three-quarters of a million people.[98] The cooperatives offered goods and services at prices well above those found in the state sector, and paid their workers much higher incomes; in 1989, average cooperative pay was over 500 rubles per month, more than twice the national average for wages and salaries (see Table 4.3).[99] High prices and high wages sparked public hostility to the cooperatives, which were charged with unfair competition by state factory workers and managers (who labored under wage and price controls that were not applied to co-ops), and with speculation.

While most cooperatives worked in light consumer goods and services and construction, some provided for-profit social services.[100] During 1987 and 1988, medical care, rest homes, child care, and other services were offered on a limited basis to users who paid fees, while doctors and other providers were given expanded rights to supplement their state salaries with private practices.[101] Privatization of social services was, however, introduced slowly and ambivalently, with resistance from local officials as well as public criticism of excessive fees, abuses, and the harmful intrusion of the profit motive. In the critical area of health care, for example, a bold liberalization of regulations on private medical practices in the fall of 1988 was quickly reversed amid charges that doctors were using state clinic facilities for their private profit. The reversal of this decision will be examined more closely in chapter 5.

Conclusion: Gorbachev's Policies Constrained

The Gorbachev leadership repeatedly drew back from measures which threatened to abrogate the old social contract. In spite of its explicit commitment to reformist labor and social policies, and its apparent readiness (in most cases) to accept and deal with the social consequences, the leadership retreated when confronted with real costs, bureaucratic resistance, and societal opposition. The record for implementation of reformist labor and social policies is one of retreats, reversals, delays, and decisions to avert most harsh consequences in the social sphere.

Reform policies did result in some erosion of labor's social contract guarantees: some workers (mostly marginal) were released from their jobs, others lost wages, and many experienced unaccustomed economic insecurity. Some social services were privatized, and retail price reforms and subsidy cuts were anticipated. But in each case, by early 1989 new decisions or concessions had limited the painful effects for workers: factories were allowed to reabsorb released workers, bankrupt enterprises were bailed out, wage discipline was relaxed, quality control for the most part was abandoned, privatization was severely limited, and retail price reform was indefinitely delayed. Though willing to cut back somewhat on social and economic security, the reformers acted as if unwilling to take measures which would cut deeply into the old guarantees or adversely affect the welfare of broad social strata. Alfred Evans reaches a similar conclusion in his study of social policy under Gorbachev: "As the Gorbachev leadership . . . more sharply sensed rumblings of discontent from those who [felt] protected by existing guarantees, it [became] more cautious and hesitant in approaching resolution of some of the tasks most essential for successful economic restructuring."[102]

This pattern of policy retreats fits the hypothesis that a social contract, conceived of as a set of societal expectations and state obligations, constrained the Gorbachev leadership from pursuing its chosen reform strategy. The reformers made extensive preparations to jettison (or radically alter) the old contract in the interests of economic and moral revitalization of the Soviet system. They made it clear that the state no longer intended to deliver the policy and allocational outcomes (secure employment, etc.) required by the contract. But in the end they proved unwilling to follow through on their stated intentions to abrogate the contract's provisions. They acted, in other words, as if constrained to deliver the package of social contract policy goods, even in the face of their own preference for different policy and allocation decisions.

Chapter 5 will analyze more closely the causes of retreat from reformist social policies in 1988 and 1989, by presenting three case studies. The evidence will show that both bureaucratic resistance and popular protest played a role in undermining reformist social policies. However, even in those cases when the leadership had adequate political instruments to push through its programs, it retreated. The case studies will buttress the argument that, ultimately, the reformers' own reluctance to violate long-established expectations and entitlements proved the critical factor in defeating the reform.

FIVE

Job Security, Medical Services, and Price Stability under Gorbachev

---

This chapter presents case studies of policy-making under Gorbachev on central social contract issues: job security, socialized services, and price stability. The first case examines policy toward insolvent enterprises, the second focuses on privatization of medical services, and the third concerns pricing policy. Each case study follows the development of policy from the initiation of reform in 1987 to a pressured decision point, at which the Gorbachev leadership faced a clear-cut choice between continued pursuit of reform policies and maintenance of the social contract. Study of these decision points should indicate whether the social contract constrained Gorbachev's policy-making.

Constraint is in effect when leaders consistently deliver social contract policy in the face of rising costs, declining resources, and pressures to make different policy and allocational decisions. I have shown that the Brezhnev leadership maintained the contract even under such stresses. There is also evidence (in the cases of full employment and price subsidies) that the Brezhnev regime's decisions were strongly influenced by concern about workers' expectations and their potential responses to the contract's violation. However, the question of constraint remains somewhat complicated by the Brezhnev leadership's self-proclaimed paternalism—its ideological and normative commitment to comprehensive state provision of welfare.

The critical decisions of the Gorbachev period provide a better test of constraint, for two reasons. First, the Gorbachev leadership did not share its predecessor's paternalism; the new leaders and their social theorists had repudiated both the ideology and practice of comprehensive state provision. Second, while the Brezhnev leadership faced increased costs and various competing pressures and claimants in its decisions to maintain the social contract, it was not clearly committed to any alternative set of socioeconomic policies.[1] By contrast the Gorbachev leadership was strongly committed to a reform program which would undercut all basic provisions of the contract.

The three case studies are designed to determine what factors drove the leadership's decisions. They are sensitive to the role of bureaucratic resistance (which is seen by many analysts as the central factor inhibiting reform), and they seek to sort out the effects of bureaucratic resistance, popular opposition, and the political leadership's own reluctance to abrogate the old contract. They benefit from the relative openness of the Gorbachev period, presenting much fuller and more detailed pictures of policy-making than in the Brezhnev-era case studies.

The Politics of Enterprise Insolvency

The bankruptcy provision of the Law on the State Enterprise is a particularly useful case for study of the reformist policy process, because its implementation was at once economically necessary, politically threatening, and measurable. Within the complex and sometimes convoluted politics of reform, enterprise insolvencies and bankruptcies are comparatively concrete and quantifiable; we can trace fairly clearly the major decisions on this issue, and see the extent of their potential and actual effects. And the policy on insolvency was one of the points in the reform program where the demands of welfare and efficiency clashed most starkly. Enterprise bankruptcies would have led to mass layoffs and dislocation of workers, thereby cutting to the core of the social contract's provisions for secure jobs and stable incomes. At the same time, bankruptcies would have served the pressing economic need to eliminate thousands of obsolete and inefficient production facilities, which tied up vast financial and labor resources.

Stage 1: Projected Impact of the Bankruptcy Provision
During the Brezhnev period, Soviet enterprises operated with a safety net which protected them from insolvency and closure regard-

less of their individual performance or profitability. In the spring of 1987, as the reformist leadership prepared its program for restructuring the management system, the Brezhnev-era practices of lax credit and cross-subsidization came under fire. At an early June economic conference, Gorbachev criticized the ministries for failing to improve performance of unprofitable enterprises, and declared that the practice of redistributing assets from the more efficient to the loss-makers must end.[2] At the Central Committee Plenum later that month, speaking of the safety net policies which had contributed to the protracted maintenance of large numbers of poorly managed, technologically obsolete plants, he concluded, "As the years went by, this system came into ever sharper contradiction with the conditions for, and requirements of, economic development."[3] Prime Minister Ryzhkov, reporting to the Supreme Soviet in late June, complained that credit was frequently used to cover "thriftlessness," and that payment discipline had badly deteriorated.[4]

The Law on the State Enterprise mandated termination of these practices, with the transition of all enterprises to economic accountability, self-financing, and self-management over the following two years. Article 23 of the law made explicit provision for bankruptcy, and specified the following conditions: "The activities of an enterprise should be terminated (1) if there is no need for its further operation and it cannot be reorganized; (2) when an enterprise has operated at a loss for a long time and is insolvent; when there is no demand for its output; and when measures taken by the enterprise and higher-level agencies to ensure profitability have brought no results."[5] It was shortly followed by the "Basic Provisions for Radical Restructuring of Economic Management," which laid out plans for a broad reform of the finance, credit-granting, banking, planning, and pricing systems.[6]

Finance Minister Gostev reported that, at the time of the enterprise law's passage, approximately 13 percent of Soviet enterprises operated at a loss, while a total of 25 percent in industry and construction were loss-making or low-profitability enterprises and "would have difficulty working in the new conditions of management."[7] Unprofitability was unevenly distributed by sector and region, with some ministries experiencing considerably higher than average rates, and some entire sectors virtually bankrupt.[8] Moreover, while the reformers preferred to stress poor management and lax workers as the main causes of low profitability, central pricing policies and obsolete equipment were at least equally to blame. Many production facilities and some whole sectors (for example, coal) were rendered unprofitable by state price controls which required enterprises to sell their output below its cost of production. Others, especially older facilities, performed badly because they had long been deprived of investment for retooling and plant modernization.

In his speech to the Supreme Soviet at the end of June, Ryzhkov set the policy agenda for unprofitable enterprises. He instructed the ministries to "elaborate specific measures and define concrete timetables for the elimination of losses at each enterprise," and recommended retooling, improvements in organization of production, and strengthening of labor discipline.[9] If such measures failed, enterprises would be reorganized or closed according to the provisions of the enterprise law. The prime minister affirmed his government's intent to eliminate loss-making by the end of the Twelfth Five-Year Plan.

The reform program was further elaborated in mid-July by a series of decrees on finance, banking, and pricing which had direct relevance to the insolvency issue. The decree "On Restructuring the Financial Mechanism" restricted the ministries' rights to engage in cross-subsidization by prohibiting confiscation and redistribution of enterprises' profits in excess of firmly set normatives.[10] The decree "On Improvement of the Banking System" instructed banks to extend financing to enterprises entirely on the basis of financial criteria of creditworthiness, and to end extension of credit to those that systematically failed to meet repayment terms. It also gave banks the right to declare insolvent enterprises which did not keep up payments, to notify their suppliers, to place them on special payment regimes, and to submit to their ministries proposals for reorganization or closure.[11] Finally, the decree "On Reconstructing the System of Prices" promised new industrial wholesale prices which would cover production costs and eliminate economically unjustified losses and profitability variations in production and sale of goods.[12]

However, as Aslund and others have argued, these decrees contained qualifications and inconsistencies which raise some serious questions about their likely effectiveness.[13] The decree on the financial mechanism proposed temporarily waiving or reducing payments for loss-making or low-profit enterprises (in effect, proposing variable normatives). The decree on banking hedged on the issue of credit to loss-makers, stipulating that superior organs might under some conditions allocate resources. Most troubling, the decree on pricing promised introduction of wholesale prices which would consistently cover production costs in 1990–91, that is, only after the full transition to self-financing had been completed for one to two years. There was also, as Hewett and others have noted, a contradiction in the reformers' policy toward the ministries: on the one hand Ryzhkov instructed the ministries to aid financially troubled enterprises with retooling and other measures, while on the other hand the reform decrees sought to restrict ministries' access to the necessary financial resources.[14] These inconsistencies were problematic for the reform but, as we shall see below, they did not prevent the newly empowered banks from pushing scores of enterprises toward collapse.

Final preparations for implementing the enterprise law went forward at the fall 1987 Planning and Budget meetings of the Supreme Soviet. Gosplan chair Talyzin laid out plans for the transition to self-financing in 1988 of enterprises producing more than 60 percent of industrial output and employing 55 percent of the work force, a vast proportion of Soviet industry; the remainder were to be transferred in 1989.[15] Gosbank chair Garetovsky stressed that credit facilities would be strictly targeted and require prompt repayment, that late loans would be recalled and financial penalties imposed, and that, based on an "analysis of credit relations within enterprises in different sectors over the last few years," he expected insolvencies and proposals for liquidation of enterprises.[16] Reformist political leaders and economists were almost unanimously enthusiastic about the prospects for self-financing. The one central official voicing cautious dissent was Chairman Shalayev of the All-Union Central Council of Trade Unions (VTsSPS), who stressed economic leaders' lack of preparation for transfer to the new management system (which was scheduled to begin for most of Soviet industry on January 1, 1988, only several weeks hence), and the fear that "a critical situation could develop in the national economy at the beginning of next year . . . many labor collectives . . . [may] find themselves in very unfavorable conditions, with all the ensuing consequences."[17]

Stage 2: Assessing and Confronting the Costs

As the central government prepared to implement the Law on the State Enterprise, local and regional leaders responded with a campaign of special pleading about the hardships it would impose on their jurisdictions, and lobbied for additional time and money. At virtually every party plenum, regional and local party conference, and Supreme Soviet session in the fall of 1987, party officials and other governmental and economic elites assessed their respective regions' "readiness" for self-financing, and found it wanting.[18] They spelled out the implications for their localities, lamenting the poor financial and technical state of many of their enterprises and arguing that it would be impossible for most of these to operate on self-financing principles in the next year or two. They named major enterprises, large-scale employers integral to their respective regional economies, which would become legally insolvent as soon as the law went into effect. The then Kazakh premier N. A. Nazarbayev provided perhaps the best statement of their common grievances:

> Comrades! Growing concern is caused by the degree of readiness of the republic's labor collectives with regard to the USSR Law on the State Enterprise, which is due to come into force. The technical standards of production are still poor at many of them . . . The Karaganda metallurgical combine is in a complex position . . . The bulk of the growth of the country's supplies of tin for the canning industry ought to be produced there, and this has a direct effect on food supplies . . . The combine is not fulfilling its profit plan. We cannot understand how the collective will work under the principle of full economic accounting and self-financing from the start of 1988. Unfortunately, there are many similar examples today.[19]

Provincial authorities insisted that many facilities would require substantial initial investment to become self-supporting, and frequently cited the center's past failures to carry out planned and promised plant modernization. They stressed the injustice and political risks of threatened plant closings.[20] Without opposing the reform directly, they lobbied against its implementation and (as Hewett predicted) engaged in a "struggle for exceptions."[21]

Such regional lobbying and special pleading was standard fare in Soviet politics, but some regional leaders did have compelling grievances against the self-financing legislation.[22] To take the most important instance, much of the Soviet fuel complex (mining, oil, timber) operated at a loss partly because state price controls kept wholesale prices artificially depressed, below production costs.[23] In a report on the problems of the fuel complex in early 1988, A. Komin, first deputy chair of the USSR State Pricing Committee, concluded, "Present prices do not permit us to transfer coal miners, timber producers, and oil extraction workers to economic accountability. We must raise wholesale prices for fuel and other raw materials, in order to allow these sectors to become profitable."[24] Such increases would in turn have to be covered by either larger state subsidies to industry or increased retail prices. But the leadership was determined to cut subsidies, and seemed unwilling to take the political risk of raising retail prices at this stage of the reform.[25] In any case, many obsolete and exhausted facilities (particularly mines) had been kept in operation for decades, creating a large accumulation of facilities which, even with price liberalization, could not become profitable.[26]

A dramatic picture of the reform's implications for regions dependent on fuel production came from the Magaden CPSU Obkom Plenum in late December 1987: the fixed assets of most of Magaden's mining and enrichment combines dated from the 1940s and 1950s, costs of production and transportation were relatively high because of the region's remoteness, and state price controls held fuel prices well below costs. The transition to self-financing in January 1988 would immediately bankrupt some 22 percent of the oblast's 198 enterprises, leading to large-scale layoffs of workers who would find few local opportunities for reemployment.[27] In other mining areas as well, particularly the Donbass, implementation of the Law on Enterprise raised the specter of regional depression.

In the winter and spring of 1988, several central government organs produced reports and investigations assessing the initial impact of self-financing on various economic sectors and regions.[28] A June 1988 report by Gosstroi (State Construction Industry) official V. A. Balakin detailed deep financial troubles in the construction industry.[29] Balakin reported that, while the ministry had managed to improve profitability in all-union construction organizations, almost one-half of trusts in the national construction complex remained loss-making or barely profitable in April 1988. In the same month, *Sotsialisticheskaia Industriia* published an assessment by Gosplan staffers of work under cost accounting in five industrial sectors. They concluded that most of the enterprises had not fulfilled their profit plans; that between one-third (in the USSR Ministry of Chemical and Petroleum Machine Building) and one-half (in the USSR Ministry of Instrument Making, Automation Equipment, and Control Systems and the Ministry of the Automotive Industry) had begun self-financing with substantial debts, shortages of working capital, and much worn and obsolete equipment; that the requirements of self-financing had, for the most part, aggravated both financial and technical problems; and that, at the time of the investigation, many of the enterprises were "on the verge of collapse."[30]

Additional evidence confirms the strained financial state in many production sectors as self-financing went into effect. Published data on the percentages of low-profit and loss-making enterprises in 1987 and early 1988 indicate that they included almost 50 percent in construction, 38 percent in machine-building, and about 30 percent in light industry.[31] Under conditions of genuine self-financing and cost accountability, virtually all of these enterprises would face severe financial strain, loss of credit facilities, and probable dissolution within the next few years.

Stage 3: Rising Issue Salience and the First Stream of Insolvencies

The transfer of Soviet enterprises to self-financing and economic accountability began on a limited basis in 1987, and was to be implemented in all sectors of material production during 1988 and 1989. The reported numerical results seemed impressive: by the end of 1988, according to Goskomstat, 19,000 industrial enterprises employing 55 percent of the total number of workers were operating on the basis of full cost accountability.[32] However, the substantive effects on industry's financing principles and operations remained limited. Few enterprises were fully subjected to self-financing requirements, while ministries continued to play a role in funding and subsidization as well as to dictate production plans.[33] Reports to the 19th Party Conference in June 1988 show that ministries were continuing to recentralize and redistribute enterprises' earnings, at once undermining the Law on Enterprise, angering managers and workers from profitable enterprises, and sustaining the substantial minority of weak enterprises.[34] For the first several months of 1988 the banks seemed to cooperate: industrial credit remained lax.

A few bankruptcies of marginal facilities were reported in the summer of that year. The Ukrainian Ministry of Local Industry closed down a sewn-goods factory which had been established twenty years earlier to provide work for surplus female labor in a mining region of Lvov Oblast. The factory had received no investment since its creation, and had a backlog of fines for short or unacceptable deliveries that had absorbed recent subsidies intended to improve its productivity for the transition to self-financing. As a marginal facility with poor infrastructure, poor-quality products, and a female labor force, it was the exception that proved vulnerable to reform pressures. Some of its shops were transferred to another factory, while the remaining workers were left unemployed. Three agricultural-machine–building factories in Saratov Oblast also went bankrupt in August. They were in a sector of poor performers, and each had additional problems of large-scale indebtedness, fines, or unsalable products. There were also reports of some bankruptcies in construction, and a few cases of recently legalized cooperatives taking over insolvent production facilities.[35]

In the late summer and fall of 1988, the salience of the unprofitability issue rose in conjunction with the issue of the recently acknowledged budget deficit. At the fall 1988 Planning and Budget meetings, the Gorbachev leadership for the first time seriously examined the patterns and causes of deficit spending, and pointed to industrial subsidies as one of the main drains on the state budget. The reformers declared their intent to reduce both deficit and subsidies, in part by eliminating enterprise loss-making. At the same time, tightening bank credit increased pressures on financially weak enterprises, and led to the first stream of reported insolvencies in September and October.

Gorbachev raised the issue of the large and growing Soviet budget deficit at the July 1988 Central Committee Plenum.[36] As is shown in Table 5.1, the deficit was rising rapidly during this period, increasing from R18 billion in 1985 to almost R50 billion in 1986, and nearly doubling again to R90 billion in 1988. (But official figures cited by Finance Minister Gostev at this time were much lower: R35 billion for 1988 and R37 billion projected for 1989.) Gorbachev insisted that measures to reduce the deficit, among them large-scale replacement of budget-financing and ministerial subsidies with bank credit, be included in preparing the 1989 plan and budget.

The Council of Ministers' Meetings on the Draft State Plan also addressed the deficit-insolvency link in September, while the State Committee for Statistics reported that combined losses from the run-

Table 5.1 USSR state budget deficit, 1985–1990

Year	In billions of rubles (nominal)	As percent of GNP
1985	18.0	2.3
1986	47.9	6.0
1987	57.1	6.9
1988	90.1	10.3
1989	91.8	9.9
1990	100.0 (est.)	10.5 (est.)

Source: Anders Aslund, "Gorbachev, Perestroyka, and Economic Crisis," *Problems of Communism,* Jan.-Apr. 1991, p. 24. Aslund's figures are based on official Soviet data; numbers for 1990 were estimated by Aslund. *PlanEcon* has different figures for estimated deficits, but in most cases the differences are not great. Gostev gave budget deficit figures of R35 billion for 1988 and R37 billion for 1989, but these are universally considered much too low. See *PlanEcon Report,* vol. 4, no. 41, Nov. 4, 1988, p. 10.

ning of factories cost the state R12 billion in 1987 (of a then-claimed deficit of R35 billion).[37] When submitting the draft budget the following month, Finance Minister Gostev stated that approximately 24,000 enterprises in various sectors were operating at a loss, and asserted that the budget deficit "is a result of . . . the policy of extensive subsidies and huge losses . . . parasitic attitudes, and passive financial policy."[38] The Council of Ministers' meeting demanded that management organs submit programs to eliminate loss-making at enterprises under their jurisdiction. For those that had no realistic prospects of operating profitably, the Council recommended amalgamation with a profitable enterprise, leasing out of equipment, or dissolution.[39] The political pressures on insolvent enterprises were mounting.

At the same time state banks, now operating under cost accounting principles, tightened industrial credit. With strong support from the Finance Ministry, the banks intensified pressures on poor performers by publishing lists of insolvent enterprises, pressing their management to meet repayment deadlines, and cutting off credit to some plants which had large and mounting debts. For example, in mid-September the USSR Industrial Construction Bank declared insolvent some fifty enterprises and organizations which had "systemati-cally violated payment discipline." The following week, the Bank for Housing and Social Construction published a list of seventeen insol-vent enterprises, referring for authority to Article 23 of the Law on Enterprise. The list continued, with a few ministries even proposing dissolution of the least viable plants under their jurisdictions. A total of some 300 enterprises were reportedly declared insolvent by the beginning of 1989, constituting the first significant stream of insol-vencies in the history of the Soviet economy.[40]

Threatened enterprises in turn sought both political and financial help from their supervising ministries and local party and govern-ment authorities. Most managed to make at least temporary deals, which kept them in operation and saved their workers from layoffs and loss of wages. In one case, both the party *gorkom* (city commit-tee) and *obkom* (oblast, or regional committee), as well as the factory manager and its newly created labor-collective council, lobbied the relevant ministry to allocate funds for the factory's transition to a new line of production.[41] In another case, the city soviet agreed to pay workers' average wages from its budget during reorganization of an insolvent local enterprise. In still a third, a ministry in effect "re-bought" one of its own insolvent plants from the bank, and returned it to operation. Others were able to arrange extension of credit repay-ment schedules, guarantees for additional loans, or other emergency funding, with local party and soviet authorities often directly pressur-ing banks to cooperate.[42] Only some of the most marginal failed to find support and were forced into outright bankruptcy and closed.

Critical Decision Point: Bankruptcies or Bailouts?

In the fall of 1988, reform policies were beginning to impose some measure of financial discipline in Soviet industry. Credit had been cut off for scores of insolvent enterprises and (in spite of intervention by local political authorities) proceedings to close, auction, or dis-solve many plants were in progress. At the same time, the leadership had declared its determination to cut the large budget deficit by cur-tailing subsidies to loss-makers. The stage was set for the reformers to make the hard decisions, to follow through with enforcement of the Law on the State Enterprise by slashing subsidies to unprofitable plants, endorsing the Ministry of Finance's tight credit policies, and forcing the financially and technically weakest enterprises into bank-ruptcy. (It might also have targeted smaller subsidies for moderniza-tion of more viable plants and for continuing support to industries hurt most by pricing policies.) At this critical decision point, as the results of the fall Planning and Budget meetings show, the leadership instead retreated from the policy course it had set.

The fall Planning and Budget meetings produced two decisions which were directly relevant to the future of loss-making enterprises. First, the budget called for maintenance of the bulk (some 70 per-cent) of state subsidies to industry in 1989. The leadership estab-lished a goal of reducing subsidies to loss-making plants by 30 per-cent in 1989, and announced its intention to phase out such subsidies entirely in 1990.[43] Thus, the hard decision was again delayed, and a theoretically "final," somewhat reduced round of state aid was appor-tioned to industry for production modernization (with some sugges-tions that it was to be repaid once enterprises had become profitable). It was assumed, against all reason, that this subsidy would be ade-quate to solve industry's problems, and that massive cuts could be made more easily next year. Second, the meetings elaborated a set of options for the reorganization and financing of those enterprises which proved incapable of eliminating losses, including merger or amalgamation with profitable plants whose revenues could cover losses and, for small and medium-size plants, conversion to lease con-tracts or cooperatives. The possibility of selling shares to members of the enterprise collective or to outsiders was added by new legisla-tion in October.[44]

The leadership decisions of fall 1988 virtually ended reports of bankruptcies. The unprofitable could continue to limp along on state and ministerial subsidies, merge, or seek private financing through conversion to lease contracts, share holding, or cooperatives (a viable alternative mainly for small, light-industry plants). Indeed, available data indicate that the reformers continued to increase industrial sub-sidies over the following two years: subsidies (to heavy industry only) grew from R6.7 billion in 1988 to R7.5 billion in 1989 and R8.5 billion (planned) for 1990.[45]

But the fall 1988 decisions relieved the pressure on insolvent enter-prises without providing either sufficient means or incentives for them to modernize and to improve efficiency and output quality. It left in place the fundamental problem of Soviet industry which reform was intended to resolve—the thousands of inefficient, overstaffed, obsolete production facilities which tied up labor, investment funds, energy, and materials. Moreover, enterprise managements soon realized that, as monopolistic or near-monopolistic suppliers, they could respond to profitability pressures by increasing prices and output of their more expensive product lines. This tactic, which was adopted on a large scale by 1989, was extremely damaging to the overall reform process because it fueled inflation and contributed to severe shortages of inexpensive consumer goods.

Reformist policy toward insolvent enterprises suffered from some fundamental inconsistencies, especially on pricing policy. It also met considerable bureaucratic and political opposition: ministerial, regional, and local authorities intervened at various points in an effort to protect threatened enterprises, first lobbying for exceptions and additional resources, then providing direct aid to plants which had come under pressure from the banks. As with layoffs, it was only the marginal enterprises that failed to find defenders and succumbed easily to reform pressures. The allies and survival strategies available to most insolvent enterprises in the face of the Ministry of Finance's tight credit policies provide a sense of the resilience of the old safety net, the density of the protective institutional network blocking reform. But this bureaucratic resistance was not decisive in blocking the reformist agenda.

In the case of enterprise insolvency, the Gorbachev leadership *did* have instruments sufficient to implement its policy to at least some extent: it had state financial institutions with the will and means to call in loans and deny operating funds to insolvent plants, and it had some control over the level of industrial subsidies. Moreover, financial instruments were beginning to have some effect in the fall of 1988, pushing significant numbers of the weakest enterprises toward collapse despite the resistance of ministries and local politicians. It was precisely at this point, confronting for the first time the real effects and costs of its policies, that the leadership retreated. In spite of its declared commitment to self-financing and deficit reduction, Gorbachev's government decided to bail out insolvent enterprises, and it proposed other alternatives to closure which left industry's fundamental problems in place. In the fall of 1988, the reformist leadership decided to preserve enterprises and jobs rather than to pursue its policies to their logical conclusions.

Some months later the reformist economist Abalkin addressed the continuing problems of insolvent enterprises. "Loss-making factories must be closed down . . . [but] the *political will* on plant closures had been lacking despite provisions for bankruptcy in legislation which came into force one year ago . . . on this wave of enthusiasm . . . we drew up our future plans . . . Everything proved much more complicated. The social and psychological situation in the country . . ."[46]

Privatization of Medical Services

I discussed in chapter 2 the accumulating problems and evidence of deterioration that existed in the Soviet health care sector by the end of the Brezhnev period. The reformist leadership clearly recognized and broadly publicized these deficiencies. Gorbachev's newly appointed minister of health, Dr. Yevgenii I. Chazov, quickly established a reputation as a harsh critic of his domain; in official speeches and interviews during 1987 and 1988, Chazov castigated the system for its poorly trained and underqualified doctors, dilapidated physical facilities, obsolete diagnostic equipment, unproductive research institutes, chronic shortages of basic supplies and medicines, incapacity to perform procedures already common abroad (for example, coronary bypass surgery, organ transplants), low pay, routine extortion of bribes, and inattentive and irresponsible attitude to patients.[47]

Chazov's criticisms were echoed by both other medical professionals and officials, and by the Soviet public.[48] Indeed, though free medical services were one of the most broadly and highly-valued policy outputs of the Soviet state in the 1970s, VTsIOM's opinion polling showed that deep public dissatisfaction with the quality of those services had developed over the following years. Table 5.2 indicates that by 1990 a large majority—74 percent—of Soviets were dissatisfied with the public health service, and that this number rose to 80 percent and more for residents of larger cities and those with higher education. Finally, the reformers' ideological critique of universal state provision and excessive egalitarianism was applied to the health sector's problems, producing claims of wage leveling among medical workers, insufficient options for patients, and much de facto privilege and corruption.[49]

In their efforts to address these myriad problems, the Gorbachev

Table 5.2 Attitudes toward the public health service, in USSR and by size of settlement, 1990

Question: Are you satisfied with the public health service in the Soviet Union?[a]	Population Point				
	USSR	Moscow, Leningrad	Oblast center	Small city	Village
Nearer to satisfied	16%	10%	10%	20%	17%
Nearer to dissatisfied	74	86	80	69	74
Difficult to answer	10	4	9	11	9

Source: Adapted from *Obshchestvennoe Mnenie v Tsifrakh,* vyp. 4, ("Sotsialnaia Zashchishchennost' glazami naseleniia"), (Moscow: VTsIOM, 1991), p. 9. Other parts of the survey showed that this pattern of attitudes was held among Soviets of all ages and levels of education; 25 to 54-year-olds were slightly more dissatisfied (77%), and those over 55 and under 24 slightly less dissatisfied (69% and 70%, respectively) than the average. Eighty-five percent of those with higher educations were dissatisfied, as were 74–75% of those with secondary and specialized secondary educations, and 69% of those with nine years of school and less. Among regions, Belorussians were significantly more satisfied (28%) than Ukrainians and Russians (11% and 16%, respectively). Information on the organization and methods used in the survey may be found on pp. 3–5 of the report.

a. Literally, "Are you satisfied with how problems of public health service in the Soviet Union are resolved?"

leadership adopted an ambitious program which involved two major components: first, large-scale increases in state funding for the development and modernization of socialized health services; and second, an increase in the provision of private medical services offered to the public on a for-fee basis.[50] In this case study I will concentrate on policy toward the privatization of medical care during 1986 through 1989, tracing the liberalization of policy and the expansion of paid services during these years and then focusing on the critical decision to restrict privatization at the end of 1988.[51]

Stage 1: Plans for Restructuring the Health Sector

In 1985, according to official sources, legally paid medical services comprised approximately 0.4 percent of overall Soviet public health services. This tiny paid sector, which had apparently been in existence since the 1920s and consisted mainly of out-patient clinics, was heavily regulated and taxed, and starved for resources.[52] The first reformist proposals for privatization of medical care spoke in terms of expanding this network of fee-for-service polyclinics. In July 1986, the USSR Ministry of Public Health announced that the volume of paid services would increase by 60 percent during the Twelfth Five-Year Plan. The ministry also announced plans for the opening of for-fee clinics in all republic capitals and all cities which had medical schools, and proposed the establishment of fee-charging chronic-care hospitals.[53] In the fall of 1987 the major pronouncement on reform of the health care sector, the "(Draft) Basic Guidelines for Development of Health Protection and Restructuring of Public Health in the Twelfth Five-Year Plan and up to the Year 2000," further stipulated that the volume of paid medical services to the population would be increased five times by the end of the year 2000.[54]

While radical in approving the principle and extending the practice of private, paid services, the planned percentage increases (from a base of less than 0.5 percent) would have affected only about 2 percent of medical services over the following fifteen years. Moreover, the Gorbachev leadership simultaneously proposed increases in state funding for medical services: The 27th Congress resolutions promised that investment in the medical system would grow by 60 percent during the Twelfth Five-Year Plan.[55] An October 1986 joint party, government, and trade union resolution allocated R3.45 billion to raise wages (and increase wage differentiation and incentive pay) for public health workers.[56] The "Basic Guidelines" proposed a long list of improvements in everything from medical education to polyclinics' physical plant, improvements which Chazov claimed would be financed by nearly tripling overall state capital investment for public health.[57] And, as with other reform policies, the leadership was defensive about privatization of medical care. In spite of the months of scathing criticism of the state system, the "Basic Guidelines" lauded free medical treatment as a great achievement of socialism, while both Chazov and other officials repeatedly promised that paid services would be used only to supplement state provision, and that "The foundation of the system will remain medical services accessible to everyone . . . social guarantees of health care."[58]

But privatized medical services were also expanding during these years by a separate route and at an unplanned rate, under the new legislation on individual labor activity and cooperatives. The Law on Individual Labor Activity, which went into effect on May 1, 1987, explicitly permitted provision of paid medical services by qualified individuals. The law required medical personnel (and all other state employees) to retain their state jobs and engage in private practice only in their free time, and only on an individual or family basis. It prohibited "medical activity in certain specialties determined in accordance with USSR legislation on public health."[59] Subsequent official commentary on the law specified that private practitioners were restricted from performing surgery, treating infectious diseases, caring for pregnant women and drug addicts, and issuing certificates of illness or disability. Shortly before the law went into effect, the Ministry of Health set down more detailed qualifications, regulations, and criteria for private practices. While these included some guidelines on fees, officials acknowledged that charges would "depend on the qualifications and prestige" of service providers, and left them effectively free of regulation.[60]

The legalization of cooperatives, which proceeded gradually during 1987 and was formalized by the May 26, 1988, Law on Cooperatives, effectively extended the possibilities for privatization to clinics, hospitals, nursing homes, and other types of collective medical practices. The law included medical services in its list of desirable fields for cooperative activity, and prohibited no specialties. It stipulated simply, "Cooperatives are entitled to engage in any kind of activity except those prohibited under USSR and Union Republic law." Cooperatives were given the right to own and lease property, including buildings and equipment, and (within limits) to employ under labor contract individuals who were not cooperative members. The law established procedures and guidelines for the formation, operation, and taxation of cooperatives, and left them free (in the cases of most services) to set whatever prices the market would bear.[61] The legalization of private economic activity, particularly cooperatives, led to a significant expansion of the network of paid medical services and fee-charging facilities, which led in turn to controversy over both the principle and size of charges for health care.

Stage 2: Growth of For-Fee Medical Services

The response of medical professionals to these new opportunities began modestly. By the fall of 1987, some 2,500 had registered for individual labor activity in medical services—a little over 1 percent of the total 200,000 individuals registered under the law.[62] Growth of medical cooperatives was more impressive: first established in 1987, their numbers increased into the thousands in 1988. Medical cooperatives, most of which were clinics offering diagnosis, treatment, or both, were established mainly in large cities, with more than half of the total located in Moscow.[63] Doctors who worked in cooperatives generally had better-than-average qualifications, with one-third reportedly holding advanced degrees. Their salaries averaged approximately R400 per month, twice that of doctors in the state sector. There is considerable evidence that public demand for cooperative services was high, both from Moscovites and among the 50 percent or more of clients who came from out of town to pay for more rapid access or better-quality service than they could get in the state system. The private services most in demand were gynecology (including abortion), neuropathology, and surgery.[64] Most of those patronizing medical cooperatives were reportedly ordinary working people. They paid, on average, 11 rubles for an office visit and 65 rubles for a course of treatment. The first private, for-fee general hospital was also opened in Moscow in the fall of 1987.[65]

All cooperatives in the Soviet context faced difficulties in securing supplies and premises, overcoming official obstructionism, and dealing with public hostility over high prices, high wages, and the perception that they were diverting scarce goods and qualified personnel from the subsidized state sector.[66] Medical cooperatives were no exception. While data from VTsIOM indicates a surprisingly high level of public support for the *principle* that paid medical services should be available as a supplement to state services, most public opinion expressed toward the medical cooperatives was hostile.[67] A *Moscow News* survey in November 1987, for example, showed an absolute majority against all aspects of requiring payment for health care. Soviet citizens complained, to newspapers and to the Ministry of Health, that the cooperatives violated their constitutionally guaranteed right to free medical care.[68] Many questioned the "social justice" of requiring pay for medical services, and questioned even more the morality of denying services to those who could not pay. Both the public and the ministry had credible concerns that the best-qualified personnel would migrate to the private sector, further impoverishing the quality of health care provided by the state.

Like other Soviet cooperatives, those in medical services were vulnerable to the crass profiteering and corruption which fed on the chronic shortages of the Soviet service sector. The most severe shortage in medicine was of advanced diagnostic equipment; the pent-up demand for access, and potential profits for those who could provide it, were commensurately great. Some medical cooperatives specializing in diagnostics worked out arrangements to lease equipment from state clinics and hospitals, and hired technicians to operate it. The cooperatives then charged substantial fees for diagnostic work (for example, 100 rubles for a CAT scan), a good part of which went back to the clinics and hospitals as lease payments.[69] This arrangement lent itself to various types of abuses. Patients complained that state clinics would no longer provide diagnostic tests, but instead would lease the necessary equipment illegally to the fee-charging cooperatives and send patients there for diagnosis. There were charges that the chief physicians leasing out equipment were often on the boards of the cooperatives and profited from their services. The fees, especially of diagnostic cooperatives, were condemned as excessive, exploitive, and resulting in effective denial of medical services to pensioners and the poor.[70] (The cooperatives' defenders replied that black market charges for access to advanced equipment were much higher.)

By the fall of 1988, medical cooperatives were developing rapidly and drawing intense criticism, and had established a union to defend their interests.[71] Patients continued to flock to them. At the same time, public disaffection grew, state clinics were threatened, and cases of abuse (including the sale abroad of scarce medicines, blood, and, in at least one case, organs) and excessive charges attracted much attention. In addition, the majority of doctors apparently shared a critical attitude toward their entrepreneurial colleagues: In mid-October, the USSR Congress of Physicians, meeting in Moscow, voted overwhelmingly for tighter regulation of medical cooperatives.[72]

Critical Decision Point: To Regulate or Prohibit Medical Co-ops?

At the end of 1988, the Law on Cooperatives had been fully in force for six months, and in the medical sector and in general, the results had been decidedly mixed. Officials were deluged with public complaints about the cooperatives, cooperators were becoming organized, and various types of abuses and corruption had developed in the sector. At this point the reformist leadership faced a critical decision: how, and how much, to regulate cooperatives? The logic of the reform program required that the leadership seek to limit serious corruption and allow the sector to continue developing until competition brought down prices and improved service. Instead, however, it further limited the activities of several types of cooperatives, placing particularly harsh restrictions and prohibitions on the provision of private medical services.

Two measures in late 1988 seriously affected the future of medical cooperatives. First, in late October, the USSR Ministry of Health issued Order No. 785, "On the Use of Costly Medical Technology," prohibiting the leasing of "expensive" and "unique" diagnostic equipment to cooperatives.[73] Health Minister Chazov, in the past a supporter of privatization, defended the order as intended only "to eliminate existing violations . . . and provide full and effective use of state equipment for . . . free qualified medical aid."[74] He cited in support of the order the decision by the Congress of Physicians, the deluge of letters claiming denial of free care, and the profiteering of chief physicians. Chazov insisted that he continued to support medical cooperatives for treatment and preventive care, but argued that diagnostic cooperatives must be prohibited because of the acute shortage of advanced diagnostic equipment and the illegality of leasing out equipment needed at state facilities.[75]

Chazov's order was followed in late December by a Council of Ministers' resolution, "On Regulating Individual Kinds of Cooperative Activity," which further prohibited or restricted the activities of virtually all medical cooperatives.[76] The resolution banned cooperatives from engaging in diagnostics, administering regular physical exams, and treating a range of diseases. Table 5.3 gives a complete list of the December 1988 prohibitions, which included the most popular cooperative services, and compares the resolution with earlier reformist legislation. (Note that some of these services had been prohibited under the Law on Individual Labor Activity, but not under the more liberal Law on Cooperatives.) The December resolution further stipulated that cooperatives could engage in medical services (besides those prohibited) only on the basis of contracts with a state organization or institution. Chazov indicated that cooperatives should be confined to convalescent and nursing care, while the government insisted that its central purpose in issuing the new restrictions was to protect society against incompetent and poorly qualified practitioners.[77]

The overall effect of these two measures on medical cooperatives

Table 5.3 Private, for-fee medical services permitted and prohibited by Soviet legislation, 1986–1989

Legislation	Services permitted	Services prohibited
Law on Individual Labor Activity (Nov. 19, 1986); Ministry of Health Regulations (Mar. 4, 1987)	Medical activities	Certain specialties, in accordance with USSR public health legislation; specifically surgery, pregnancy, infectious diseases, drug addiction, issuing of certificates of illness or disability
Law on Cooperatives (May 26, 1988)	All types of medical activities	Activities prohibited by USSR or republic law
Ministry of Health Order No. 785 (Oct. 1988)		Leasing and use of diagnostic equipment
Resolution "On Regulating Individual Kinds of Cooperative Activity" (Dec. 29, 1988)	Medical activities only on basis of contract with state institution	Diagnostics, exams; specialties including surgery, pregnancy, abortion, infectious diseases, cancer, mental illness, preparation of medicines, drug addiction

Source: Pravda, Nov. 21, 1986, pp. 1, 3; June 8, 1988, pp. 2–5; *Isvestiia,* Sept. 9, 1987, pp. 2–3; Nov. 17, 1988, p. 3; Dec. 23, 1988, p. 3; Dec. 31, 1988, p. 2.

was dramatic. *Argumenty i Fakty* reported that at least 40 percent of cases seen in medical cooperatives would now be prohibited.[78] A half-dozen diagnostic cooperatives in Moscow were immediately closed, while representatives of the Union of Health Cooperatives gathered in emergency session and protested the new measures as punitive.[79] In the longer term, the number of medical cooperatives continued to grow, but at a very modest rate in comparison with both their rate of growth during 1988, and the continuing rate for several other types of cooperatives. There were also allegations that abuses, including the leasing of advanced diagnostic equipment and the buying up of scarce medicines by cooperatives, continued under the contract provision of the December resolution.[80]

Here again is the pattern of liberalization and retreat on a reform policy which threatened the social contract: the reformers encouraged development of private, paid medical services to supplement state services which were admittedly inadequate in quantity and quality, then returned to a policy of almost exclusively state provision. Several interests and powerful actors were opposed to medical cooperatives, including much of the public, the majority of doctors, and administrators of the public health sector who stood to lose control over personnel, resources, and clients. Indeed, the cooperative movement overall generated enormous resistance from state workers and administrators who were threatened by privatization. How can the influences of bureaucratic self-interest be distinguished from social contract concerns in this critical decision?

First, consider why medical cooperatives were restricted more severely than all but a few other types of cooperative enterprise (specifically, education, publishing, and such patently illegal activities as weapons production) by the December 1988 resolution.[81] Bureaucratic forces were opposed to all types of cooperatives; indeed, the most powerful groups of industrial ministries and managers opposed production cooperatives, not the social service co-ops which were hardest hit by the new restriction and prohibitions. Thus, the argument that this decision was primarily a response to bureaucratic pressures seems weak in accounting for the specific content of the decision. Next, consider the reasons cited by Chazov, a prominent and vocal reformer, in justifying the policy turnabout: Chazov stressed concerns about "social justice," the proven potential for private practitioners to exploit the shortages and inadequacies of the state sector, and the public discontent over privatization and especially its abuses. The pattern of the decision—the singularly harsh restrictions on privatization of health care and education—suggests strongly that considerations of state responsibility for, and societal entitlement to, free social services did weigh heavily.

The decision to restrict privatization of medical services was, in effect, a decision to leave most of the funding burden for health care on the state. Privatization had been one element of the reformers' ambitious program for improving Soviet health care, and had been intended to accompany (and supplement) large increases in state funding. Privatizing medical services would have had the advantage of mobilizing resources at no cost to the state (and of absorbing some of the population's excess cash). When privatization was restricted, the state was left to fund its health program mainly through growing state subsidies. The level of state spending on medical care continued to grow during the Gorbachev years, increasing from R17.6 billion in 1985 to R24.6 billion in 1989, and R26.7 billion (planned) in 1990. The Soviet health sector remained seriously underfinanced, both in terms of admitted need and by comparative international standards.[82] Nevertheless, the Gorbachev leadership continued the Brezhnev-era practice and fulfilled the social contract guarantee of regular (if modest) yearly increases in state spending for the universal socialized provision of health care.

Retail Price Reform

Retail price reform constitutes something of an exception to the general pattern of reform policies. As was discussed in chapter 4, while the Gorbachev leadership announced its intention to implement a comprehensive price reform, insisted that this measure was critical to the viability and coherence of perestroika (particularly to self-financing, which began in January 1988 for most of Soviet industry), and reported that it had begun drafting plans, no retail price reform was enacted for nearly four years.[83] In addition, Gorbachev and other officials promised repeatedly that price reform would not impose costs on the "working people," that the state would compensate low-income and average consumers for any increases. Finally, instead of retreating from an enacted policy (as in the other cases), the leadership delayed, then indefinitely postponed, price reform. And in a significant move backward from the reformist agenda, a move I will define as the critical decision in this case, the reformers strengthened administrative controls over prices in early 1989.

In the case of price reform (as with privatization of medical care), a decision to delay or avoid retail price increases was effectively a decision to keep the subsidy burden on the state budget. In the years 1986 through 1990, the Gorbachev leadership *decided* to retain the social contract's guarantee of retail price stability (backed by a rising level of state subsidies) rather than to pursue its reform agenda, but unanticipated consequences of its policies nevertheless abrogated that guarantee.

Stage 1: Confronting the Dilemmas of Price Reform

What made the retail price issue so politically difficult that the leadership held back from even enacting a policy? First, the proposed price reform meant abandoning policies which had kept the cost of necessities nominal throughout most of the Soviet period. Subsidized, low, and stable prices for necessities had been one of the reliable, tangible, and valued policy goods which Soviets received from the state, and as production and procurement costs for most goods had risen throughout the Brezhnev period, the increases had been covered by ever-higher state subsidies (especially for food). To eliminate subsidies and rationalize prices, the reformers would have to pass on to consumers, all at once, the accumulated increases, at least doubling the costs of many food products and other basic goods. In spite of the leadership's assurances about compensation and protected living standards, the increases would inevitably hurt consumers, especially low-income groups whose money is spent disproportionately on basic goods.

More to the point politically, raising prices and cutting subsidies would impose new costs on virtually all urban strata of Soviet society simultaneously, especially groups that enjoyed privileged access to state-subsidized goods under the old distribution system. Soviet economists A. Bim and A. Shokhin made the trenchant points on the likely effects of retail price reform in their October 1986 article in *Kommunist*:

> In addition to low- and fixed-income individuals, the "losers" would include the populations of many large cities, industrial centers, and economically developed areas, workers in large enterprises, and numerous categories of administrative and managerial personnel, i.e., categories which today either purchase meat and dairy products at state stores or have priority in obtaining them (through rations, public catering, or ordering at enterprises and offices, etc.). No income compensation can encompass the full variety of existing consumer markets and differences in "value" of earnings of different categories of working people.[84]

Bim and Shokhin here suggest the central factor that distinguished price reform from other policy areas and that accounts for the leadership's singular caution on this issue from the outset of reform: by raising prices and cutting subsidies the reformers would impose new costs on virtually all members of several critical urban strata, including industrial workers, simultaneously. By contrast, reformist policies on employment and wages, for example, would impose costs on more limited strata and would, at least in theory, produce both winners and losers. In the worst-case scenario, price reform could provide a source of grievance linking discontented industrial workers with the broader urban population. Just such a linkage had occurred in 1962 in Novocherkassk, when food price increases sparked industrial strikes which were suppressed, with loss of life.[85] The reformers were clearly cognizant of the potential parallel: When Goskomtsen head V. Pavlov was asked about the 1962 reform and its repercussions during an interview in the fall of 1988, he replied, "We have been thoroughly analyzing the negative factors of [the 1962] price rise . . . so as not to allow anything similar to happen."[86]

There are additional reasons to believe that concern about public response deterred the reformers from moving ahead with price reform—concern not only about protest and unrest, but about alienating the population from the whole project of perestroika. It is important to remember that, in 1987 and early 1988, there was large-scale popular support for perestroika (however vaguely conceived), and hopes for the success of economic reform were high. The leadership also knew that Soviet public opinion was overwhelmingly hostile to price increases and completely unswayed by reformist arguments on the issue. While public opinion surveys were not yet common at this point, letters to the editors of various publications provide an unambiguous reading of the popular response: most readers' letters to both *Pravda* and *Izvestiia* criticized the proposed price increases. At *Literaturnaia Gazeta* all but a dozen of 1,500 letters on the subject expressed opposition.[87] A review of readers' letters to *Nedelia* revealed that only about 3 to 4 percent of letter writers favored price increases, and that only one letter in dozens supported the official position on price reform. The reviewer concluded, "Price reform . . . is unacceptable, and could produce . . . massive opposition to restructuring."[88] These informal indicators of public opinion provided evidence to the Gorbachev leadership that the Brezhnev-era social contract had left Soviet society with a sense of entitlement to a stable cost of living, and an expectation that the state should assure price stability.

During the first years of reform, the Gorbachev leadership chose to avoid the political costs and risks of violating that expectation. The leaders held back from raising prices and cutting subsidies because they did not want to turn the people against reform by imposing very tangible new costs on the entire urban population before reform policies had delivered any tangible benefits. Between June 1987 and the fall of 1988, officials of the government and Goskomtsen regularly asserted that they were preparing a price reform, but no draft policy documents appeared. The delay did considerable damage to the overall coherence of the reform program. In the most important instance, during 1988 more than half of Soviet enterprises were transferred to self-financing, and maintenance of the old, administratively depressed prices for their products (along with myriad other factors) contributed to the failure of this critical reform measure.

Stage 2: Price Increases without Price Reform

Beginning in the fall of 1988, the state consumer sector was nevertheless beset by rising prices, the disappearance of common, inexpensive goods, and severe supply disruptions. In September the press reported price increases, and in October food and other goods shortages, as well as higher prices, were reported in state retail trade in 140 cities, with worse deficits in smaller towns.[89] Over the following year the situation grew progressively worse, with inflation rising from an estimated 7 percent in 1988 to well over 10 percent in 1990, while shortages continued.[90] The decline in price stability and basic provision came not as a result of straightforward policy decisions—indeed, the leadership continued to delay retail price reform and maintain subsidies—but largely by default, as unintended and unanticipated consequences of reform policies.

A number of factors contributed to the inflation and shortages. Enterprises in the consumer goods sector which had been transferred to self-financing often responded by raising prices for their goods. While state price controls generally remained in effect, enterprises had been given limited authority to raise prices for certain categories of new, higher quality, or especially fashionable goods (sold under special labels), and to sell some goods at contract prices.[91] By late 1988, large numbers of consumer goods with (at best) cosmetic improvements were being sold at higher prices under the new categories; in September *Izvestiia* claimed that virtually the entire R3 billion increase in retail value of goods produced by the Ministry of Light Industry had come from increasing production of such "improved" or "fashionable" goods.[92] Enterprises also raised profits by phasing out inexpensive product lines, including many everyday items which had been produced at state-controlled "socially low" prices. As

Goskomtsen deputy chair A. Komin explained, "In light industry . . . The desire to put their finances right by increasing prices pushes economic leaders to erode the cheap range [of goods], which also leads to an increase in average prices."[93] The result was to impose on customers more expensive commodities in place of cheap ones.

The reformers had (with few exceptions) failed to anticipate that many Soviet enterprises, placed under pressure to show profits, would take advantage of their position as monopolistic or nearly monopolistic suppliers and raise prices or switch to more profitable product lines. Table 5.4 shows the resulting growth in Soviet enterprises' profits from 1987 through 1989: they increased steadily and rapidly, especially during 1988, when first and fourth quarter profits exceeded those of corresponding periods in 1987 by more than 11 percent. These profit levels were achieved mainly by raising prices, with little increase in productivity. As I have already noted, enterprises used some of these easy profits to put into effect wage increases which then contributed to excessive growth in workers' monetary incomes, further fueling inflation.[94]

Another factor contributing to inflation and shortages was the cooperative sector, which was expanding fairly rapidly under the liberal legislation of May 1988. It was for the most part free of state price controls, and it generally charged prices well above those in state stores. In theory cooperative producers and suppliers should have proliferated, producing competition within the cooperative sector and between cooperatives and state enterprises in the consumer sector, and thereby driving down prices in both. In practice cooperatives faced a range of obstacles, including official obstructionism and problems with access to work space, supplies, and credit, which limited

Table 5.4 Growth in profits of Soviet enterprises by quarter, 1987–1990 (percent growth over corresponding quarter of pervious year)

	1987		1988				1989		1990
	I–II	III–IV	I	II	III	IV	I–II	III–IV	I
Percent profit growth (nominal)	4.4	5.6	11.8	10.0[a]	8.0[a]	11.4	7.4[a]	0.6	–7.4

Source: PlanEcon Report, vol. 6, no. 16, Apr. 20, 1990, p. 4 (some figures are averaged).
a. Figure estimated on basis of partial data for year.

their opportunities for market entry and expansion.[95] On the other hand, cooperatives which did manage to get established could take advantage of their freedom from price controls, and the population's excess demand and money, to charge prices which were often far above their own costs, and extremely high in comparison to (often-subsidized) state prices for comparable goods. In addition, from the fall of 1988, unprofitable state enterprises often were taken over by cooperatives and run profitably, largely because cooperativization freed them to charge higher prices.

All of these factors, as well as the serious ethnic unrest in 1988, caused shortages and supply disruptions in the state retail sector. Shortages of state-sector supplies forced consumers to rely on higher-priced goods from cooperatives and farmers' markets. Collective farm market prices in turn began to increase dramatically, reportedly rising almost 10 percent in 1989 (and an additional 30 percent in 1990, with meat prices up nearly 50 percent).[96] Chronic supply disruptions also encouraged the buying up of available state goods for profitable resale (by both cooperators and illegal speculators) or hoarding, and increased efforts by enterprises and organizations to secure "closed distribution" for their employees. Rumors of impending official price increases, which persisted despite the leaders' denials that price reform was imminent, also sparked panic buying and hoarding and further aggravated tensions in the consumer market.[97]

From the fall of 1988, the reformist leadership was left with neither price stability nor a comprehensive and rationalizing price reform. Price increases had come as unintended and unanticipated effects of industrial reform measures, rather than as intended and (at least somewhat) controlled effects of a consciously crafted price policy. Those on low and fixed incomes were severely affected, both by inflation and by the disappearance of cheap mass-consumption goods. Moreover, consumers who were already confronting inflation and shortages would presumably be even less willing than before to countenance reform policies which would bring additional, *planned* price increases and subsidy cuts. Price reform, economically necessary but politically difficult from the beginning, became even more difficult in conditions of a deteriorating consumer market. While the Gorbachev leadership delayed an essential price reform to avoid the political costs, its other economic policies inadvertently undermined price stability. As a result, it began to pay the political costs of increased prices without reaping any economic benefits.

Critical Decision Point: Strengthening State Price Controls

Faced with uncontrolled inflation (though at a level which was still modest by international standards) and serious shortages, the Soviet government prepared in the fall of 1988 to strengthen state-administrative controls over both prices and product mixes. By the end of October, Goskomtsen and state ministries and departments were elaborating "measures to curb negative phenomena in price formation, and measures aimed against the 'erosion' of cheap goods."[98] In late December the radical reformist economist Nikolai Shmelev, (to this point a strong supporter of price increases) advocated that price reform be delayed until the market improved and could be saturated with consumer goods, lamenting, "We simply cannot possibly 'win' the 'price campaign' under the present conditions . . . it can only discredit perestroika in people's eyes."[99]

In the first weeks of 1989, Gorbachev's government moved to formalize its program of price stabilization through the reassertion of state-administrative controls. In early January the Politburo authorized various restrictions to be placed on prices in both the state and cooperative sectors.[100] Goskomtsen chair Pavlov cancelled most of the new indexes which were being used to justify increases in consumer prices, and banned the application of supplements or contract prices to socially priced goods for children and the elderly. Pavlov remarked that the government might have tried using "economic methods," (for example, taxation) to stabilize the consumer market, but said that, in the interest of settling the problem quickly, "We have taken the line of administrative regulation."[101] Cooperatives offering goods or services at prices not exceeding state retail prices (for comparable goods and services) were given priority for supplies, credit, taxes, and benefits.[102] Finally, on February 3, the Council of Ministers adopted a decision, "On Measures to Eliminate Shortcomings in the Prevailing Practice of Price Formation." It stipulated that, beginning in 1989, "state orders" to light industry would cover "the manufacture of the most important groups of goods at socially low prices for children and older people"; it limited temporary price increases for goods of improved quality to 15 percent against the regular retail price; and it called for establishment of a unified all-union system of price controls.[103]

The democratization of Soviet political life in 1988 and 1989 contributed to the pressures for stabilization of prices and market conditions. Deteriorating market conditions helped spark labor unrest, and striking workers demanded controls on prices and cooperatives as well as improved supplies of state-subsidized goods. Shortages, supply disruptions, and high cooperative prices were among the central grievances in the massive miners' strikes of the summer of 1989; the degrading soap shortage stands as a symbol of their discontent.[104] In late summer and fall, the newly radicalized official trade unions began an aggressive campaign for price controls (and simultaneously against a proposed wage freeze). In collaboration with emerging conservative organizations, particularly the United Front of Working People, the unions staged large demonstrations in a number of major cities for price controls and economic stabilization.[105] These and other groups lobbied the newly empowered Supreme Soviet. (Labor politics relating to these and other reform issues are discussed further in chapter 6.)

The Supreme Soviet, the first (somewhat) democratically elected and empowered legislative body to function in the Soviet polity, quickly acted to further strengthen state controls over prices, production, and cooperatives. Its fall 1989 session, which concentrated on problems of the consumer market, did make some efforts to design financial levers and regulatory measures to replace the old, heavy-handed administrative controls, but it relied mainly on new restrictions and subsidies. Its decisions included the resolution, "On Certain Measures to Encourage Production of Goods for the Old at Socially Low Prices," which increased price subsidies and created a special network of "veteran's stores"; a decree, "On Putting the Activities of Cooperatives in Good Order and Regulating Prices," which established permissible levels of prices and markups for cooperatives; and a revision of the Law on Enterprise which suspended the articles concerning the setting of contract prices for food products and "socially important" items.[106] The legislature also banned price increases for specific foodstuffs and clothing for the poor, put into place rigid "state orders" for basic goods, and discussed rationing of necessities. In late November 1989, the government approved a comprehensive stabilization program which relied on a range of administrative measures (though it did avoid rationing).[107] Prime Minister Ryzhkov declared 1990 a year of extraordinary measures to stabilize the economy, and formally postponed price reform.

Why did the reformist leadership decide to reassert state-administrative controls over prices at the end of 1989? The reformers, in spite of their stated commitment to price reform, were from the beginning loathe to take responsibility for increasing retail prices. When those prices began to increase anyway as a consequence of the development of cooperatives, some liberalization of rules on price setting in the state sector, and profitability pressures brought by the Law on the State Enterprise, the leadership was confronted with both bureaucratic and popular pressures to halt the increases. The ministries, which had engaged in every imaginable subterfuge to retain control over production through the "state order" system, must have welcomed this additional justification to reassert their somewhat-eroded authority over consumer goods. Indeed, bureaucratic interests and standard operating procedures seem to have played a major role in this decision: the government, confronted for the first time with open inflation, fell back reflexively on its established practice of administrative controls, in the process shoring up both the work load and the authority of the ministries and state committees. There is some evidence of attempts by reformist economists and the Supreme Soviet to design economic levers for stabilization as well as some potentially effective taxation policies, but for the most part the reformists lacked the necessary knowledge and institutional framework to design and implement such regulatory measures.

It also seems that the reformist leadership found uncontrolled prices intolerable because they undermined stable living costs and popular welfare. Concern about reduced production of inexpensive mass-consumption goods and its effect on the welfare of the poor, pensioners, and large families with low per capita incomes, pervaded the political dialogue. Discussion about the exploitive practices, speculation, and illegitimacy of (and moral outrage toward) entrepreneurs—and for that matter state enterprises—who made large and easy profits at the population's expense, was also pervasive. The underlying assumption that the state held responsibility for provision of basic goods, especially to the poorer sectors of the population, fueled the discussion.

Gorbachev's government, moreover, backed up its rhetoric with measures to increase supplies of socially priced goods, through new controls and new subsidies. The pattern of policy decisions on the price issue, with its stress on controlling costs of necessities and supplies of goods for low-income groups, supports the argument that leaders were genuinely concerned with social welfare and provisions. The couching of debates and discussion in the Supreme Soviet around these same concepts of social justice and popular welfare further suggests that the ethic of Brezhnev's comprehensive welfare state was deeply entrenched in Soviet political culture. The reformist critique repudiated this ethic with a barrage of compelling arguments, but when prices and profits actually began to rise, the sense of injustice and violation of socialist norms proved more compelling, even to reformist leaders and economists. Democratization and the rise of labor activism soon added the voices of workers and others to the debate, and popular pressures weighed heavily in favor of stabilization. As with wage reform and quality control, democratization added obstacles to retail price liberalization.

The decision to postpone retail price reform was, in effect, a decision to keep a massive subsidy burden on the state budget. Indeed, budget expenditures for food and consumer subsidies rose more rapidly than any other category of state spending during the years 1985 through 1990 (Table 5.5). Decisions in 1989 to further increase subsidies for production of some socially priced goods added to the upward trend. Food subsidies alone increased almost R40 billion over these years, from R56 billion in 1985 to an estimated R95.7 billion in 1990, with the largest single increase (more than R20 billion) between 1988 and 1989. Overall, consumer subsidies exceeded R100 billion in 1989. As with medical services, the reformist leadership did not manage to reduce the level of state support for consumer price subsidies, or even to slow its growth.

Conclusion: Reform and the Social Contract

Despite its commitment to welfare state retrenchment, the Gorbachev leadership continued (or at least tried to continue) delivering on the old social contract. The reformers took measures to impose financial discipline and cost accounting on Soviet enterprises, but

Table 5.5 Soviet state budget expenditures for consumer and food subsidies, social insurance, and health care, 1985–1990

Type of expenditure	1985	1986	1987	1988	1989	1990[a]
	In billions of rubles (nominal)					
Total state expenditures	386.5	417.1	430.9	459.5	482.6	488.2
Consumer subsidies	58.0	65.6	69.8	89.8	100.7	110.5
Food subsidies	56.0	58.0	64.9	66.0	87.7	95.7
Social insurance and health care	83.6	89.3	94.5	102.5	105.5	117.2
	As percent of GNP					
Consumer subsidies	7.5	8.2	8.5	10.3	10.9	11.6
Social insurance and health care	10.7	11.2	11.5	11.7	11.4	12.3

Source: Anders Aslund, "Gorbachev, Perestroyka, and Economic Crisis," *Problems of Communism,* vol. 40, nos. 1–2, Jan.-Apr. 1991, p. 25.
a. Estimated figures.

when confronting bankruptcies they decided to bail out or reorganize the insolvent. They legalized and encouraged the privatization of medical services, then restricted it when prices rose and the best personnel and equipment migrated to fee-charging facilities. They delayed a retail price reform which was critical for their overall reform strategy, and retracted policies of limited price liberalization in the state consumer sector (and to some extent in the cooperative sector as well) when prices rose and supplies of inexpensive goods disappeared. In each case their intentions and efforts to reduce state expenditures and responsibility for societal provision were largely abandoned. The leadership might have let society bear the costs of layoffs, price increases, and service cuts (as the postcommunist leaders of Poland, Hungary, and eastern Germany have done), in the hope that continuing liberalization would solve the problems of monopoly and shortage. Instead they moved backward, constrained by entrenched concepts of state responsibility and societal entitlement, by fear of alienating workers and other urban strata from the overall project of perestroika, and later by pressures from activist workers and new political and legislative organizations.

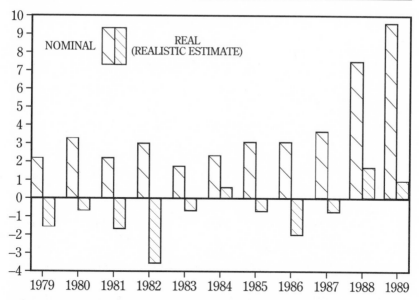

Figure 5.1 Nominal and real monthly wages, 1979–1989 (annual change in percent). *Source:* "Soviet Economic Performance in 1989," *PlanEcon Report,* vol. 6, no. 7–8, Feb. 21, 1990, p. 7.

Paradoxically, while the Soviet leadership was retreating from the effects of these reformist policies, other reform policies did result in a breakdown of the state's delivery on central provisions of the social contract. While the leadership's decisions *were* constrained by the social contract, its mistakes were not so constrained, nor was the effectiveness of its decisions to retreat assured. The central fact remains that reform policies had undermined workers' protected cost of living, producing a significant decline in real wages, despite continuing increases in nominal wages. Figure 5.1 shows that real wages declined, or increased at a lower rate than inflation, during the reform years. The Gorbachev leadership was failing to deliver critical policy and allocational outcomes promised by the social contract. The state's failure to maintain price stability and basic welfare provision for workers, combined with some erosion of income equality and employment security, constituted a significant breakdown of the Soviet social contract.

Soviet Workers and Their Discontents: The Emergence of Labor Activism and Unrest

The present chapter tracks the growth of working-class activism during the reform period, from the grievances and appeals of workers released by the Belorussian Railroad in 1986, to the explosive mass strikes by Donbass and Kuzbass miners in the summer of 1989 and protests by official and unofficial workers' organizations in major cities of European Russia in the fall of that year. The record created by this activism—especially the demands of striking workers and the protests and programs of unofficial, grass-roots workers' organizations—is the first substantial source of direct information we have about Soviet workers' conditions and aspirations. After years of informed speculation, extrapolation from émigré surveys (of questionable representativeness), and inference from behavior patterns, this is real information about Soviet workers' discontents, dissatisfactions with, and attitudes toward labor and social policies. Careful sifting and analysis of this record reveals much about workers' responses to both past and present regimes.

First of all it should say something about workers' actual attitudes toward Gorbachev's reform policies. Existing evidence and scholarly speculation on this question present a somewhat confusing picture. The view in mainstream Sovietology (based on the assumptions of the social contract thesis) has been that blue-collar workers would more or less uniformly oppose reforms which undercut social security and egalitarianism.[1] A second view, proposed by some specialists on Soviet labor, anticipated a divided response from workers. The labor specialists argued that Soviet workers' attitudes had become differentiated according to education and skill levels, and that the better-educated upper strata (which Blair Ruble calls the "working middle class") would likely support reform measures.[2]

Evidence from the mass strikes of summer 1989 flies in the face of both these views; the coal miners, a predominantly blue-collar group, demonstrated broad support for enterprise independence and self-financing, a central part of the reform program. In other instances, too, actual workers' responses were both varied and differentiated in ways that neither the Sovietologists nor the labor specialists anticipated. An analysis of the demands and programs of striking workers will paint a clear picture of the attitudes held by at least some groups of workers toward reform, explain those attitudes, and reveal how and why they differed from what was expected. Most important, tracking the upsurge of labor activism will provide new information for the assessment of the social contract thesis.

The Gorbachev leadership implemented policies which led to an erosion of social contract guarantees in employment policy and (unintentionally) to an abrogation of the contract in the spheres of basic state provision and price stability. According to the contract thesis, the leadership's failure to deliver the expected policy goods should have led to deterioration in the system's legitimacy and political stability. Did the decline of employment security and price stability in fact lead Soviet workers to withdraw consent and compliance from Gorbachev's regime?

At first cut, it seems that the answer is clearly positive: the rise of working class activism did coincide with the erosion and breakdown of the social contract. However, during 1988 and 1989 the Soviet system also underwent a profound democratization, with a lifting of repressive controls over political expression and organization. Workers could now express their grievances much more freely, at much lower cost and risk than in the past, and they should therefore have been more inclined to do so. If Soviet workers harbored any discontent, the loosening of controls alone should have produced some increase in organizing activity, protests, and strikes.

Because the loosening of controls came at the same time as the breakdown of the social contract, the effects of these two factors on workers' behavior cannot be clearly separated; both likely contributed to the increase of open discontent. In assessing their relative significance, however, it is useful to ask this *key question:* did Soviet workers use their new rights in substantial measure to protest erosion and breakdown of the old contract, and to demand revival of the old policies of state control and provision? If so, that would constitute evidence that the social and labor policies and allocational outcomes provided by the Brezhnev regime met workers' preferences and coincided with their agendas. Such evidence would support the case that the provision of an acceptable package of benefits explained in significant part past labor quiescence.

The growth of working-class activism in the reform period went through several stages of development:

1. 1986–1987: increasing numbers of labor disputes, grievances, and appeals over employment rights;
2. fall 1987–1988: sporadic collective protests at the workplace, work stoppages, and localized strikes;
3. spring-summer 1989: strikes in mining regions, culminating in the mass strike of July and August 1989;
4. fall-winter 1989–1990: continued strikes and growth in grassroots, working-class organizational activities.

For each stage, I will examine the patterns of workers' activism, paying attention to the sources of grievance, the scale and types of protests, specific demands, official responses, and resolutions. Soviet workers did frequently protest the progressive erosion and breakdown of the social contract during the reform period: price stability, basic provision, and income stratification were prominent issues in the workers' movement. At the same time, there were groups of workers who strongly supported central aspects of the reform program. And from some sectors of the working class can be heard a deep, accumulated anger and disaffection which were clearly rooted in the deterioration and failures of regime performance long before Gorbachev.

1986–1988: Protests over Layoffs and Pay Cuts

It will be useful first to establish the context for the growth of workers' activism by reviewing major developments in labor policy and regime performance during the years 1986 through 1988. A number of reform policies were implemented in this period. In 1986, the party adopted an economic modernization plan calling for large-scale reductions in the use of manual labor. In June of 1987, the Law on the State Enterprise was passed; it mandated both self-financing and self-management, and became effective for 60 percent of Soviet industry on January 1, 1988. These policies produced some layoffs, financial pressures on enterprises, and a few bankruptcies. Wage reform and state quality control were also introduced during this period, affecting levels of pay and bonuses for some workers.

The first measurable increase in labor discontent came as a response to staff reductions. In the first large-scale experiment, the release, retirement, or transfer of 12,000 workers during reorganization of the Belorussian Railroad in 1986, a substantial number of workers appealed to the trade unions to block their dismissal, twenty-six took legal action for reinstatement, and five were reinstated because of infringements of labor regulations in their release.[3] From this modest beginning, dismissals and transfers of workers led to increased complaints and appeals about violations of labor legislation, disputes over rights to employment and procedures for dismissal, and pressures on trade unions to protect their members' jobs. In late 1987, the industrial press reported a growing number of lawsuits brought by dismissed workers seeking reinstatement, and characterized the atmosphere in labor dispute commissions as "increasingly strained."[4] Chairman Shalayev of the All-Union Central Council of Trade Unions (AUCCTU) reported growing conflict in the factories because of indifference and abuses toward workers during staff reductions. Z. P. Pukhova, chairwoman of the Soviet Women's Committee, stated at the 19th Party Conference that her organization had received "tens of thousands" of appeals on employment rights, indicating once again that the dismissals had fallen particularly heavily on women.[5] Workers sent complaints about dismissals to ministries, party organizations, trade unions, and newspapers.[6]

Workers' protests against layoffs were limited mostly to individual grievances and appeals through established, official channels. Dismissals had long produced a low level of grievance in the system, and they now became a source of more serious tensions and conflict in industrial relations.[7] One result was to complicate, and occasionally block, the process of releasing workers; enterprise managements were required to consult with workers and gain approval of trade unions in dismissals, and they could encounter bureaucratic delays and court-mandated reinstatement of some who appealed. Another result was to push trade union cadres into a more activist stance in defending workers' rights, at least in a legalistic sense, and thus to set up unions somewhat against management, a small step toward the radicalization of the official unions. Workers' response to dismissals remained mild and politically innocuous, with no reports of overt resistance or protest outside official channels. This response is understandable given that the effects of release were mitigated for most workers by reassignment within the enterprise, and that actual layoffs were largely confined to marginal workers, that is, women and those at or near pensionable age, groups not prone to conflict and confrontation. Their appeals, while often poignant, were usually powerless.

In the fall of 1987, the Soviet press began reporting sporadic collective protests, work stoppages, and strikes by Soviet workers. These strikes appeared most often (or perhaps were simply most visible and therefore most reported) in the transport sector, mainly among bus drivers, but also in manufacturing and other sectors. The following characterization is based on accounts of some twenty strikes reported in the Soviet press and other sources between the fall of 1987 and the end of 1988.[8]

The strikes were (as far as can be determined) spontaneous, uncoordinated, and localized. In most cases, workers struck to protest reductions in pay which had resulted from introduction of either new wage-determination schemes or state quality control *(gospriemka)*. In a few cases, working conditions, regimes, or rules were the central issue. Secondary grievances about social conditions, especially inadequate housing, were common. As strikers set forth their demands and elaborated their positions, complaints about obsolete equipment, poor management of production, and the indifference of managers to working conditions came to the fore most frequently.

In a typical strike at a bus manufacturing plant in the Moscow suburb of Likino, for example, workers stopped the assembly line when they lost bonuses because state product-acceptance workers had rejected part of their output. The workers recognized and lamented the poor quality of their products (which one assembly-line worker described as often "like a ragged forgery of a bus, 40–50% incomplete" but blamed obsolete equipment and a long history of underinvestment.[9] A discussion among the Likino plant's workers, managers, and quality control inspectors about the source of the conflict included the following remarks:

Previously the plan was achieved by promises of money. Whether they earned it or not, they still received it . . . Now the money has to be earned. How do you earn it with old equipment? . . . In the pressing shop, some of the machine tools are more than 40 years old. How can you talk of quality? . . . production organization [is] utterly archaic . . . Radical reconstruction was needed even two five-year plans ago. The people work normally, but the bus does not meet the present state standards. But are the workers who produce such a bus to blame?[10]

Workers, pressed between new quality and performance standards and old, substandard technical and working conditions, saw their wages fall and stopped work. However receptive to Gorbachev's exhortations to work hard and earn their income, they saw no "social justice" in losing pay because of conditions beyond their control.

In virtually every case, the strikes brought a rapid response from local party and government (and sometimes higher-level) authorities, who negotiated with the workers or their chosen representatives, generally agreed to meet demands, and frequently replaced managers. Whole shops, factories, or depots seem to have gone out on strike; there were no reports of splits in workers' ranks. Nor were there reports of repression or punishment of strikers, though strikers sometimes complained of efforts at intimidation. Indeed *Pravda,* commenting in July 1988 on the "now-common occurrence" of strikes, offered the relatively mild rebuke: "The strike fever is too high a price for us and perestroika . . . It's a terrible blow to the country's economy."[11]

The partial democratization of the Soviet system at once emboldened the strikers and disoriented the authorities. Workers appealed to proreform and prodemocracy slogans of "labor collectives' initiative and independence" and to their newly conferred rights of self-management to justify their actions.[12] The responses of factory trade unions were mixed and confused; some supported the workers, others stood aside and further discredited themselves. Workers were galvanized to strike over pay cuts (as in the Brezhnev period, to prevent loss of ground rather than to make new demands), but most recognized that long-term failures of management and ministries underlay their grievances. Democratization also played a critical role in their calculations, as suggested by the following excerpt from the discussion at Likino: "It seems . . . that the shop stopped work out of desperation. Of course, before we did not take such a risk, but these are now different times."[13]

Despite their proreform slogans, though, the strikers clearly opposed reform policies on wages and quality control. Where these policies imposed immediate and tangible costs on collectives of male blue-collar workers, they met bold and effective resistance. The strikes, moreover, brought into relief some of the difficulties and contradictions in those policies. It made little sense, for example, to impose higher quality or performance requirements (or self-financing requirements) on entire industries without substantial planning or preparation. Again, a representative of the state acceptance system at Likino makes the salient point: "Virtually everything [in the pressing shop] needs to be replaced . . . It was neither physically nor technically possible to change the situation from October 1986, when the state acceptance system began functioning as an experiment, up to January 1987 when we were already operating officially."[14]

On the whole, the workers seem to have won. Authorities generally acceded to their demands, and during 1988 both quality control and wage reform policies were virtually abandoned. By the end of that year, wages were reportedly growing more rapidly than productivity in more than half of Soviet enterprises.[15] Uncontrolled wage increases in turn contributed to inflationary pressures, which were to become a source of future labor unrest.

In the Slavic regions, through 1988, worker discontent remained confined to the factories and to production relations (and did not spill over into politics). Meanwhile nationalist unrest, including sustained mass strikes, had begun in other regions, especially in the Caucasus. And in the RSFSR and the Ukraine, the sporadic local strike pattern of 1987 and 1988 was soon eclipsed by the beginnings of a massive strike movement among miners in the Soviet Union's major coal basins.

The Miners' Strikes of Spring and Summer 1989

The most dramatic and significant labor unrest of the Gorbachev period erupted among miners in July of 1989, engulfing the major Soviet coal basins and affecting production for much of the summer. The summer strike movement followed several months of small, localized mine strikes, and collective appeals to both local and national authorities for attention to the miners' grievances. It began on July 10 in the Western Siberian Kuznetsk Basin (Kuzbass), with 1,000 miners striking for a thirty-point program.[16] Within a week, more than 100,000 Kuzbass miners were on strike and production in the basin was paralyzed. Unrest spread to the Donetsk Basin in the Ukraine (Donbass), to the Arctic city of Vorkuta, and to other regions, involving some half million Soviet miners by early August.[17] Their grievances were many, and their lists included demands for a mix of traditional, social contract policies and implementation of reforms.

The strikes spawned grass-roots leadership and organization, as well as oblast-level committees which coordinated actions, worked out unified demands, and bargained on behalf of the strikers. The miners largely bypassed local trade union and party cadres, and apparently eschewed efforts of other political groups to assume a role in the strikes. Thus, their movement provides the best evidence we have of self-activated, unrestrained workers' voices, largely unadulterated by official formulations, expressing their attitudes and demands. At the same time, the strikers represent only one sector of the industrial labor force, a sector clearly distinguished by three features of the mining socioeconomy which are critical to an understanding of the strikes' patterns and program:

1. the concentration of miners in workers' settlements where they do hard and dangerous work, which contributed to their solidarity and militance;
2. the low profitability of the coal industry caused by state price controls;
3. international demand for coal, which can potentially be sold for hard currency on international markets.

In my examination of the strikes, I will look first at some salient economic and political background factors, then at the actual development of unrest and the strikers' demands.

Economic Background Factors

The coal strikes were partly fueled by worsening conditions in the social spheres of the mining regions. I discussed in chapter 4 the general deterioration of supplies, price stability, and distribution networks in the consumer sector during 1988 and 1989. The effects of this deterioration were especially acute in some of the mining regions. In the Ukraine (which includes most of the Donbass), retail prices were increasing for several months preceding the strike, the production of inexpensive necessities was shrinking, the gap between purchasing power and the availability of goods was widening, and shoppers were experiencing unaccustomed shortages and stoppages in sales of essential goods. The soap shortage, which was to become a symbol of the miners' grievances, was itself largely a result of the reform's dysfunctions: rumors about planned price increases had led to increased demand, then to panic buying and hoarding of soap in 1988.[18]

In October 1988, the Central Committee of the Ukrainian Communist party reported severe deterioration in the supply to the population of meat and dairy products. In its January 1989 examination of the republic's social and economic development, the Ukrainian Council of Ministers reported poor progress in construction of housing, facilities for health service and education, and new production facilities in light and local industries which produce nonfood consumer goods.[19] There is ample evidence that such problems extended to other mining regions and settlements, where they were often superimposed on a poor and long-neglected social infrastructure.[20]

Reform policies also caused problems for miners in the production sphere. As in other industries, new cost accounting procedures sometimes meant loss of wages or bonuses because of conditions which were beyond the miners' control.[21] The coal basins had been transferred to self-financing in January 1988, in spite of the fact that much of the sector had long operated at a loss and that state price controls perpetuated the mines' unprofitability. Loss-makers were especially concentrated in the Donbass, the oldest of the mining regions, which suffered from a long-term lack of state investment, obsolete technology, exhausted mines and declining output.[22] Under self-financing, these mines faced the potential threat of insolvency and closure. At the same time, the mines' administrations could not raise coal prices so long as the old price policies remained in effect and the ministry continued to control the level and disposition of their output (nor could they boost profitability by changing their product mix and increasing output of expensive "improved" goods, the common ruse of manufacturers of consumer goods). But if the regime's half-hearted implementation of reform was exacerbating problems in the coal basins, the miners envisioned an opportunity to resolve those problems through genuine implementation of the reform policies, and they struck in part to support, indeed to demand, those policies.

Political Background Factors

Glasnost also contributed to the miners' mobilization. Mining is by nature hard and dirty work, but the policy of "openness" brought to light the extraordinarily poor, difficult, and dangerous working conditions of Soviet miners. Press exposés, official reports, and special investigations focused on the coal industry, detailing its worn and obsolete equipment, its lack of safety regulations and procedures, the poor health of miners in comparison with other sectors of the population, and the ecological devastation of the basins.

In the fall of 1988, for example, *Sotsialisticheskaia Industriia* ran a series titled "Life of a Miner," poignantly describing these hardships, which were then widely discussed in the industrial press.[23] In early 1989 an official of the State Mining Safety Inspectorate published a long article in *Ekonomicheskaia Gazeta,* providing statistics and specific information about working conditions, and citing figures from a Special Collegium of the USSR Prosecutor's Office on the high rate of occupational injuries and violations of safety regulations in the coal industry.[24] Commissions sent to mining settlements to investigate fatalities publicized reports on local conditions contributing to accidents and recommended dismissal of responsible managers. Ecological issues, including air quality, chemical contamination, and the detrimental effects of pollution on the health of miners and their children, came to the fore as major issues. All this discussion and attention no doubt contributed to the common consciousness of grievances in the mining communities and, more important, defined these grievances for the first time as legitimate political issues.

The democratization of politics also formed an important part of the background to the strikes. In March 1989 the first elections allowing for some popular initiative and competition were held, to choose delegates to the Congress of People's Deputies (which would in turn elect a national legislature, the Supreme Soviet). In the Russian and Ukrainian republics, numbers of high-ranking Communist party officials were defeated in these elections, demonstrating unequivocally that democratization allowed for popular repudiation of party leadership. Moreover, mining towns and settlements elected their own deputies, in many cases rank-and-file workers or individuals with a history of opposition to the political establishment.[25] The elections and the convening of the legislature thus provided the miners both with assured access to the national leadership through their deputies, and with an audience of an unprecedented type for their actions and demands. The summer strikes in fact coincided with the first meeting of the new legislature, and deputies from mining regions played an important role in presenting and defending the strikers' grievances in Moscow. Finally, in early May a draft Law on the Rights of Trade Unions, including a tentative right to strike, was published, placing workers' grievances and rights squarely at the center of the national political agenda.[26]

Development of the Strike Movement: Spring 1989

Open discontent among Soviet coal miners was first reported in March and April 1989. It took the form of localized strikes which usually involved a single pit and limited demands for better wages and working conditions. About a dozen strikes were reported during the spring months. They affected the Kuzbass, Donbass, Vorkuta, and Norilsk mines, and lasted from several hours to several days. The largest by far included 1,000 miners.[27] The leadership responded by sending high-level officials to meet with the aggrieved workers; Coal Industry minister M. Shchadov, Nonferrous Metallurgy minister V. Durasov, chair of the State Committee on Labor and Social Issues I. Gladky, and A. Melnikov, the first party secretary of the Kemerovo Oblast, were all sent out to settle various of the strikes. The center's representatives typically accepted the miners' demands as justified, and they made (or promised) concessions on most issues.[28]

While the spring strikes remained limited in terms of their size and demands, they nevertheless represented an escalation of labor unrest over earlier strikes, for several reasons. First, they were concentrated in a single sector and made very similar demands; so while localized, they no longer had the sporadic and disconnected pattern of the earlier strikes. Second, the miners displayed a much stronger antiadministrative bias, often calling not only for dismissals of directors but also for substantial reductions in managerial and technical personnel. And third, while the earlier strikes were settled by local authorities, those in the mining regions commanded central intervention. Striking miners were generally contemptuous of their official trade unions and other "social organizations," and bypassed all local and regional authorities (party, soviet, and industrial) to negotiate with emissaries from the central government.

Indeed, the miners struck only after having petitioned the lower-level authorities in vain. In turn, the common inertia and indecision of union and other local officials in the face of the strikes further discredited these authorities. M. A. Srebny, chair of the Coal Industry Workers' Union, commenting on the effects of the spring strikes, admitted, "The strikes have shaken both the directors and the trade union leaders."[29] The crisis of authority would deepen. In June, as the newly elected deputies were gathering in Moscow, the miners sent them collective petitions. Still receiving no response, they set a strike deadline.

The Mass Strikes of Summer 1989

The summer coal strikes began on July 10 in the mining city of Mezhdurechensk in the Kuznetsk Basin (Kemerovo Oblast, western Siberia), where 1,000 miners refused to work and presented a list of thirty-five demands. Within a week the strike had spread to eight additional Kuzbass cities, involved more than 100,000 miners, and closed down virtually the entire coal basin.[30] The miners demonstrated in town squares—often joined by others from the local population—maintained order, discussed their grievances, and elected representatives to local strike committees. Within a week, they had organized an oblast-level strike committee headed by T. Avaliani, an enterprise deputy director who had been persecuted under Brezhnev for suggesting in a letter that the aged and incompetent general secretary resign, and had been recently elected as a people's deputy from the basin.[31]

In the next several days, the Kemerovo Oblast Strike Committee met with two high-level commissions sent by Moscow: the first, headed by Minister Shchadov and AUCCTU chairman Shalayev, to discuss the miners' immediate demands; the second, a Supreme Soviet commission chaired by N. Slyunkov, a member of the Politburo and the Central Committee, and including L. A. Voronin, first deputy chair of the Council of Ministers, to look into the oblast's broader socioeconomic problems.[32] The miners also instructed their deputies to address the Supreme Soviet on their behalf, and the strikes filled a substantial part of the legislature's agenda in mid-July. By July 20 a thirty-six–point protocol had been signed by members of both commissions and the oblast strike committee, promising fulfillment of most of the miners' demands and specifying concrete deadlines and those responsible for fulfillment. Gorbachev reported to the Supreme Soviet on the Kuzbass strikes with qualified sympathy, and a telegram signed by Gorbachev and Ryzhkov committed the leadership to the protocol.[33] Avaliani's committee called for an end to the strike, and on July 21 most Kuzbass miners were back at work.

However, the strike had spread on July 17 to the Donetsk Basin, on July 19 to Vorkuta in the Pechora Basin (in the Arctic Circle), and on subsequent days to Karaganda (in Kazakhstan) and other regions. What had begun as a regional strike, now turned into an industrywide one affecting all major coal mining areas of the Russian, Ukrainian, and Kazakh republics. The breadth of the strike, which broke out in rapid sequence in cities and basins separated by hundreds and thousands of miles and interrupted most of the country's coal supply, created a national crisis. The leadership hastened to extend the Kuzbass settlement to all miners and mining regions, and promised to negotiate any additional grievances and demands. The miners demanded guarantees. After another round of meetings between regional strike committees and central emissaries, Supreme Soviet discussions, and assurances from Gorbachev and local deputies, the Donbass, Vorkuta, Karaganda, and other miners returned to work. By the end of July the strikes had abated everywhere, consignments of goods were arriving in mining settlements, some demands over pay and work scheduling had been met, and much else had been scheduled for delivery or discussion.[34]

The national miners' strike of summer 1989 confronted both national and local leaders with unprecedented challenges. Gorbachev's government approached the strikes without any legal provisions or constituted procedures for arbitrating collective labor conflicts; indeed, the Soviet Union's first draft Law on Labor Disputes was submitted to the Supreme Soviet during the strike.[35] The government developed ad hoc procedures, bending to the miners' insistence that top-level national leaders travel to the basins and negotiate with strike leaders, and providing multiple institutional guarantors (including

Council of Ministers, AUCCTU, soviet, and regional CPSU committees) to the strike agreements. Local soviet, trade union, and party
authorities were further (perhaps finally) discredited by the strikes,
and Moscow's management of the negotiations left local authorities
largely irrelevant to their settlement. National leaders criticized their
local counterparts for having ignored the miners' accumulating grievances, and in many localities striking miners called for the resignation of local leaders and immediate new elections for party, soviet,
trade union, and workers' committees. Condemnation of the trade
unions was particularly harsh; as a fairly typical news commentary
put it: "The strike revealed the total bankruptcy of many trade union
functionaries."[36]

In place of these authorities, the strikes produced a new grass-
roots leadership which seemed to command respect from both above
and below: the strike committees got large concessions from the government and were generally able to control the miners (that is, to
call an effective end to the strikes). They continued to function as
workers' committees after the strikes had ended, monitoring fulfillment of the miners' demands and retaining the authority to call new
strikes if those demands were not met.

The Miners' Demands and Reform

At first perusal the strikers' demands, which were presented to the
government in lists of thirty, forty, and more, seem to indicate that
Soviet miners were aggrieved about everything—living conditions,
work regime, the slow pace of reform, some of the effects of reform,
management, and environmental pollution. A typical list included demands for improved pay, pensions, and holidays; better provision of
food and industrial goods; more housing construction; consumer,
municipal, and medical services; more investment in modernization
of the mines; cuts in the administrative apparatus; more rights for
labor collectives; and other political, ecological, and job-specific demands.[37] Initially, most attention was focused on the fact that the miners supported the central element of the industrial reform—transition of their enterprises to economic autonomy and self-financing.
Gorbachev, presiding over the Supreme Soviet when the strikes began, welcomed strikers' demands as evidence of grass-roots worker
support for reform. However, careful assessment of their demands

will show that the miners were both conditional and somewhat ambiguous in their support for reform.

The strikers' central demand was that their mines be transferred
to economic independence and self-management by the labor collective, in accord with the provisions of the Law on the State Enterprise.
But they also set a number of conditions for the transfer: increases in
coal prices; lower plan (or state contract) targets; the right to control
disposition of above-plan output, including the right to market output
abroad, retain foreign currency, and use it for local development; the
right to manage profits; reduction of the managerial apparatus; and
autonomy from the ministry.[38]

Passage of the Law on the State Enterprise, and the ensuing discussions of cost accounting, self-financing, and potential insolvency of
loss-making enterprises, had focused the miners' attention on their
sector's sorry financial state and its sources. They realized (or
learned) that their coal was valuable both at home and in hard currency markets abroad, and that mines often made little or no profit
because the state depressed domestic wholesale and retail prices below the cost of production and kept hard currency earnings from
foreign sales in the central budget. As a consequence, mining regions
had few resources for either production or social development, and
often had to depend on ministerial subsidies. As one striking miner
succinctly stated the case, "Miserly sums are left [for us] by comparison with the solid profits earned [by us]."[39]

The miners saw an opportunity to resolve their problems through
genuine enterprise autonomy and self-financing. Autonomy from
ministerial diktat and state pricing restrictions would allow miners
more control over pricing and marketing. They could raise artificially
depressed domestic coal prices to cover both the costs of production
and profits. They could also sell part of their output on the international market, earn hard currency, and use it to modernize production and to improve social infrastructure and the supplies of consumer goods. As an *Izvestiia* article on the strikes in the Kuzbass
explained: "The miners believe that they have the right to sell coal
at contract prices . . . the prices for [coal] are such that enterprises
. . . make low profits or a loss, and have insufficient funds for the
renewal of equipment and technology and the accelerated development of housing construction and the social and consumer infrastructure. Therefore the demand is being advanced to grant coal industry

enterprise collectives full economic independence and to increase deductions into the local budget."[40]

The conditions the miners demanded for the transition to self-financing (including higher coal prices and lower production plans) would, however, unilaterally increase their claims and advantage while raising energy costs for all domestic consumers. And while the miners envisioned a self-supporting future, a significant part of their program amounted to short-term demands for improvements in delivery of traditional social contract policy, including subsidized consumer goods and social services, state investment in housing construction and technical renovation, and various benefits for rank-and-file production workers. When the leadership conceded to most of these demands, the miners were in effect promised more autonomy, higher coal prices, fewer production demands, and more subsidies. As economists soon began to point out, these concessions increased strains on the general economy and budget. The package the government promised the miners was estimated by Ryzhkov to cost more than R2 billion and would contribute to both inflation and the deficit.[41] Soviet leaders and scholars have looked upon the miners' strikes as evidence of unexpected support for reform among industrial workers that would likely strengthen Gorbachev and his policies. However, it seems that their implications for reform were ambiguous. The strikes did demonstrate worker support for core reform policies, but Gorbachev's settlement with the miners had high costs for the state budget and for the regime's already tenuous control over the reform process.

One should stop here to consider the miners' basic orientation toward the political economy. Their program implied an image of an economy in which the state controls less and self-managed enterprises seek prosperity through the market's supply-and-demand prices. While this is not a pure market program it should give one pause, because it calls into question long-held assumptions about the inherent conservatism and dependent psychology of Soviet blue-collar workers. The coal miners, without the benefit of official or intelligentsia leadership (though they were obviously inspired by the center's reform program), developed and supported a program based on autonomy, workers' democracy, and markets, because they believed that such policies would serve their collective self-interest.[42] They responded to the new information and new political and economic opportunities apparently offered by reform with a straightforward assessment of their rational self-interest. There is little to suggest that traditional and dependent values or belief systems confined their options or behavior.

I should also point out that the miners' support for reform policies depended on their occupation of a particular niche in the Soviet economy that, in turn, defined the structure of their opportunities. The miners stood to benefit from reform policies because of the nature of their product, the presumed demand for coal on both domestic and international markets. Their proposed solution to their poverty and low profitability depended on their ability to sell coal on hard currency markets, and to buy products and services on these markets for local development, and it was therefore not generalizable in Soviet industry. While a similar strategy might work for other raw-material producing sectors (for example, oil, gas, perhaps timber), it would provide little benefit for the vast majority of Soviet enterprises whose products were not salable on international markets. Most Soviet workers did not share the miners' prospects of profiting from economic autonomy, and so they should not be expected to share the miners' proreform policy preferences.

Evidence from the mine strikes casts serious doubt on the validity of Western assumptions about Soviet workers. Blue-collar workers in traditional heavy-industry sectors were expected to oppose marketizing reforms, and instead the most aggressive support for such reforms is found among miners. Policy preferences were expected to be differentiated according to education and skill levels, but there is little evidence of such differentiation among the miners; instead there are strong suggestions of a different basis for differentiation, according to sector and economic opportunity structure.

The Miners' Demands and the Social Contract

A careful study of the summer strikes makes it clear that the miners' concerns ranged well beyond the immediate reform program. Many also harbored deep dissatisfactions with the pre-Gorbachev state's delivery on the central aspects of the social contract, particularly housing, medical care, and municipal services. Striking miners claimed insistently that their settlements suffered from problems that had accumulated in the sector over decades, "the neglected state of the social sphere . . . long years of arrogant neglect of people's basic needs."[43] The Kemerovo Oblast party secretary A. Melnikov echoed these claims, saying of development in the Kuzbass, "In the cities facilities were provided according to the village system: an enterprise with a small workers' settlement, badly appointed, without municipal amenities," while both government and trade union officials acknowledged that deep and long-standing grievances about living standards underlay the miners' militance.[44] Descriptions of conditions in mining cities and settlements support the claims of long-term neglect of the social sphere. Many miners lived in dilapidated housing, including barracks which had been built during the 1930s and 1940s for convicts and victims of repression (especially in the Arctic regions). The shortage of hospitals, nurseries, cultural institutions, and schools was characterized as "catastrophic," with schools in many towns operating indefinitely in multiple sessions. Municipal services in settlements were extremely poor, with water and electricity often supplied during limited hours and sewage inadequate. Pollution and related health problems were severe and medical care was poor, with little available treatment for diseases and injuries common to miners.

Such claims (and confirming descriptions) of long-term neglect of the social sphere in the coal basins raise some questions about whether the Brezhnev-era social contract extended to the whole of the Soviet working class. Of course the quality of services provided by Brezhnev's welfare state was universally poor, and many of the miners' grievances (specifically, inadequate housing and poor health care) were common throughout Soviet society. Nevertheless, there is evidence that the miners benefited considerably less from the social contract than did some other groups of workers, particularly those in urban regions of the western RSFSR and Ukraine. For example, an official report to Central Committee of the Ukrainian Communist party in August 1989 provided the following statistics on housing conditions and municipal amenities for Donbass miners: 20 percent of residences lacked running water; 26 percent were not connected to a sewage system; 28 percent lacked central heating; 63 percent lacked hot water; 49 percent lacked gas.[45] By contrast, Mervyn Matthews's study of poor (that is, low-per-capita-wage) Soviet families from urban areas (interviewed after emigrating) found that virtually all had had running water, sanitation, gas, and electricity, while higher percentages (85 percent and 68 percent, respectively) had had central heating and hot water.[46] Although miners enjoyed relatively high wages, their housing conditions were markedly inferior to those of even poor urban families. While more comprehensive statistics are needed to make the case conclusively, these data on amenities indicate that coal miners have long been less than full beneficiaries of state spending for social provision.

There are other reasons to think that the mining settlements were relatively deprived of funds for social services and infrastructure even during the Brezhnev period. Beginning in the early 1960s, Soviet energy policy turned away from primary dependence on coal to much heavier reliance on oil and gas. Planners also shifted investment within the coal industry, away from the old and exhausted Donbass mines to the newer coal fields of the Kuzbass, while declining labor productivity and increasing transport costs strained resources throughout the industry. As a consequence, the Donbass was seriously deprived of funding and suffered deterioration of both production facilities and social infrastructure, which contributed to dangerous working conditions and poor health. At the same time, production in the Kuzbass was built up rapidly, with little investment in the social sphere. As the population grew, shortages of housing, schools, health care, and other service facilities became acute.[47]

This evidence strongly suggests that the Brezhnev-era social contract did not extend evenly to all sectors of the Soviet labor force. Coal miners were relatively deprived of state provision, though they did benefit from high wages and stable employment (whereas a competitive, profit-driven economy would likely have closed down many Donbass mines). Sovietologists have long recognized inequalities in Soviet society, but have tended to regard the social contract as a more or less undifferentiated deal for workers. The striking miners' claims indicate that there were large and prolonged disparities in the Soviet state's delivery of benefits to different sectors of the working class, disparities which in turn affected levels of discontent among different groups of workers. One senses that the miners were much more deeply aggrieved about their accumulated problems, and much less interested in statist solutions, than were their worker-activist counterparts in other sectors.

Labor Activism after the Summer Strikes

In the months after the summer 1989 coal miners' strikes, two central developments characterized Soviet labor politics: the state's delivery on core provisions of the social contract deteriorated further, and working-class activism grew. Breakdown of the state's side of the contract took place mainly in the consumer economy, in the forms of worsening inflation, shortages, and distortion and corruption of distribution networks. The growth of workers' activism took several forms:

Strikes, though not on the scale of the summer, remained a constant feature of the labor scene.

New, informal organizations emerged to proclaim themselves defenders of workers' interests in the reform period.

The militance of the official trade unions increased markedly.

Workers engaged in organized protests in many regions, and official and unofficial workers' organizations lobbied the newly established legislature (the Supreme Soviet) on labor and social issues.

With regard to the development of labor activism in this period, I wish to focus on two questions. Did the activism and protest of different groups of workers focus on common grievances and demands? And did social contract issues have a prominent place among workers' discontents?

Continuation of Strikes

The conclusion of the miners' strikes in early August left a tense atmosphere in the country's coal basins. A kind of dyarchy emerged in most mining towns, with local party, soviet, and trade union authorities on one side, and strike committees on the other. Already discredited, local officials were now faced with mass votes of no confidence. Some were replaced by new elections; more were effectively supplanted by the strike committees. Distrust and disputes between management and strike committees arose often, sometimes paralyzing managers and everywhere obstructing the return to a normal pace of work. Most important, strike committees retained the right to call for renewed work stoppages if the agreement between government and miners was not honored. The July protocol, which was formalized as Council of Ministers Resolution No. 608, left the government overcommitted, while regional strike committees in each basin became "committees of workers' control" over its implementation.[48] The stage was set for renewed conflict.

In the months after the strike accord, the miners' committees repeatedly raised grievances about the government's delivery on Resolution 608 and threatened or held brief warning strikes. As there was still no national organization to represent the miners, government commissions, led by Deputy Prime Minister P. M. Riabev, traveled to the various coal basins throughout the winter and spring to respond to these grievances. Though the Riabev commissions had the power to adapt decisions and settle disputes, and negotiations with the miners typically went on for weeks, nowhere were the problems resolved, and threats of renewed strikes were frequent.[49]

The miners' strike had a demonstration effect on other producers of energy resources, who saw similar opportunities in sectoral independence. In the spring of 1990 oil and gas workers in the Tyumen region, which provided 60 percent of Soviet output of these resources, threatened a strike over demands for improved living standards and the right to sell a portion of their product abroad and keep the hard currency earnings. After emergency talks, the government acceded to most of their demands in what was called the Tyumen Protocol. This settlement, too, led to protracted disputes over the workers' claims of nonfulfillment, and repeated strike threats.[50] Belorussian potassium miners demanded that they be given the same rights and benefits as the coal miners, and other workers followed the miners' lead in striking over ecological demands.[51] There were also numerous strikes and strike threats in the transport sector, both national and local, which would continue and worsen.[52]

The government responded to the continuing unrest by trying to establish "rules of the game," that is, a legal framework for industrial conflicts. On October 9 the Supreme Soviet adopted the resolution "On Procedures for Settling Collective Labor Disputes," which both established and limited the right to strike for Soviet workers. The resolution mandated procedures and time frames for registration of grievances, labor-management negotiations, arbitration, and notification of intent to strike. It also provided for government postponement or suspension of strikes under certain conditions, prohibited strikes in a number of sectors and circumstances, and gave the courts the task of ruling on strikes' legality.[53] Gorbachev, citing the "emergency" situation in industry, sought a fifteen-month ban on all strikes, but was rebuffed by the Supreme Soviet.[54]

The legislation was first applied to a protracted strike in Vorkuta which had closed the Pechora Basin's largest mine for more than five weeks. The strikers had several grievances: slow progress in implementing Resolution 608, refusal of the city *ispolkom* to register the strike committee, and burdensome requirements for receipt of bonuses for work in the north. On October 27, the Komi ASSR Supreme Court ruled that three labor collectives and their strike committees were in violation of the resolution on collective labor disputes, and threatened fines and other sanctions.[55] The issue of the strike's legality now became a central focus, politicizing the conflict and leaving the miners outraged and intransigent. It continued for several more weeks, with escalating demands and appeals to higher courts, and was finally settled after numerous concessions from the authorities.

In sum, the democratizing Soviet state was weak and vulnerable in the face of grass-roots challenges from labor. No longer willing to repress workers' grievances in the mode of its authoritarian predecessor, it also lacked the established democratic state's legal and institutional framework for labor negotiation. Moreover, its hurried efforts to create rules for dealing with industrial conflicts failed; miners and others rejected the legislation, and its application served only to politicize the labor movement.

Emergence of Informal Workers' Organizations

During the summer of 1989, another type of working-class activism emerged in the cities of the western USSR: some (mainly Russian) workers joined a network of informal political organizations known as the United Front of Working People. The United Front originated in Leningrad, where its constituent congress was held in mid-June. More local chapters were quickly set up, and in mid-July representatives of workers' fronts (Interfronts) from the Baltics, Moldavia, Ukraine, Moscow, Leningrad, and other RSFSR cities met in Leningrad to establish a coordinating body. In early September an official umbrella organization, the United Front of Russian Working People (which I will designate by its Russian acronym, OFT) held its founding congress in Sverdlovsk, with 110 delegates representing twenty-nine Russian cities and Russian groups in other republics, and appointed V. A. Yarin chair.[56] The OFT was not a spontaneous or autonomous workers' organization; Communist party officials sponsored the creation of local chapters and sat on coordinating councils, and the newly militant AUCCTU subsidized meetings and communications.[57] Moreover, the Front had explicitly political and nationalist agendas. Nevertheless, unlike the other mass nationalist movements involving workers, the OFT was centrally concerned with economic policy and labor issues, and it provided the most visible and articulate opposition to the reformist assault on the social contract.

The OFT's politics may best be characterized as conservative, Russian nationalist, and antireform (though the organization itself was a product of democratization). It favored social unity on the basis of "Soviet patriotism," and opposed nationalist and linguistic autonomy movements, especially in the Baltics and Moldavia. The OFT declared that its aim was "to unite the efforts of working people . . . in the struggle to implement perestroika and improve the people's life on the basis of Marxist-Leninist principles and socialist ideals," and claimed to fear "change of the CPSU's social and class nature."[58] Its members lamented the decline in the number of working-class deputies elected to the new Supreme Soviet and advocated changes in the electoral law that would increase representation of industrial workers. It had ties to conservative and nationalist circles among the intelligentsia, and constituted the main opposition to the proreform Popular Fronts and other liberal, informal, mass organizations in the western cities of the USSR.[59]

Because party and trade union officials from the beginning played a substantial role in this conservative organization, many observers and analysts of the Soviet political scene saw the OFT as essentially a front for antireform officials—as, in Andrei Sakharov's words, "a way of manipulating the working class in the interests of the apparat."[60] Critics asserted that it was begun by Leningrad party officials and pro-Communist worker-activists to shore up their power after their defeat in the March 1989 Congress of People's Deputies elections, and that the changes in electoral laws advocated by the OFT were calculated to increase the representational weight of industrial workers whose votes the party could control.[61] The OFT's criticism of economic reform was likewise interpreted as a cynically self-interested ploy by the apparat to maintain its power and prerogatives. However, it should not be assumed that workers who supported or participated in the OFT were simply objects of elite manipulation. Some workers may have seen it as an organization which genuinely represented their interests and, particularly in its economic platform, gave voice to their views on reform.

The OFT objected to the basic principles of Gorbachev's economic reform and saw them as antithetical to the interests of workers. The Front opposed the move toward market socialism, with its "inherent price rises, unemployment, and stratification of society"; the leasing of state production facilities, which it saw as a step toward the reinstitution of private property; the use of profit indicators; and the revival of "exploitation of wage labor."[62] It was highly critical of the cooperative movement and demanded that the government create equal conditions for workers in state enterprises and cooperatives. It called for popular control over the creation of joint enterprises, and vowed to "combat the transformation of the USSR into a raw material appendage of other states and the rapacious exploitation of its natural and manpower resources."[63] It decried the effects on workers of four years of reform—shortages, rationing, price increases, unemployment, inflation, and speculation—and demanded that the government lower prices, control excessively high incomes, and reorient the economy away from profit. While the negative effects of reform on workers' living standards were generally acknowledged by late 1989, government officials and economists attributed the problems to inadequacies and half-measures in implementation. The OFT blamed directly the essence of the reform.[64]

Radicalization of the Official Trade Unions

During the first years of Gorbachev's reforms, the AUCCTU supported the government's economic and labor policies. Chairman Shalayev frequently repeated the leadership's promise that workers would be shielded from the negative consequences of reform or adequately compensated for losses. The AUCCTU's leadership accepted the prospect of large-scale layoffs and committed their organization to overseeing the process, guiding displaced workers to job retraining, and guaranteeing reemployment. (Shalayev did, however, encourage use of laid-off workers within their own enterprises through increasing the number of shifts—that is, the "redistribution of labor within the enterprise"—which, as I discussed in chapter 4, minimized displacement.) Shalayev accepted the need for price reform, with the provisio that workers on low incomes and large families must be compensated (as Gorbachev promised, in any case). Union officials criticized excessive wage leveling. They supported development of the cooperative sector, with strict state control over prices.[65] In each of the major areas where reform policies threatened the social contract—employment security, price stability, egalitarianism—the union leadership gave at least qualified assent.

By late 1988 the reform's costs for workers had become clearly visible, and the union leadership responded by adopting a more critical posture. Union sources began to criticize abuses and violations of labor legislation during staff cuts, and factory committees were more often in conflict with managers over workers' rights to legal protection in dismissals. As the effects of self-financing on prices and the goods mix became evident, the unions advocated reinstitution of state plans for low-priced goods for children and the elderly. Shalayev complained that lease-contracting collectives violated labor laws and protections. Still, the AUCCTU's criticisms of reform policies remained moderate and piecemeal throughout the spring of 1989. This moderation was clearly reflected in the agenda which the trade unions presented to the Congress of People's Deputies in early June, a fourteen-point program which confined itself mainly to traditional, noncontroversial labor relations issues, and spoke to reform issues only in calling briefly for more controls on prices and cooperatives.[66] By this time much more extreme critiques of the basic reform program were being voiced, both by local trade union officials and by the workers' United Front forming in Russian cities.

The miners' strikes destroyed the complacency of the official unions, demonstrating at once workers' deep discontent and their complete lack of confidence in the local trade union representatives. The rise of independent miners' organizations, moreover, threatened the AUCCTU's monopoly, raising the specter of repudiation and replacement by a democratic labor movement organized from below. Shalayev, who went out to the coal basins as a member of a government commission, defended the strikers and blamed his union for "failing to ensure that the workers' legitimate demands were examined and satisfied." Promising that "the lessons of the strike will not be wasted," he initiated a period of self-criticism, self-flagellation, and reassessment which resulted in the AUCCTU's adopting a much more militant posture, activist politics, and an antireform agenda.[67]

In the weeks after the strikes, the trade unions thoroughly examined their failings. In late July, the AUCCTU Presidium concluded its report on the strike: "Gross violations of the legal interests of workers . . . indifference to their needs, were the objective preconditions [for the strikes]. Many trade unions . . . resigned themselves to sluggishness and serious omissions in the resolution of socioeconomic problems . . . and as a result lost authority and trust in the collectives."[68] Others went further, identifying the causes as much more than tactical or personnel problems. Shalayev, discussing the miners' decision to bypass the trade unions in organizing the strikes, said: "Many trade union committees . . . displayed timidity, and yielded the initiative to other social forces . . . unions have gradually become somehow built into the administrative-economic system, and distanced from their main responsibility."[69]

At the Sixth AUCCTU Plenum in early September, Shalayev redefined the trade unions' tasks and program, instructing them to shift their emphasis from production issues to protecting the rights of the working people. He proceeded with a harsh critique of reform, charging that it "carried an entire array of negative manifestations directly harming the interests of workers," and requiring the unions to defend those interests more aggressively.[70] He detailed some of the reform's real costs for workers, including layoffs, price increases, and competition from cooperatives. And he set official labor's new agenda with two policy statements, "On the Growth in Prices and Goods in Short Supply and on the Soviet People's Standard of Living," and "On Serious Distortions in the Cooperative Movement."[71] These statements effectively threw the AUCCTU's weight against economic reform, demanding a price freeze, a return to stringent price controls, and severe restrictions on cooperatives and privatization. Shalayev also criticized in principle the leasing of state enterprises, and warned of the looming threat of unemployment. With this radicalized program, the official trade unions became for a time an active, militant antireform force in Soviet politics.

In the aftermath of the Sixth Plenum, trade union committees began to engage in more activist politics. Union officials organized worker rallies in several major cities, including Moscow, Leningrad, and Kiev, to demonstrate support for the plenum's policy statements.[72] According to newspaper accounts, thousands of workers turned out to protest high prices, inflation, and profiteering by cooperatives, and to demand price controls and other administrative restrictions on economic activity, including suspension of operating rights for cooperatives that exceeded state prices.[73] The AUCCTU (as already noted) aided in establishment of the workers' United Fronts, providing subsidies and communication facilities, while the Fronts endorsed and supported the trade unions' policy line. The unions also began to lobby the government and legislature on social and labor policy. In debates over the comprehensive stabilization program in the fall of 1989, they strongly supported new administrative controls over prices and production, but rejected measures to control wages.[74] (The stabilization program was put into effect in December, without much success.) In the early months of 1990, the unions succeeded in delaying or obstructing new reform initiatives, most significantly the adoption of critical wholesale price increases.[75]

While the OFT and the radicalized trade unions did mobilize some working-class support and activism for their antireform agenda (and gained some recognition from Gorbachev), their influence remained extremely limited among workers in the Slavic republics.[76] The Interfront movements were quite successful among Slavic workers in the Baltic states and Moldavia, where they combined economic conservatism with opposition to the Popular Front movements for linguistic and political autonomy in those republics. But in Russian and Ukranian cities, the OFT fared poorly in the competition with other emerging popular organizations. Polls conducted in Moscow in early 1990, for example, showed the OFT at the bottom of the popularity scale.[77] One such poll, reported in early 1990, found that the liberal Interregional Group of Deputies was supported by 56 percent of respondents, the Moscow Popular Front by 34 percent, the nationalist-extremist Pamyat by 30 percent, and the OFT by 19 percent with the rest dismissing it as an "insignificant organization."[78]

More significantly, the results of elections to republic-level and local soviets in the early months of 1990 confirmed these low support levels: the conservative, antireform OFT finished near the bottom everywhere, while a liberal, proreform consensus seemed to dominate across social strata.[79] (Within months the AUCCTU restructured itself and moderated its policy line; see chapter 7.) It seems likely that the OFT was discredited, and its potential for winning support among workers undermined, by its more or less open association with old party and trade union bureaucrats. Nevertheless, keeping in mind that the OFT positioned itself as the best available defender of the social contract, its failure to gain significant support among workers has important implications.

Assessing the Social Contract Thesis

Does the erosion and breakdown of the contract that began in 1987 *explain* the rise of working-class activism? Were Soviet workers before Gorbachev quiescent because they were getting an acceptable package of benefits from the state, and did they become restive because they were no longer getting an acceptable package? Or were they quiescent before because of controls and repression, as others have argued;[80] becoming activist only because those controls had been lifted? Did Soviet workers use their new rights in substantial measure to protest the breakdown of the old contract and to demand revival of the old policies of state control and provision?

The evidence is ambiguous. On the one hand, deterioration and breakdown of the Soviet state's delivery on the contract was an important cause of rising worker discontent. Workers struck against wage reforms and quality controls which threatened their security of income, and pressed for wage increases to cover inflation. Rising prices, "uncontrolled" incomes in the cooperative sector, profit-driven distribution networks, and shortages of subsidized and price-controlled goods were central targets of workers' protests. In the summer and fall of 1989, some workers joined or supported the anti-reform OFT and even the official trade unions managed to organize large protest meetings against rising prices and cooperatives. Striking miners demanded improved delivery of selected social contract goods. Clearly, some groups of activist workers demanded a return to social contract policies and allocations, including stable, state-controlled prices, strong state regulation of distribution networks, repressed income differentiation, and guaranteed employment. Erosion of their protected economic position was a key factor in motivating workers' activism.

On the other hand, there is considerable evidence of workers' support for reform policies and leaders. First, as far as can be determined, the majority of workers in large cities of the Slavic republics supported proreform Popular Front organizations and candidates in the elections of late 1989 and early 1990. The OFT received comparatively weak support, despite its strong defense of social contract policies. I am led to the tentative conclusion that a return to the old contract (at least under the old party and trade unions) was not the preference of most workers. Second, the miners did support central elements of the economic reform, specifically self-financing and economic independence. They envisioned a self-supporting future, which suggests their eagerness (at least in the long term) to forgo the contract in exchange for control over their own production and product. They, along with other fuel and raw materials producers who could sell their products in international hard currency markets, faced a different structure of opportunity than the bulk of Soviet workers (whose output was not salable abroad), opportunity which led them to proreform positions.

The social contract thesis has other important weaknesses and limitations in explaining workers' behavior. It fails to take into account some of the major causes of discontent within the core of the working class. Many Slavic workers clearly had job-specific grievances—over working conditions, regulations, relations with administrators—which were unrelated to social contact issues. Many also harbored deep dissatisfactions with the quality, quantity, and consistency of the pre-Gorbachev state's delivery on some aspects of the contract, especially housing and living conditions. In other words, protests against the detrimental effects of reform policies on workers' well-being were inextricably mixed with grievances about the inadequacies or deterioration of the late-Brezhnev welfare state. Evidence from the miners' strikes makes it clear, moreover, that the contract was not an undifferentiated deal for all workers, that in fact the state delivered much more effectively to some worker groups (particularly those in large urban areas) than to others. Even if the Gorbachev leadership had continued with the old contract, it would likely have confronted serious discontent among some workers.

Finally, as I have noted, Soviet political democratization must be appreciated as a critical independent factor contributing to the increase of open working-class discontent. Because the loosening of political controls coincided with erosion of the social contract, the effects of these two factors on workers' behavior cannot easily be separated. Soviet workers used their newly acquired rights to some extent to protest the breakdown of the social contract and to demand its restoration, but this was not the sole focus of their activism. Overall, on the issue of Soviet workers' support for reform versus the social contract, the evidence remains mixed.

In February 1990, when the CPSU renounced its claim to a monopoly on political power in the Soviet Union, the conditions for the social contract ceased to exist. The party no longer held sole control over, or responsibility for, policy and allocational outcomes, and no longer demanded political compliance or quiescence. Elected legislatures and officials already influenced policy outcomes, while trade unions were free to lobby and workers were free to press their claims through strikes. In a critical sense, study of the social contract ends here. Nevertheless, because there was substantial continuity in the political leadership and policy agenda through the end of the Gorbachev era, in the following chapters I wish to examine the continuing breakdown of the social contract, and labor's response to it, during 1990 and 1991, and to consider the attempts by both Gorbachev and Boris Yeltsin to construct a new "social partnership" with labor.

SEVEN

Failure of the Social Contract:
Labor and the Soviet Collapse

The emergence of working-class activism, independent trade unions, and competitive political processes transformed labor and social policy-making in the Soviet Union. By 1990 workers and unions had become major players in these processes, influencing legislative drafts and debates, policy decisions, and allocational outcomes. With the collapse of the Communist party in the aftermath of the August 1991 coup attempt, elected officials and independent organizations were left to restructure labor relations in the absence of authoritarian controls or paternalistic obligations. This chapter covers both structures and policy in 1990 and 1991, with some consideration of the continuing effects of the social contract in Gorbachev's last year and in Yeltsin's Russia.

The newly-established General Confederation of Trade Unions (GCTU), the reformed successor of the old All-Union Central Council of Trade Unions (AUCCTU), emerged as the most significant labor organization in this period. As was discussed in chapter 6, the AUC-CTU adopted a radical, antireform program in the fall of 1989. It soon abandoned this obstructionist strategy, however. In the course of 1990 the centralized AUCCTU transformed itself into an independent confederation, and sought a constructive role as labor's representative in the reform process. It set forth a policy agenda which focused on jobs programs and income maintenance, the core of the old social contract. The GCTU, along with its republic-level affiliates, played a role in policy-making from early 1990 onward.

Social Policy

Employment

In 1990 Soviet authorities admitted the existence of long-term structural unemployment, variously estimated at 2 to 8 million and concentrated in central Asia and the Transcaucasus. The threat of unemployment in Slavic regions as a consequence of reform remained marginal, affecting primarily women and youth seeking to enter the labor force.[1] However, economic performance continued to deteriorate dramatically because of the general collapse of the state planning mechanism, the collapse in trade with former Eastern European client states, strikes, and ethnic conflicts. Transition toward a market economy became broadly accepted as inevitable, and government and labor leaders anticipated that it would produce high levels of labor displacement in the near future. Projections of 5 to 30 million unemployed by the early 1990s became common (echoing the projections made in 1987 and 1988) and motivated both popular fears and a new round of legislation (the 1988 Law on Employment having been disregarded and apparently forgotten).[2] The observer cannot escape the sense of familiarity and frustration, as Gorbachev's government again poured energy into detailed preparations for the effects of a reform it would never implement.

The Basic Law on Employment for the USSR and the Republics was passed in January 1991, after a year of consideration and debate. The GCTU played a major role in the legislative process, submitting its own draft of the law which called for a more liberal definition of "unemployed," higher benefit levels, longer periods of eligibility, and early retirement provisions; by its own calculations, the trade unions' version would cost R12 to 15 billion, against R5 to 6 billion for the government's.[3] The final measure was a compromise, setting guidelines for registration and compensation of unemployed workers which the republics were to follow in designing their own legislation, and creating a State Employment Service. Those who qualified were to receive benefits for several months, job referrals, and opportunities for retraining. The law was to go into effect on July 1, 1991, to be funded by a 1 percent tax on the wages fund of all employers.[4]

All republics with large Slavic work forces (the RSFSR, Ukraine, and Kazakhstan) passed legislation which met or exceeded the all-union guidelines, and began registering the unemployed in the summer of 1991. The eligibility criteria for benefits were somewhat restrictive, requiring (for example, in the Russian republic) an individual to have worked 36 weeks in the previous year, to have lost his or her job involuntarily and not for cause, and (at least in Moscow) to hold a residence and work permit. At the same time, considerable compensation was provided to those who qualified, including 75 percent of their former base salary for three months, and declining percentages for nine months more.[5] Others could register for job referral services only. Even allowing for the inadequacies of the services and the available data (which are generally considered to seriously underestimate joblessness), the number of registered unemployed workers provides at least a crude indicator of the scale and growth of layoffs in these regions from mid-1991 onward. The data indicate clearly that the scale remained quite modest: in December 1991, the Republic of Russia had 450,000 registered unemployed workers, with 51,000 receiving benefits, while the state employment services reported 1 million persons registered as "not engaged in labor activity and seeking employment" in the USSR overall.[6] Discussions with Russian labor experts confirm that even the most modest projections of unemployment levels did not materialize.[7]

As Elizabeth Teague has pointed out, these statistics clearly do not reflect the massive shakeout of surplus labor which real market pressures would bring. Indeed, it seems reasonable to ask here how the Soviet economy managed to maintain such high levels of employment despite serious disruptions of production in many sectors and a decline of 17 percent in real gross domestic product during 1991.[8] Three factors would seem to account for the continuing relatively low levels of job loss in the Slavic regions through 1991:

1. *Transfer of labor from the state to the private sector.* State sector employment did decline somewhat, but was partly counterbalanced by absorption of workers into cooperatives, joint ventures, and other private sector jobs. A major International Monetary Fund (IMF) study found that while employment in state enterprises and organizations fell 7.9 percent from 1990 to 1991, it increased 100 percent in leased enterprises, 189 percent in economic associations, 374 percent in joint ventures, and 146 percent in joint stock enterprises over the same period.[9]

2. *A growing level of "hidden unemployment" of a new type.* Enterprises which had neither sufficient supplies to employ the labor, nor

wages to pay their workers, put those workers on part-time or gave them extended leaves rather than laying them off. The level of such hidden unemployment remains indeterminate, but RSFSR minister of labor A. Shokhin characterized it as a major factor in explaining the low levels of reported unemployment in the fall of 1991.[10]

3. *Continuing government subsidies and lax bank credit to state-owned enterprises.* Despite the insistence of reformers that loss-making plants must be closed, and the serious declines in productivity and overall production of Soviet industry, government subsidies continued to grow at least through 1990. The same was true for bank credit: short-term credit to enterprises increased by 145 percent in 1991.[11] These subsidies and credits allowed managers to retain most of their work force (though, as noted above, not always 100 percent of the workers at full-time) and were the key to the low level of job losses through 1991.

In sum, the Gorbachev administration continued to repudiate in principle the old social contract guarantee of full employment, but continued to deliver on its substance for most Slavic male workers. While perhaps 10 percent of workers in the urban-industrial economy had moved into private sector employment by the end of 1991, the vast majority continued to work for the state. The newly assertive trade unions exerted some pressure for continued job security, placing every available legal and procedural obstacle in the way of plant closings and layoffs.[12] But this was not the critical factor; it was rather the anticipated magnitude and unknown consequences of plant closings that paralyzed the reformers. Additionally, as the economy deteriorated, more and more enterprises fell into the ranks of loss-makers, until it seemed that a substantial part of the economy would close down without subsidies.

Prices and Wages

In 1990, the trend of increasing prices and wages continued. Retail prices rose slowly but steadily throughout the year, growing 10 percent overall from January to December according to the official price index (see Table 7.1). At the same time the consumer market deteriorated rapidly with severe shortages and imbalances, few products regularly available in state stores, and declining availability as well as increasing prices in kolkhoz markets. Some local authorities

Table 7.1 Soviet retail price index, January 1990–September 1991
(Jan. 1990 = 100%)

1990		1991	
Month	Percent	Month	Percent
Jan.	100	Jan.	120
Feb.	101	Feb.	127
Mar.	101	Mar.	131
Apr.	102	Apr.	197
May	102	May	200
June	103	June	200
July	104	July	200
Aug.	105	Aug.	200
Sept.	106	Sept.	203
Oct.	108		
Nov.	109		
Dec.	110		

Source: PlanEcon Report, vol. 7, nos. 43–44, Dec. 9, 1991, p. 14. (Percents are rounded to nearest whole number.)

turned to food rationing, distributing coupons which were then required for purchase of scarce goods.[13] Despite declining productivity and output, wages and incomes also rose, with overall money income increasing 16.9 percent in 1990.[14] The gap between incomes and available supplies of goods and services continued to widen, contributing to inflationary pressures.

In April 1991, the Gorbachev government finally initiated its long-promised retail price reform. The reform was intended to stabilize the consumer market, reduce (but not eliminate) subsidies, and move the economy toward market determination of prices. Officials claimed that it would increase prices for necessities 60 percent on average, and that the state would compensate the population for 85 percent of the increase with increments to wages and transfer payments.[15] The reform legislation established three price categories:

1. Basic consumer goods and services were subject to uniform price ceilings or maximum increases, though the allowed increases would double or triple the cost of many common food items (averaging, for example, 130 percent for dairy products and 200 percent for bread and meat products).

2. Other specified consumer goods were to be sold at regulated retail prices, with maximum limits or scales for increases or other regulatory procedures.
3. A third list of domestic and imported consumer goods would be sold at contract or free prices.

According to State Pricing Committee chairman V. Senchagov, initially prices for 15 percent of goods turnover would be regulated while free prices would be set for 30 percent, with the sphere of free price formation to expand gradually.[16]

Like the reformers' earlier treatment of price reform (discussed in chapter 4), the April 1991 legislation seemed to devote more attention to the compensation package than to pricing policy. It specified in great detail compensation levels for workers, families with children, students, pensioners, and others, and provided some new benefits for children, as well as supplements to savings accounts. However, the immediate compensation provided to most workers and pensioners was 60 to 65 rubles per month, an amount sorely inadequate to cover the steep price increases triggered by the reform. The new price legislation went into effect on April 2, with dramatic effect.

Retail prices increased more than 50 percent for the month, including 175 percent for light industrial goods and 240 percent for foodstuffs. (See Table 7.1, which shows an increase of 66 points in the retail price index for April.) Real wages fell more than 25 percent.[17] As one academic economist stated in a report to *Izvestiia*, "Any illusions about new retail prices being compensated by 60–65 ruble supplementary payments were dispersed at once."[18] Though rents and some other expenses remained stable (bringing the overall increase closer to the government's claim of 60 percent), the effect on poorer strata who spent much of their income on food was severe, and the number living close to or below the poverty line increased markedly. At the same time the price reform failed to satisfy market-oriented economists, who argued (correctly) that it did not fundamentally change the mechanism for price formation, but retained much of the old administrative controls and limits which distorted prices.[19]

Workers responded to these increases with new industrial strikes, strike threats, and calls for the government's resignation. Miners, already engaged in a protracted strike, grew more intransigent. Here it can clearly be seen that the social contract had broken down: the state allowed, indeed sponsored, large retail price increases which produced a precipitous drop in real incomes; as a consequence labor unrest increased. A massive strike in the cities of Belorussia continued through most of the month, while a strike movement in Ukraine was defused only through immediate concessions by the republic's government. Altogether, more than 8,000 strikes were reported throughout the Soviet Union in April and May.[20] The GCTU also played a major part in the protests over price increases, demanding full state compensation to the population for all expenditures occasioned by the reform.

Gorbachev's government quickly caved in to these pressures, introducing almost immediately a series of stop gap measures to increase compensation to specific groups. Over the following months it adopted a package of income maintenance measures, while factory managers independently increased their workers' wages. Both helped to restore pre-April real wage levels by August, and to supersede those levels by the end of the year.[21]

Social Services

During 1990 and 1991, several categories of state spending on social services increased. Wage levels for workers in education, health, social security, and cultural institutions were raised, transfer payments to children, invalids, and pensioners were increased, and normatives for maintenance of citizens in hospitals, rest homes, and other facilities were raised.[22] However, most of these increases were provided to compensate for rising prices during and after the April 1991 price reform and were simply absorbed by inflation. They did not, for the most part, increase either the real wages of social service workers or the quantity and quality of services provided. To complicate matters further, republics began to establish and fund much of their own subsidy and social service policies during this period. It is therefore impossible to compare meaningfully the level of expenditures in these years with earlier expenditure levels.

There is clear evidence that, at the same time, a number of factors contributed to the deterioration of social services. First, the health care system suffered from severe shortages of medicines and medical supplies. The Soviet Union had long relied heavily on its Eastern European trading partners for these goods, and when Council on

Mutual Economic Assistance (CMEA) trade links broke down in 1989 and 1990 it was left to find both new suppliers and hard currency for medicines. To make matters worse, environmental activists within the Soviet Union had closed down numerous chemical factories which produced critical raw materials for the limited domestic pharmaceutical industry.[23] Second, the appearance of AIDS within the population and the health effects of Chernobyl and lesser contamination problems added significantly to the normal burden of infectious and degenerative diseases. Third, in 1991 strike threats and brief strikes by teachers and medics became frequent. Though both wanted higher wages, medical personnel stated as their primary grievance the lack of the most basic supplies needed to treat patients.[24]

Gorbachev's government tried to maintain its commitment to state provision of medical care and other social services. Besides raising wages and transfer payments, it exempted medicines entirely from the 1991 price increases (one of the few products so exempted), maintained subsidies, and allocated additional hard currency expenditures for purchase of medical supplies. It kept most social service facilities (clinics, schools, child care facilities) in operation, and provided special subsidies to cushion the impact of food price increases on these institutions. There were some claims of improvement in health indicators such as infant mortality.[25] However, the weight of available evidence indicates deterioration in the state's provision of social services despite increasing allocations, largely because of uncontrolled inflation, severe shortages and black market control of scarce goods (including medicines), and labor unrest. Moreover, introduction of private medical insurance was under active consideration. In the area of social services too, the social contract was failing.

Labor Organization and Unrest

From early 1990, the Soviet labor movement basically split between militant, strike-prone independents in energy and transport sectors and reformed official unions, which sought a constructive dialogue with government. The following section examines the efforts of both reformed officials and militant independents to press their demands on Gorbachev's government during 1990 and 1991, and shows that the Soviet state proved a weak manager of the newly emergent and newly assertive labor interests.

The Reformed Official Unions: Seeking a Constructive Dialogue

In the course of 1990 the AUCCTU transformed its structure, moderated its policy line, and sought a constructive role as labor's representative in the reform process. These changes were formalized at the 19th AUCCTU Congress in October 1990 (though most had already been adopted into practice before that time). The Congress replaced the union's old, centralized structure with the General Confederation of Trade Unions, which declared itself an independent and voluntary organization.[26] Several GCTU-affiliated, republic-level Federations of Independent Trade Unions (FITUs) were also established, the largest and most important in the Russian republic, the FITU(R). The GCTU refuted reformists' assertions that it was simply a whitewashed AUCCTU, and credible arguments could be made on both sides. The continuity in leadership was undeniable: V. Shcherbakov, first chair of the GCTU, had been deputy chair of the AUCCTU, and Ye. Klochkov, chair of the FITU(R), was a former AUCCTU secretary. Further, the GCTU simply adopted the old union's membership lists, claiming to represent 140 million workers (most of the Soviet labor force) at its founding.[27] On the other hand, the GCTU no longer took orders from above; its policies and tactics were driven by the imperative to survive in a democratizing polity.

The General Confederation now recognized the need for economic reform and declared its "conditional support" for a market economy with a diversity of ownership forms, but it demanded that the transition program include social guarantees. It adopted a policy agenda which focused on jobs programs and income maintenance. Insisting that employment remain the state's responsibility during reform, the GCTU pressed for liberal unemployment compensation, state programs for retraining and resettlement, and special (essentially public works) programs for the anticipated 5 to 10 million workers who were to be displaced by the end of 1991. It also demanded that the state maintain living standards (against increasing costs and inflation) through regular indexation of all wages, pensions, and transfer payments; the guarantee of a subsistence minimum; and increases in the minimum wage.[28] On the basis of this program the GCTU set itself up as a "constructive opposition" to the reformist government, submitting alternative policy drafts to the Council of Ministers and Supreme Soviet, wrangling over the specific provisions of labor legislation, demanding legal guarantees of trade union rights, and generally behaving as a good institutional citizen of the new democratic order.

Over and above its specific policy agenda, the GCTU sought to formalize and institutionalize its role as a direct, permanent participant in the policy-making process. Modeling its approach explicitly if imperfectly on corporatist principles (see the discussion in chapter 1), it pressed Gorbachev's government to create a permanent negotiating structure which would work out a comprehensive annual socioeconomic agreement among the state, labor, and managers/entrepreneurs. The GCTU would act as the designated national representative of labor in this negotiating structure, while the FITUs would engage in similar bargaining at the republic level.[29] FITU(R) chair Klochkov summed up this program with his call for "legislative enshrinement of the role of unions at the republic level in the elaboration, realization, and supervision of measures on the transition to a controlled market economy and social guarantees."[30]

The GCTU, in this way, sought a "constructive dialogue" with government over the specifics and mechanics of the reform program. While claiming in principle the right to strike, the union eschewed confrontation and insisted that all issues relating to reform could be peacefully negotiated through consultation and compromise. It is important to note here that the union sought protection not for workers alone but for virtually the entire population: pensioners, students, children, all recipients of state transfer payments. It defined its constituency broadly, focusing especially on the "economically vulnerable," while the independents represented narrower sectoral interests.

Through late 1990 and early 1991, as increasingly radical reform programs were debated (especially Yavlinsky's 500 Days program), inflation and social tensions rose, and energy and transport workers regularly issued ultimatums backed by strike threats, the GCTU promoted its moderate program of "reform with social guarantees" and worked to institutionalize a "social partnership" with government. Yet experience of the miners' movement would seem to indicate that confrontation was a winning union strategy: strikes had brought large concessions from the state and real authority among the rank-and-file workers. Why, then, did the GCTU adopt such a conciliatory stance toward Gorbachev's faltering government?

The GCTU was, in a sense, a bodiless head—it had a large apparatus of functionaries with a very limited mass base. Numerous public opinion polls and surveys show that the official unions had long since ceased to inspire mass confidence or loyalty. In a March 1989 survey by the All-Union Center for the Study of Public Opinion, for example, more than 75 percent of urban respondents gave a negative evaluation of the trade unions' role in "protecting the rights of workers in our country," with 52 percent assessing the unions' performance as "fairly low" or "very low."[31] Trade union affiliation had long been an involuntary formality for the tens of millions of members unions claimed, and the legacy of rank-and-file distrust and hostility toward union functionaries could not easily be overcome.[32] For most members, the unions' only use was as distributors of social security and other benefits.

On the other hand, the GCTU still faced little or no competition from independent unions in most sectors. And even where it did face competition, as in mining, officials of the independent unions claimed that fear of losing GCTU-administered benefits kept workers from switching.[33] If the General Confederation could establish itself as the authorized bargaining agent for labor in state councils at this point, it would be in a position to bind members through delivery of more benefits and policy goods and, potentially, to preempt other challenges from below. And the GCTU was hedging its bet on Gorbachev's government by seeking to establish similar bargaining structures at the republic level.

In essence, the GCTU was trying to preserve its dominant position by integrating into the democratized Soviet state as the "peak" or "chartered" representative of labor. In this effort it had considerable advantages. First, it was well connected with government leaders, most notably through the recent promotion of its past chair, G. Yanaev, to the position of vice president. Second, much of the reformist leadership doubted the morality and feared the social consequences of mass unemployment and uncompensated price increases, predisposing it to the GCTU's agenda. Third, the independent unions had so far brought only months of fruitless meetings, nonnegotiable demands, and disruptive strikes, while the GCTU held out the promise of labor peace. Finally, the notion of a corporatist approach had some cachet because of its association with practices in the industrial democracies.

By the fall of 1990, both the central and republic-level governments had in fact begun holding regular consultations with the reformed official trade unions over employment, income, and other labor and social policies. In October, Ryzhkov declared his government ready for a social partnership with the GCTU, which he acknowledged as representing 140 million workers. He and his successor, V. Pavlov (from January 1991), met with Shcherbakov to discuss a draft general agreement between the union and the Council of Ministers for 1991. After some foot-dragging on the part of the government, the agreement was approved in April 1991.[34] Russian republic leaders Yeltsin and Silayev also met with FITU(R) chair Klochkov, confirmed the need for close collaboration and mutual responsibility between the unions and the new republic-level organs of power, and began negotiations. The republic government deferred to the FITU(R)'s demand for social guarantees and for a permanent role in the planning and implementation of reform, and made a draft socioeconomic agreement for 1991 with the union's presidium.[35] Talks over increasing social protections also began between Ukrainian leaders Kravchuk and Koralevsky and the FITU(Uk).

There were some problems inherent in the Soviets' use of a corporatist approach to managing labor relations. Deputy Prime Minister V. Shcherbakov identified the central one in his comments about meetings on a general wage agreement for 1992: "In the civilized world . . . such agreements are signed by employers with trade unions, and the government plays the role of arbiter. The situation is different in our country: the government is the controlling authority, and 90 percent of the property is in the hands of the state. That means that the Cabinet of Ministers signs the agreement as a representative of the owner—the state—along with the trade unions, whose interests are represented by the GCTU."[36] While Shcherbakov also spoke of a "third force," the Science and Industry Union, which nominally represented managers and entrepreneurs, he admitted that it represented mainly state enterprises and was "not yet endowed with the powers that would make it a responsible participant in the talks."[37]

There are actually two distinct problems here. First, as Shcherbakov recognized, there was no significant, independent entrepreneurial or managerial group. Management was collapsed into the state, still largely subordinate to government ministries, and still dependent on subsidies from the state budget. Further, if management were brought into the bargaining process as a full participant (as it would be later, under Yeltsin), it would have stronger interests in increasing allocations from the state (perhaps in collaboration with labor) than in holding down costs. Second, the Soviet economy, with the exception of the embryonic cooperative sector, had no market features; the state largely controlled and bore responsibility for wages, prices, and production. The state could not credibly claim the hard budget constraints or profitability pressures which set limits on concessions of owners in market systems. There was, in short, no independent market or economic elite to shield it from responsibility for economic outcomes and their social costs. The state thus became not a mediator, but the direct object of union demands. Decisions on most socioeconomic issues were regarded by the unions (and much of the population) as wholly political. This protocorporatist arrangement left Gorbachev's government much more vulnerable to union pressures than would be the case for a democratic government involved in genuine three-way bargaining subject to real market constraints.

Soviet corporatism was plagued by another problem: the GCTU could not deliver labor's compliance. In spite of some feeble attempts to support the miners' economic demands, the General Confederation had no hope of gaining cooperation from the new independent unions in the coal basins. Nor were the sporadic strike movements in the energy and transport sectors during 1990 and early 1991 subject to its control. The transport strikes were mainly local wildcat actions, while the oil and gas workers' demands and strike threats were supported by sectoral unions nominally under the GCTU umbrella but clearly not bound by its commitments to cooperate and negotiate with Gorbachev's government. And while government leaders may have hoped that the GCTU had more authority in quieter sectors, data on workers' attitudes toward the union and a broader rash of strikes in the spring of 1991 contradicted these hopes.[38] The GCTU's lack of authority among rank-and-file workers made it a weak representative of labor, one which could not deliver on its promises of labor peace in exchange for social guarantees.

The Militant Independents: Strikes and Nonnegotiable Demands

Into the early months of 1990, the miners' committees continued to raise grievances about the government's fulfillment of the original 1989 strike accord, Resolution No. 608. The government insisted that it had implemented most of the promised measures, citing large supplemental payments for miners' wages, allocations for development of mining districts, and new pension legislation. But it was delivering very little of what the miners most wanted—coal price increases, independent rights to market abroad, and autonomy.[39] The government was hamstrung on these issues: domestic coal price increases, in the absence of a general price liberalization, would raise costs throughout already-troubled production sectors with no rationalizing effect. Expanded marketing rights for the miners could deprive the state of critical energy resources and hard currency, while autonomy for a single sector held multiple complications.

The miners' demands for control over production, pricing, and marketing thus brought them directly into conflict with the state and led to politicization of their movement. By the spring of 1990 the miners' committees had concluded that Gorbachev's government would not accede to their demands for autonomy, and began pressing for elimination or replacement of state structures and governmental authorities which they saw as obstacles. In July 1990, the Regional Council of Strike Committees called a twenty-four-hour political strike to demand resignation of Ryzhkov's government, the end of party control of enterprises and central institutions, and nationalization of party and AUCCTU property. Strike documents charged that the government was "unwilling or unable to ensure economic autonomy or to lead the country out of economic crisis" and that other targeted institutions were "obstructing liquidation of the command-administrative system."[40] Ryzhkov promised greater efforts to implement the original strike agreement, but the miners no longer trusted his government to deliver on its promises. Instead they turned to the newly autonomous republic-level governments for satisfaction of their demands, and began seeking independence through transfer of the mines to republic jurisdiction.[41] From this point on, the miners' movement added to the pressures for dissolution of the central Soviet government and state structures.

Strikes and strike threats also continued during 1990 and early 1991 in the oil and gas sectors and in transport, and broke out sporadically in other sectors.[42] The most serious was in the fall of 1990, when railway workers threatened an all-union warning strike, to be followed two weeks later by a genuine strike if demands were not met. Though the government insisted that the strike would be illegal under existing statutes, it conceded to most of the demands.[43] Indeed, Ryzhkov's government typically responded to labor unrest with easy concessions followed by poor delivery, setting a pattern which led repeatedly to protracted disputes with mobilized sectors of the labor force, and which further undermined the state's authority.

Spring 1991: Labor and Fragmentation of State Power

The spring of 1991 brought an upsurge of pressures and challenges from both independent and reformed official unions. The April price reform played a central role in these developments, and the GCTU responded with increased pressures for income indexation and other measures for social protection. The price increases also precipitated new strike movements and complicated efforts to settle an ongoing miners' strike.

STRIKES

In the first week of March, Soviet miners began a national political strike. Though the three organizations which initiated the strike, the Council of Kuzbass Workers' Committees, the Regional Council of Donbass Strike Committees, and the Independent Trade Union of Coal Miners, shortly set up an Interregional Coordinating Council in Moscow, the strikers displayed less organization and unity than in 1989.[44] Approximately one-third of all mines were participating in the strike at any one time, and while this was accomplished partly by design, the miners' varied demands, deadlines, and stated conditions for return to work indicate there was lack of unified leadership. The strikers made two central demands: wage increases of 100 to 150 percent with improved pension benefits, and the resignation of Gorbachev and his government. The political demands were not universal—miners in Vorkuta were demanding negotiations with Gorbachev's government while those in the Kuzbass called for its ouster—and a range of other economic and political demands were voiced by various groups from various regions.[45] Nevertheless the work stoppages continued for many weeks and imposed heavy economic costs, reaffirming the independents' ability to call a protracted and damaging strike.

The central government's efforts to deal with the miners' strike both highlighted and exacerbated its crisis of authority. First the Supreme Soviet, applying the provisions of the Law on Collective Labor Disputes, ordered a two-month suspension of the strike and arbitration. The miners rejected and ignored the legislature's order, as they did subsequent court rulings that their political demands were illegal and anticonstitutional.[46] After a three-week standoff between the strikers and the government, the Supreme Soviet pressed Prime Minister Pavlov to negotiate. Though completely rejecting the political demands, Pavlov agreed to meet with miners' representatives on economic issues. In early April he agreed to deep concessions, including a staged increase which would double miners' wages over the following year, additional compensation for price increases, the right to sell an increased portion of output at contract prices, and other benefits.[47] Most striking miners nevertheless rejected the agreement, largely because the simultaneous retail price increases undercut its significance; as one spokesman from the Donbass stated their position: "High prices have nullified everything the miners have achieved during the three years of strike struggle."[48] Many also continued to insist on the government's resignation.

While the miners defied the authority of central legislative and executive bodies, their strike provided an opportunity for the further encroachment of republic governments on the center. Even before the outbreak of the strike, Russian authorities held talks with their miners about a "republic-level settlement," while in Kazakhstan strikes were preempted by such a settlement.[49] Though initially put off by the miners' excessive wage demands, Yeltsin gave qualified support to the miners' struggle with the central government, and offered his government as an alternative bargaining partner. They found common ground in an agreement to demand transfer of the mines from central to republic jurisdiction, with the republic promising the miners economic independence. The strikes were finally ended by the center's accession to this demand.[50] The republic government thus scored a substantial victory against Gorbachev by demonstrating its ability to end the protracted strike and gaining control over major economic resources. The political ramifications were clearest in the Russian republic, where the miners' movement, Yeltsin, and the liberal political party Democratic Russia formed something of an alliance.[51]

CONCESSIONS

The GCTU did make some ineffective efforts to encourage compromise in the coal strikes. Its affiliated Coal Industry Trade Union supported the miners' economic demands but criticized the strike as an extreme measure organized by "political adventurers" who were splitting workers' solidarity, and insisted that both sides negotiate.[52] But the General Confederation devoted most of its energies to pressuring Gorbachev's government into an agreement on social protections (particularly employment and income indexation) for 1991. Frustrated with government foot-dragging over these issues, the GCTU (or its republic affiliates) threatened more than once to call strikes unless its measures were adopted, but it never actually did so. Instead, its threats invariably produced more meetings and unsteady progress toward agreement. When the April price increases were announced, the GCTU demanded that they be delayed until a law on income indexation had been adopted, and pressed for immediate and full compensation. When the price increases nevertheless went into effect on April 2, it condemned the government's compensation package, claimed that the higher prices were pushing large numbers of Soviet workers below the poverty line and that the minimum living wage had increased nearly two and a half times (from R130 to R320 per month), and added to its agenda demands for a wage increase of 70 to 100 percent in base industries by the end of 1991.[53]

On April 20, less than three weeks after the price increase went into effect, Gorbachev's Council of Ministers and the GCTU signed an agreement on labor and socioeconomic policies for 1991. The agreement committed the government to raising some categories of wages, lifting controls on others, drafting legislation on income indexing, and augmenting compensation for the price increases. It promised a staged increase in minimum wages and retirement benefits and substantial increases for wages in basic sectors and for employees in health care and education, and it gave enterprises independence in setting wage levels (above the guaranteed minimum) by repealing upper limits.[54] The legislation removed all restrictions on factory and shop floor managers, who had since 1988 been granting large wage increases in order to pacify and retain their workers. Such increases by managers were a critical, independent factor pushing wages upward and undermining state control.

The terms of this agreement made it clear that the Gorbachev government would not or could not impose wage and income restraint (as several of its Eastern European counterparts had under similar circumstances). Pressed by the GCTU, along with more amorphous popular dissatisfaction and some increase in strike activity, the government jettisoned its own modest compensation program and agreed to an extremely costly and inflationary package of income maintenance measures. Over the next two months, a minimum consumer budget was established and a draft Income Indexation Plan was prepared with the participation of the GCTU. Indexation of pensions, social allowances, grants, and wages in state organizations was to be carried out every three months on the basis of the consumer price index. Economists estimated that 1 percent growth in the price index would cost R3.55 billion nationwide. Labor and Social Issues minister Paulman held out against indexation of all wages, arguing that it would produce hyperinflation.[55] In any case wages continued to grow. These measures proved extremely costly for the Gorbachev government and its reform program, contributing to (though not alone causing) a wage-price spiral which would see average wages increase 1,000 percent over the next year and prices, in many cases more.

The agreement with the GCTU did not bring labor peace. The Confederation did not organize strikes, but neither could it prevent them; its affiliates were often pushed into supporting labor militance in an effort to establish some credibility with their rank and file. In May, air traffic controllers and pilots threatened strikes, with the FITU(R) supporting at least some of their demands.[56] The government responded with prosecution and new legislation declaring transport and political strikes illegal, increasing sanctions against wildcat actions, and giving the president the right to postpone or suspend strikes. But in the event, the controllers gained wage increases of 60 percent and other concessions, threatened future strikes if the remainder of their demands were not met, and formed an independent union. November and December brought another wave of strikes, though not on the scale of the spring's.[57]

Costs of Unrest and Concessions

In sum, Gorbachev's government made large concessions to labor without quelling unrest, and paid the costs of both. Coal production decreased 11 percent in 1991, and that of coking coal 20 percent. The coal strike also had a "downstream" effect on metallurgy, contributing to a 12 percent decline in steel output and a 13 percent decline in iron ore production in the first three quarters of 1991.[58] Millions of labor days were lost to strikes in 1990 and 1991 (though days lost to economic and political strikes cannot be separated statistically from the even larger numbers lost to strikes motivated by conflict between ethnic groups).[59] The economic effects of these strikes on production, while serious, should not be exaggerated, however; there were multiple sources of disruption in the Soviet economy by this point, including the large-scale breakdown of supply and exchange linkages. The socioeconomic and political consequences of labor activism and the state's weak responses to it were far more significant.

As Table 7.2 shows, average wages and salaries took off in the

Table 7.2 Growth of Soviet wages and salaries with percent growth over corresponding quarter of previous year, 1990–1991

Growth	1990				1991		
	I	II	III	IV	I	II	III
	Growth of wages						
Average wages, salaries[a]							
Rubles/month	257	257	257	309	285	336	351
Including bonuses					300	406	467
Increase (%)	9.4	7.5	8.4	22.6	10.9	30.7	36.6
	Change in income						
Population's money income (%)	13.3	12.5	17.3	24.9	23.8	63.2	120.0

Source: PlanEcon Report, vol. 7, nos. 43–44, Dec. 9, 1991, p. 9.
a. Nominal, nonagricultural, state sector.

second quarter of 1991, increasing 30.7 percent in that quarter (over the corresponding quarter of 1990) and 36.6 percent in the third quarter. The population's money income grew even more rapidly, increasing 63.2 percent in the second quarter (over the corresponding quarter of 1990) and 120 percent in the third. These increases were the combined result of direct compensation payments from the state, state-mandated wage increases for some workers, and easy raises given by managers who were under pressure from workers and subsidized by the state budget. Inflation, however, grew even more rapidly: the retail price index increased from 120 in January 1991 (with January 1990 set at 100) to 203.4 at the end of the third quarter of 1991 (see Table 7.1). As a result real wages and incomes declined significantly, producing pressures for further wage and subsidy increases.[60] Government spending to meet these pressures, along with drastically declining revenues, produced a burgeoning budget deficit for 1991 estimated at approximately 20 percent of GDP.[61] The Gorbachev government's inability to control either the inflationary spiral or the restive workers further obstructed its economic reform program and helped undermine its remaining authority, contributing to the rapid disintegration of the state in the aftermath of the abortive coup attempt of August 1991.

Conclusion

Could the Soviet state have managed emergent labor interests more effectively? A large part of its problem was structural: a democratizing state which owned and controlled most of the economy was especially vulnerable to labor's demands, and to the politicization of strike movements. But the state also influenced labor's organization and access to the policy process by recognizing the GCTU as the national representative of Soviet workers and treating it as a partner in the formulation of labor and social policies. Such official sanction gave the GCTU considerable advantage over challengers by putting it in a privileged position to negotiate and deliver policy goods to workers. General Confederation unions not only retained their role as distributors of social benefits, but also got the government to increase the benefit pool. And in addition to Gorbachev's government, the more staunchly reformist Yeltsin and Kravchuk governments also accepted the GCTU's affiliates (the republic-level FITUs) as "peak" representatives of labor. As a result, while the GCTU lost some members and significant independent unions formed in a few sectors, the large majority of Soviet workers remained within the Confederation and its affiliates in August 1991.[62]

The government's purposes might have been better served by refusing such recognition to the GCTU. The Confederation could not deliver on its no-strike pledge in any case, and there is reason to believe that few workers would have responded to its threatened strike calls. If the government had called the GCTU's bluff in the spring of 1991 and refused to conclude the agreement on wages and income indexing, it might have held down the costs of compensation and the inflation rate. Indeed, Gorbachev's government might have been better advised to encourage the diversification of unions, rather than recognizing a single union which was heavily oriented toward protecting workers and others likely to lose from reform. New unions in some sectors would have been likely supporters of reform measures (as was true to some extent for the independent miners' movement).[63] On the other hand, without the GCTU-initiated income indexing and other measures, social tensions over price increases might have reached explosive levels, and the human costs would surely have been greater.

EIGHT

Labor, Democracy, and Reform in the Post-Soviet Transition

The weight of evidence presented in the preceding chapters supports the social contract thesis. The Brezhnev regime consistently provided (with the few qualifications noted) full and secure employment, egalitarian wage policies, retail price stability, and subsidized social services. It produced this set of policy and allocational outcomes even in the face of rising costs, declining resources, and pressures to deliver other policy goods to competing claimants. At pressured decision points it acted as if constrained to maintain the contract, repeatedly committing additional resources, or abandoning other policies at significant cost, to do so. In sum, the Brezhnev leadership delivered on the social contract—though never as fully as officially planned, promised, or claimed, and at a declining level in its later years.

Moreover, the social contract thesis accounts for Brezhnev-era labor and social policy better than competing explanations do. Some economists argue that full employment and job security, central elements of the social contract, were products of soft budget constraints on Soviet managers. But in fact multiple political and legislative interventions were necessary to secure and maintain employment for certain groups of workers whom managers considered marginally productive. Bureaucratic-politics explanations also seem ill-suited to explain some welfare-oriented policies (for example, on employment and prices), which mainly benefited unorganized and poorly represented societal groups: marginally productive workers and urban consumers, respectively. And the pattern of regular increases in per capita spending for social services through much of the late-Brezhnev period of stringency seems inconsistent with the bureaucratic model, which should give primacy to the claims of the industrial ministries. Overall the social contract thesis, with its stress on the central leadership's direct commitment to social welfare, provides a more cogent explanation for the consistent pattern of policy results over time.

Some scholars point to the leadership's paternalism, or its commitment to socialist ideology, as the source of these policies. The case studies I have presented indicate that fear of a popular response to violations of the social contract was a more important factor: the Brezhnev leadership sought universal full employment, but was more active and thorough in assuring this outcome for cadres of young urban males, whose discontent could threaten stability, than for isolated groups of unemployed women in provincial towns. And in the debate on increasing food price subsidies (especially the last, most costly round of increases in 1982), concerns about social justice were explicitly mixed with fears about the response of workers and urbanites to rising retail prices. The Brezhnev leadership was genuinely committed to providing social security and distributive equality, but when it became especially difficult or expensive to maintain these policies, fear of alienation and protest among urban and male workers weighed heavily in the outcome.

According to the social contract thesis, the Brezhnev leadership traded policy goods for workers' political quiescence and compliance with authoritarian rule. On the basis of available evidence, the pattern of workers' collective political behavior during the Brezhnev years does fit the thesis: workers remained generally quiescent so long as the regime delivered on the contract; strikes and unrest increased in the early 1980s, when delivery had measurably deteriorated. Social contract issues played a role in at least one-half of all reported strikes, and grievances over food shortages were central in the 1980 and 1981 strikes. Moreover, attitude surveys of Soviet émigrés showed that a large percentage valued state provision of social services and welfare (indeed, that this was consistently the single most positively evaluated feature of the system), providing further evidence that these policies were an important source of popular acceptance of the regime.

Alternative explanations for workers' political compliance stress repression, political controls, and bureaucratic manipulation of benefits to segment the working class. The use and threat of repression certainly played a role in maintaining labor quiescence during the Brezhnev period, but it cannot account for variation in the level of open discontent. This level did increase (despite a presumably steady level of repression) when delivery of social contract benefits declined. It may be concluded, then, that threatened repression was inadequate to maintain quiescence in the absence of a minimal level of workers' satisfaction with the regime's substantive provision of social welfare. Quiescence is also seen as a result of bureaucratic domination and manipulation, which segmented and divided workers, undermining class solidarity and the potential for collective action. In fact, however, labor policy during the Brezhnev years tended to increase equality and extend universal legal and normative protections to workers, presumably restricting the discretionary and discriminatory powers of managers and others. Again, the social contract provides a more cogent and convincing explanation for the pattern of workers' behavior.

Before moving on to consider the Gorbachev period, it will be useful to consider some of the legacies left by the Brezhnev-era social contract, this pattern of exchange which continued over two decades and more. First are the normative legacies: the strong popular sense (evidenced in many surveys) of collective entitlement to basic provision, and the leaders' correlative sense of responsibility to satisfy basic needs. Following from this is the population's long-standing orientation to substantive (rather than procedural) output from government as the basis for political legitimation. The political legacy is a governmental system that focused so exclusively on maintaining control and quiescence that it created no mechanisms for genuine communication, bargaining, or mediation with its society, but that did construct massive bureaucratic organizations with at least formal claims to represent societal interests (most significantly, the All-Union Central Council of Trade Unions, or AUCCTU).

Last and most important are the structural legacies of the social contract policies. These include the massive accumulation over many years of social service subsidies, especially retail food price subsidies, and critical networks of state-run health care, child care, educational, and cultural institutions which would (for the most part) collapse if the state withdrew support. They include many thousands of aging, obsolete, overstaffed, and loss-making production facilities, which would have been forced to close down gradually in a market economy, and which employ a high proportion of manual and manufacturing workers. Finally they include several thousand "company towns" whose local economies would essentially collapse with the closure of their major enterprise, creating pockets of depression throughout the territory of the Soviet Union. These are the legacies of a declining authoritarian regime, rigid and repetitive in its policy-making, lacking the energy or imagination to modernize its economy, paying out ever-growing subsidies to pacify its population.

Gorbachev's Reforms and Democratization

The Gorbachev leadership introduced reforms that were intended to accelerate economic growth, but at great cost to economic security and stability. Labor force restructuring and self-financing legislation (the Law on the State Enterprise) threatened to displace tens of thousands of blue-collar workers from previously secure jobs. The 1986 wage reform reversed the leveling tendencies of Brezhnev-era wage policies, while quality control and other measures increased performance pressures in industry. Privatized, for-fee social services were introduced. Proposed price reforms threatened state subsidies which had kept retail prices of necessities at stable levels throughout much of the Soviet period, while legalization of a private cooperative sector reduced state control over pricing and income distribution. In addition the Gorbachev leadership explicitly repudiated the paternalism of its predecessors and rejected the basic principles of egalitarian distribution as fundamentally unjust, morally debilitating, and detrimental to scientific and technological progress.

While Gorbachev intended to stop delivery of social contract policy outputs to Soviet society, he at the same time ceased to demand society's political quiescence and compliance with authoritarian controls. In stages, beginning with glasnost in 1986 and proceeding with competitive elections and the seating of a genuinely empowered legislature in 1989, and the end of the CPSU's formal political monopoly in early 1990, Gorbachev democratized the Soviet system. Though his motives here were multiple and complicated, central among them was his frequently stated belief that democratization would strengthen support for economic reform. Gorbachev and others in his administration argued that holdover bureaucratic and political authorities were the central obstacles to economic restructuring, and that democratization would liberate society's proreform energies and commitments and help overcome entrenched bureaucratic resistances.

It is interesting to consider how democratization might have facilitated economic reform. First of all, it could have led to a substantial mobilization of reform-minded elements within Soviet society who shared the leadership's urgency about the economic decline and its criticisms of excessive egalitarianism and social security. I have noted arguments that both the constituency and the normative bases for Brezhnev's social contract had weakened.[1] The traditional working class, which was its chief beneficiary, had declined in both size and importance. Intellectuals and policy specialists had defected from the contract's norms, and the growing educated professional classes in Soviet society wanted a more meritocratic, competitive, and stratified reward system and would likely be receptive to the reformist agenda. Competitive elections would logically have favored the emergence of an articulate, politically ambitious new leadership from this proreform constituency, while marginalizing the less educated and resourceful (for example, manual workers), who stood to lose most from reform. Newly empowered democratic institutions could then have served as a proreform counterweight to the entrenched bureaucracies.

On a more conceptual level, democratization could have facilitated reform by diffusing some of the responsibility for economic and distributive decisions from the political center. The fusion of political and economic institutions in the pre-1988 Soviet system constrained policy because it made the party-state leadership fully responsible for the costs of economic reform. Democratization devolves decision-making power to individuals and bodies which are selected by at least partly democratic procedures, introducing into the system new mechanisms of accountability and legitimation. It has the potential to create a polity in which the hard choices and social costs of reform are legitimated by a combination of economic efficiency criteria and democratic choice. Popular discontent might then express or diffuse itself in organizational and electoral activity, rather than by the blunt instrument of strikes and riots against an authoritarian regime. This is in part how democratization has facilitated reform in the more successful cases in Eastern Europe, where prime ministers fall frequently but privatization moves unsteadily forward.

Why, then, did Soviet democratization fail to facilitate Gorbachev's reforms? First, Gorbachev initiated his economic reform program (in 1987 and 1988) as an authoritarian leader completely lacking any democratic mandate or input. Reform policies were therefore identified with him and his chosen advisers, and Soviets broadly held him responsible for the reform's results and costs. Second, competitive elections in 1989 and 1990 could hardly have been expected to produce proreform majorities. While many reformist candidates were elected in large western Soviet cities, proreform constituencies were too concentrated geographically, and too unorganized politically, to carry the day. Throughout most of the Soviet Union the Communist party remained the only organized political force (both before and after the end of its legal monopoly) and dominated election outcomes. As a consequence, a critical mass of those elected (though by no means all Communist party members) held to the old norms and expectations. (As we have seen, the first All-Union Supreme Soviet strongly supported the retrenchment and stabilization program of the fall of 1989, and the first Russian Supreme Soviet, elected in 1990, continues as of this writing to resist Yeltsin's reform efforts.

Third, among Slavic workers the newly conferred democratic rights were used most often to protest reformist labor policies, highlighting the tension between economic reform and political democratization. Workers, given rights to organize and strike, soon began to protest the erosion of their living standards brought on by quality controls, wage reforms, and incipient inflation. By 1989 strikes among raw-materials, transport, and other workers, with both old and reform-related grievances, had become frequent. Soviet democratization mobilized first and foremost not the proreform professionals, but the industrial workers whose security and income were directly threatened by reform. In this process, the policy preferences of intellectuals and the attitudes of the Soviet middle class mattered less than the specific responses of workers, who displayed a tenacious commitment to their accustomed security, stability, and low performance standards. The Gorbachev leadership lacked both institutionalized mechanisms and competence for bargaining with organized workers, and in the event made empty promises which alienated the mobilized sectors of the labor force. Grass-roots activism, finally, pushed the AUCCTU into militant defense of workers' interests, increasing the pressure on Gorbachev's government to provide full compensation for the costs of reform.

Gorbachev thus confronted the social contract and its legacies in several dimensions. As head of the party-state, he inherited his predecessor's obligations to maintain social provision, but in a declining economy. Democratization came too late and too tentatively to devolve much responsibility from the political center, self-interested bureaucracies resisted reform, and democracy led mainly to the mobilization of societal resistance as well. However, these resistances were not (in many cases) decisive in defeating reform. The Gorbachev leadership had the policy instruments necessary to implement at least some of its reforms, particularly in the areas of enterprise insolvency, quality control, and pricing, despite bureaucratic resistance. And before mid-1989, workers' protests were neither large nor well organized enough to force policy retreats.

Reform policies did result in some erosion of workers' social contract guarantees. Some workers were released from their jobs, others lost wages, and many experienced unaccustomed economic insecurity. Some social services were privatized, and retail price reforms and subsidy cuts were anticipated. But in each case, by early 1989 new decisions and concessions had limited or averted the painful effects for workers: factories were allowed to reabsorb released workers, wage discipline was relaxed, quality control was largely abandoned, privatization was severely limited, and retail price reform was delayed.

This pattern of policy retreats leads to the conclusion that the social contract constrained the Gorbachev leadership from pursuing its declared reform strategy. The fear that workers (and others) would withdraw consent and compliance from the state if the expected social contract policy goods were not delivered drove the leadership's decisions. The old social contract defined broadly accepted standards of what the state should provide—of society's entitlements. Though it faced a variety of resistances, the Gorbachev leadership's apprehension about the social and political consequences of violating the old contract was the critical factor, common across policy areas, constraining the reformers' decisions, even when bureaucratic resistance could have been overcome and popular mobilization was not yet significant.

It is important to appreciate the enormity of the task which Gorbachev confronted in seeking to dismantle the old system. Especially significant were the structural legacies: the price, industrial, and labor force structures produced by long-term adherence to the contract. In order to liberalize prices, Gorbachev would have had to pass on to consumers the accumulated production and procurement price increases of two decades and more. The effects of such liberalization on industry, with its arbitrarily set state prices and convoluted system of profit redistribution, were incalculable. Even more problematic were the obsolete industrial infrastructure and the poorly skilled labor force inherited from Brezhnev. Perhaps Gorbachev and his advisers only came to understand the likely magnitude of the effects of their proposed policies—the bankruptcy of perhaps 25 percent of Soviet enterprises, and job loss for at least that percent of the labor force—from the policy debates of 1987 and 1988.[2] Such immense social costs, when combined with its residual paternalism and its democratic commitments, left the Gorbachev leadership unwilling to forge ahead with its original reform strategy.

It is perhaps more interesting to ask why the reformers failed to modify their policies, why they so often returned to the *status quo ante,* rather than trying to achieve at least some of their goals. Instead of continuing blanket subsidies to industry in the fall of 1988, they might (as suggested in chapter 5) have targeted smaller subsidies for plant modernization and more selective support of enterprises. Instead of severely restricting medical cooperatives, they might have sought measures to limit serious corruption, while otherwise allowing the sector to develop. Even in the case of price and consumer policy, more supple regulations and use of taxation to create differentiated incentives (for example, to encourage production of "socially useful" goods) might have provided an alternative to reassertion of administrative controls. Some Soviet officials were clearly conscious of such possibilities; as noted in chapter 5, then–Goskomtsen chair V. Pavlov suggested in early 1989 that the government could have tried economic methods such as taxation to stabilize the consumer market, but had instead reverted to administrative methods to settle the problem quickly. The Supreme Soviet also tried to design financial levers and regulatory measures to influence prices, wages, and production patterns, but in the end reverted to restrictions and subsidies.[3] The system and its leaders lacked the requisite knowledge and institutions to design and carry out such measures (as they lacked the institutional framework to bargain with striking workers). This lack of policy flexibility and regulatory capacity, which Charles Lindblom called "thumbs where one would want fingers," was yet another constraining legacy of communism.[4]

By 1990, political mobilization both by workers within and ethnic groups outside the Russian republic was overwhelming the Gorbachev regime, and its economic reform policies retained little coherence or efficacy. The one major reform initiative taken after this point, the price increase of April 1991, was in fact met by a large-scale strike movement (see chapter 7). In its aftermath, the leadership quickly conceded to General Confederation of Trade Unions (GCTU) demands for compensation and income indexing, initiating a wage-price spiral and demonstrating clearly that it could not impose income restraint. Through its agreements with the GCTU in 1991, the Gorbachev administration essentially replaced the tacit social contract with an explicit, negotiated agreement which gave organized labor privileged status and influence in economic and social policy-making. Though this agreement, along with the GCTU, became irrelevant with the collapse of the Soviet Union in the aftermath of the failed coup attempt in 1991, Yeltsin's government in Russia had already adopted a similar policy toward organized labor.

From the Social Contract to Yeltsin's Social Partnership

Today, as the democratically elected president of a now independent Russia, Boris Yeltsin should in principle be free from the constraints of the old social contract. By the time of his election in June 1991, Yeltsin was well established as a proponent of radical economic reform. In the preceding summer, he had declared his commitment to the 500 Days plan for rapid transition to a market economy (a plan that was ultimately rejected as too radical by Gorbachev and the All-Union Supreme Soviet). He had recruited many of Gorbachev's well-known, by then disillusioned advisers. He was elected to the presidency by a veritable landslide. Yeltsin had a seemingly incontrovertible democratic mandate to enact radical economic reforms.

Yet Yeltsin's administration has continued to be hamstrung by the same issues and arguments that defeated the 1987 Law on the State

Enterprise—the need to cut state subsidies and end soft credit to unprofitable enterprises, and to deal with the plant closings and mass layoffs which would inevitably follow. Also, reformist demands for fiscal austerity (in the face of threatening hyperinflation) have continued to confront serious pressures for wage and income maintenance. The legacies of the social contract have remained very much in evidence, despite Yeltsin's apparent commitment to reform and the absence of authoritarian controls. Why should this be so?

First, the political-institutional support for markets and privatization in Russia has remained weak. The conservative Supreme Soviet resisted central features of Acting Prime Minister E. Gaidar's "shock therapy" reform program. In addition, because Yeltsin has chosen to distance himself from party identification, he lacks clearly defined or disciplined support, much less a strong parliamentary coalition. In any case, liberal, proreform forces have shown strong tendencies toward internal division and fragmentation; party loyalty and cohesion remain extremely weak. The failure of this first elected government and parliament to deal with the ongoing economic crisis has already eroded public confidence in the efficacy of democratic government and the competence of leadership which emerges through electoral processes. Russia's democratic institutions have not aided Yeltsin by facilitating and legitimating reform.

Second, Yeltsin has allowed organized labor a position of some influence over his government's economic and social policies. As the Soviet Union collapsed in the fall of 1991, his government formed a "social partnership" with the Federation of Independent Trade Unions of Russia, or FITU(R), the successor to the old official RSFSR branch of the AUCCTU. Yeltsin promised to consult with the FITU(R) and other trade unions before adopting any major legislation on social and economic issues, and to conclude an annual agreement with the union on these issues. He thus incorporated the FITU(R) directly into the policy-making process, assigning the union, and by implication labor, a privileged position in the state. Yeltsin's likely motives here were to stabilize labor relations and avoid further unrest, and he was clearly influenced by the European liberal-corporatist model of state-labor relations. But such an arrangement would inevitably slow and complicate the economic transition; the FITU(R) had declared its qualified commitment to economic reform and its willingness to cooperate with a reformist government, but its primary goal would necessarily be to protect the jobs and incomes of its members.

In January 1992, Russia's government formed a Tripartite Commission on the Resolution of Labor and Social Disputes. The commission brought together representatives of government, the FITU(R) (with minor representation of the Independent Miners' Union and others), and management (represented mainly by the Russian Union of Industrialists and Entrepreneurs [RUIE], an organization dominated by managers of large state enterprises and led by Arkadii Volsky). The Tripartite Commission was to set wages, monitor working conditions, and mediate industrial disputes; in other words, it was to provide an institutional framework for managing labor discontent during market reform.[5] Along with organized labor, the commission extended to organized management a privileged position in the making of industrial and labor policy.

In practice, both the FITU(R) and Volsky's RUIE have used their privileged positions to press Yeltsin's government for concessions on wages and subsidies, and against rapid privatization, price liberalization, and fiscal austerity. Under pressure from the unions, the government has effectively bought off militant sectors of the labor force with double- and triple-digit wage increases; partially indexed most wages, pensions, and transfer payments; and continued some price controls. Under pressure from Volsky's union, it has reduced taxes, maintained subsidies, and tolerated extension of substantial bank credits to failing enterprises. The commission has, at the same time, effectively mediated labor disputes in a number of cases, contributing to a marked decline in strike activity and relative labor peace.

This corporatist approach to state-labor relations seems ill-advised for a government which wants to implement radical economic reform, including privatization, price liberalization, and fiscal stabilization. Essentially the same coalition of management and labor interests which combined against quality controls and the Law on Enterprise (though now claiming some enlightenment about the need for reform) has been institutionalized in the Tripartite Commission. In principle, the government's representatives are supposed to mediate between those of management and workers in commission meetings. In practice, managers of state enterprises and the unions which represent their workers are less often adversaries than allies in claiming resources (or resisting demands) from the state and opposing reform efforts. "More often than not," according to one well-placed observer of commission meetings, "the businessmen's lobby found itself on the same side as the unions, both ganging up against the government."[6] As Yeltsin's deputy minister of labor and employment Pavel Kudiukin explained in an interview, Russian workers remain very dependent on their enterprises, while labor and management share dominant corporative interests in making claims on the state, including interests in maintaining jobs, subsidies, and wage levels.[7] Volsky's RUIE has sought labor's support in its aggressive, and partly successful, defense of these interests.

In sum, Yeltsin remains constrained, not by an implicit social contract but by parliamentary and governmental institutions (the latter partly of his own creation) which defend vested interests in established policy and allocational patterns. It seems almost inescapable that these two interests—organized management and organized labor—should have emerged as influential in a democratizing Russia. They are the most coherent and resource-rich interests in a slowly and tentatively emerging civil society, mainly because of their critical positions in the economy, and in the case of labor, because it had a broad membership organization (the AUCCTU) which empowered itself to some extent after 1989. Management and labor are also, in an important sense, organizational legacies of the old social contract. They constrain Yeltsin's reform, but without their cooperation he would be governing in a near vacuum, with no firm organized links to major societal interests.

As Russians grew disillusioned with Yeltsin's failure to effect reform, it became for a time a common opinion among the politically knowledgeable that Arkadii Volsky would emerge as the power broker and the man with solutions. This opinion indicates an attribution of political and economic competence to the managerial elite (while such an attribution is largely denied to the political elite, reformist or otherwise). It is also a measure of how weakly democratic institutions and procedures have taken hold, even among Muscovites, and of many people's potential willingness to accept (with democratic trappings) the governance of a leadership which emerges through some form of elite co-optation and which may well claim the need to reimpose some elements of authoritarian control to achieve economic stabilization.

Democratization and Reform: Comparative and Conceptual Approaches

In theory, there are three possible relationships between democracy and economic reform in postcommunist states: democracy may facilitate and legitimate reform; democracy may lead to popular opposition and protest which blocks reform; or democracy may give way to a new authoritarianism under the weight of popular disaffection with reform. In the cases of the several Eastern European and post-Soviet states, the outcomes to this point have generally been divided between the first two: democracy has facilitated reform in Poland, Hungary, the Czech portion of former Czechoslovakia, and the Baltic states; it has produced opposition or policy paralysis in Russia, Ukraine, and the Slovak portion of Czechoslovakia. Yet all of these states had been governed, at least since the end of World War II, by a Communist party which subscribed to the principles of the social contract. Why has democracy allowed some but not others to escape from the constraints of state socialism?

In approaching this question, one should examine a number of factors. Some might suggest that their lack of national authenticity so discredited Communist regimes in Eastern Europe and the Baltic states that even their provision of social and economic security was not valued (though there is considerable survey data to suggest otherwise). More readily comparable factors might be the distribution of attitudes toward markets and entrepreneurial activities in these states. Perhaps in some cases democratization reveals a proreform consensus in the society, while in others it reveals an antimarket, antireform consensus. Here cultural and historical factors may play a role. In the case of Russia and Ukraine, perhaps there is simply not enough potential support in society to make reforms by democratic means.

Or perhaps the sequencing of political and economic reforms, and the specific responses of various elite and mass constituencies, matter more than the distribution of attitudes. Surely in all cases some groups, including industrial blue-collar workers, lose in the reform process. It may be that in the successful cases democratization precedes economic reform and creates governments dominated by technocratic modernizers and professionals who favor a more competitive, stratified, economy. These modernizers can then move forward rapidly with reform, creating both winners and losers, and generating both support and opposition. The losers will be least temporarily marginalized in the reform process, and may express their opposition through labor strikes and protests, while subsidies are cut and factories closed. At the next election they may support candidates who will moderate reform (as they have in Poland and Lithuania), but the reform will have taken on a dynamic, and already there will be fewer benefits left to defend. Moreover, the reform will have created winners as well—and quite possibly articulate political defenders who are broadly perceived as competent and effective in designing and implementing their policies.

In terms of such a hypothetical sequence of events, the Soviet reform effort was ill-fated. Gorbachev came to power as an authoritarian leader and fully identified himself with costly economic reforms before initiating democratization. The first elections were held while the party remained in power and militated against the full-scale emergence of a proreform technocratic/professional political elite. When the first elected USSR Supreme Soviet met, it was immediately confronted with the costs of Gorbachev's policies (inflation, shortages in consumer markets, and hostility to cooperatives). The reform imposed costs on industrial workers and consumers before it produced material benefits for anyone, mobilizing an antireform constituency which used its new democratic rights largely against the reform. Gorbachev and his prime ministers and prominent economic advisers proposed, debated, then abandoned a succession of reform policies and programs, thereby convincing most Soviets of their gross political and economic incompetence.

The organization of societal interest groups, and their access to the policy process during democratization and reform, must also influence the outcome of reform efforts. In the Soviet and Russian cases, the old official trade unions adapted their posture and role to the defense of workers against reform, and with the cooperation of Gorbachev, Yeltsin, and other leaders, emerged as influential institutions. It would be useful to know what role industrial trade unions have played in the successful cases of reform, and whether their members gained corporative representation in their new democratic states. Perhaps the old unions were simply discredited by their role under communism, or were less adaptive and aggressive than their

Soviet counterparts. Or perhaps new democratic leaders have done their best to exclude the trade unions, refusing to bargain with them or to channel policy goods to workers through them. It is easy to imagine that less cooperative leaderships could have successfully marginalized the old Communist unions.

Finally, it would be useful to see how workers in particular have responded to the postcommunist transitions in other states. Have they organized to defend their old social contract benefits, through old or new unions, or political parties? Have they engaged in strikes or other forms of labor protest, and if so, have they successfully pressed their demands? Workers in several of the states have experienced significant unemployment and loss of income. Why have they failed to defend their apparent interests more effectively? Do most see themselves as losers or potential losers in the reform process? Have many redefined their aspirations and expectations in accordance with the reform agenda? (For example, do many hope and expect to become small entrepreneurs?) Can a successful reformist leadership so influence significant numbers of those who suffer from reform in the short term that they will expect to ultimately gain?

These are questions for future research. We have now in Eastern Europe and the former Soviet Union a large number of states passing through broadly similar transitions, from authoritarian, socialist welfare regimes to more or less democratic and market-based systems. The potential for comparative analysis is great. These states should reveal much about the relationship between democracy and markets, and the effects of both on popular welfare. Some will presumably become stable democracies, some unstable, and some may revert to authoritarianism. Some will probably find successful strategies for integrating into international markets and will prosper, while others will not. The situation offers a valuable opportunity for studying the relative effects of their histories and political cultures, resource bases, class and political structures, and economic and political strategies, in determining the outcomes.

I am left, finally, with the Yeltsin government and its uncertain future, with constrained reforms, and with the legacies of the social contract. It may be useful to consider the singular depth and enormity of those legacies for the former Soviet Union. The Communist party was in power longest here, and the industrial base it built in the 1930s,

1940s, and 1950s is older and larger than those built by other socialist states. That base is distributed over a vast territory, including several thousand remote settlements and cities which were created to exploit mineral resources or engage in military production. The withdrawal of state subsidies from the industries which support these cities would cause social displacement of a different kind and scale than that faced by smaller postcommunist states.[8] The Brezhnev leadership ruled this country for nearly twenty years and during that time introduced few significant innovations in the economic structure. Large strata of the population—the poorly educated, the unskilled, manual and manufacturing workers—will suffer unrecoverable losses if reform policies are fully implemented. In both a moral and a political sense, no government can easily impose such costs on its population, and a democratically elected government that does so may well face popular repudiation. Yet the costs of maintaining the present system are also prohibitive. The legacies of the social contract continue to burden a reformist leadership that both wants and needs to escape them.

Notes

Index

Notes

1. The Social Contract Thesis

1. See Walter D. Connor, "Workers, Politics, and Class Consciousness," in Connor, *Socialism's Dilemmas: State and Society in the Soviet Bloc* (New York: Columbia University Press, 1988), pp. 67–85; Ed A. Hewett, *Reforming the Soviet Economy: Equality versus Efficiency* (Washington, D.C.: Brookings Institution, 1988), esp. pp. 39–50; Seweryn Bialer, *Stalin's Successors: Leadership, Stability, and Change in the Soviet Union* (New York: Cambridge University Press, 1980), esp. pp. 158–165; Gail W. Lapidus, "Social Trends," in Robert F. Byrnes, ed., *After Brezhnev: Sources of Soviet Conduct in the 1980s* (Bloomington: Indiana University Press, 1983), esp. pp. 188–192; George Breslauer, "On the Adaptability of Soviet Welfare-State Authoritarianism," in Erik Hoffman and Robbin Laird, eds., *The Soviet Polity in the Modern Era* (New York: Aldine Publishing Company, 1984), esp. pp. 220–222; Peter A. Hauslohner, "Managing the Soviet Labor Market: Politics and Policy-Making Under Brezhnev" (Ph.D. diss., University of Michigan, 1984), esp. chap. 1. Not all of these authors use the term "social contract," but all describe a trade-off of social welfare benefits for workers' quiescence, which is the essence of the thesis.
2. Hauslohner, "Managing the Soviet Labor Market" (1984), has made the most extensive examination of the social contract thesis, but it remains a subtheme and not a central subject of his fine study. Skepticism about the thesis among political scientists outside the Soviet field is evident from discussions, particularly at the Conference on Soviet Politics and Economics sponsored by Peter Hauslohner and David Cameron at Yale University in March 1989. I used many criticisms and suggestions raised at that conference in designing this study.
3. For an overview of Gorbachev's social and labor policies, see Peter Hauslohner, "Gorbachev's Social Contract," *Soviet Economy,* vol. 3, no. 1, 1987, pp. 54–89. Hauslohner describes these policies as a "new social contract,"

whereas I see them as an effort by the Gorbachev leadership to abrogate the old contract at its core.

4. Refer to sources in note 1, especially Connor, "Workers" (1988); Lapidus, "Social Trends" (1983).

5. For central controversies about these claims, see the sections on Competing Explanations for Social Policy Outcomes and Competing Explanations for Workers' Political Quiescence, later in this chapter.

6. Bialer, *Stalin's Successors* (1980), pp. 160–161.

7. For a more general discussion of the predominantly substantive (versus procedural) character of political legitimation in communist states, see R. N. Berki, "The State, Marxism, and Political Legitimation," in T. H. Rigby and Ferenc Feher, eds., *Political Legitimation in Communist States* (New York: St. Martin's Press, 1982), pp. 146–169; Stephen White, "Economic Performance and Communist Legitimacy," *World Politics,* vol. 38, Apr. 1986, pp. 462–482.

8. Quote is from David Lane, *Soviet Labour and the Ethic of Communism: Full Employment and the Labour Process in the USSR* (Boulder, Colo.: Westview, 1987), p. 229.

9. For example, Breslauer applies the concept to the whole of the regime-society relationship; Connor, exclusively to the regime and working class; Lapidus and Hewett, somewhat ambiguously to both.

10. On intellectuals' dissent and aspirations under Brezhnev, see especially Peter Reddaway, comp., *Uncensored Russia: Protest and Dissent in the Soviet Union: The Unofficial Moscow Journal, a Chronicle of Current Events* (New York: American Heritage Press, 1972); Ludmilla Alexeyeva, *Soviet Dissent: Contemporary Movements for National, Religious, and Human Rights* (Middletown, Conn.: Wesleyan University Press, 1985); George Saunders, ed., *Samizdat: Voices of the Soviet Opposition* (New York: Monad Press, 1974). The significance of nationalist aspirations among non-Slavs in the Brezhnev period was much debated in the Sovietology literature, but the explosion of nationalist-autonomy movements and communal conflicts since 1987 can leave no doubt about the breadth and depth of those aspirations.

11. I am grateful to David Cameron and Peter Hauslohner for advice on this aspect of the study.

12. The period 1965–1985 covers the brief Andropov and Chernenko transitions as well, but data for 1985 mainly reflect economic planning and performance under Brezhnev.

13. For the official statement declaring that the party had abandoned its claims to political monopoly, recognized the "sovereign will of the people," and accepted political pluralism, see the platform published at the conclusion of the February 1990 Central Committee Plenum, "Toward Humane, Democratic Socialism (CPSU Central Committee Platform for 28th Party Congress). Draft Approved by CPSU Central Committee February (1990) Plenum," *Pravda,* Feb. 13, 1990, pp. 1–2, esp. sections IV and VII.

14. Most of these data are available in a variety of Soviet statistical sources, and many of them have been analyzed and assessed by Western social scientists.

The most useful secondary sources treating relevant Soviet data are in works by Alastair McAuley, Morris Bornstein, Alec Nove, Gertrude Schroeder, and Janet Chapman. The journal *Soviet Economy* and periodic handbooks on the Soviet economy published by the Joint Economic Committee of the U.S. Congress (JEC) are also extremely valuable, especially *USSR: Measures of Economic Growth and Development, 1950–1980: Studies Prepared for the Joint Economic Committee, Congress of the United States* (Washington, D.C.: U.S. GPO, 1982), which assesses and critiques much of the relevant Soviet data. For strains on the social contract in the 1980s see Lapidus, "Social Trends" (1983); White, "Economic Performance" (1986).

15. My sources for this part of the study include a range of official Soviet party and government documents and Soviet press reports, including stenographic reports of party congresses, resolutions, leaders' speeches, press discussion, and discussions in professional journals and publications of ministries and state committees that deal with the policy decisions specified. Secondary literature is also useful for some of the cases.

16. There are some problems with data for this part of the study. Information about labor unrest during the Brezhnev period is incomplete and problematic. There may have been considerable unreported industrial conflict, and available information on the grievances and demands of strikers is incomplete and perhaps unrepresentative. However, valuable sources are available, as evidenced, for example, in Betsy Gidwitz, "Labor Unrest in the Soviet Union," *Problems of Communism* vol. 21, Nov.–Dec. 1982, pp. 25–42. I have checked and improved the accuracy of my information through research and interviews with Soviet labor experts.

17. The significance of any correlation between working-class unrest and declining delivery on the social contract under Gorbachev is complicated by the simultaneous democratization of the Soviet polity, which contributed independently to the increase in expression of popular grievance and discontent. I will return to this issue in chapter 6.

18. For an analysis that stresses paternalism as a source of Soviet social policies, see Ferenc Feher, "Paternalism as a Mode of Legitimation in Soviet-type Societies," in Rigby and Feher, *Political Legitimation* (1982), pp. 64–81; for one that stresses ideology, see Lane, *Soviet Labour* (1987).

19. Lane, *Soviet Labour* pp. 4, 16.

20. For the concept of soft budget constraints, see Janos Kornai, *The Socialist System: The Political Economy of Communism* (Princeton: Princeton University Press, 1992), pp. 140–145. Kornai himself actually does not hold that the budget constraints on wage expenditure are soft, though he does hold this view for the budget constraints on a firm's total expenditure (p. 217). For an explicit argument about soft budget constraints producing labor hoarding, see Philip Hanson, "The Serendipitous Soviet Achievement of Full Employment: Labour Shortage and Labour Hoarding in the Soviet Economy," in David Lane, ed., *Labour and Employment in the USSR* (New York: New York University Press, 1986), pp. 83–111.

21. For a discussion of overmanning and its tenacious causes in the Soviet econ-

omy, see Vladimir G. Kostakov, "Zaniatost: Defitsit ili Izbytok?" *Kommunist,* no. 2, 1987, pp. 78–79; Linda J. Cook, "Gorbachev's Reforms: The Implications of Restructuring for Workers' Employment Security," in Donna Bahry and Joel Moses, eds., *Political Implications of Economic Reform in Communist Systems* (New York: New York University Press, 1990), pp. 197–223.

22. For models of Soviet policy-making that focus on the interests and interplay of bureaucratic actors (though they differ from one another on the distribution of power and dynamics of the policy process) see: Jerry F. Hough, "The Soviet System: Petrification or Pluralism," in Hough, *The Soviet Union and Social Science Theory* (Cambridge: Harvard University Press, 1977), pp. 19–48; Paul Cocks, "The Policy Process and Bureaucratic Politics," in Paul Cocks, Robert V. Daniels, and Nancy W. Heer, eds., *The Dynamics of Soviet Politics* (Cambridge: Harvard University Press, 1976), pp. 156–178; Darrell P. Hammer, *USSR: The Politics of Oligarchy,* 2nd ed. (Boulder, Colo.: Westview, 1986), esp. pp. 225–240.

23. See Jerry F. Hough, "Policy-Making and the Worker," in Arcadius Kahan and Blair Ruble, eds., *Industrial Labor in the USSR* (New York: Pergamon Press, 1979), pp. 367–398; Hough, "The Soviet System" (1977).

24. Hough, "Policy-Making" (1979), p. 375. Hough does explicitly state elsewhere that "politicians take the danger of popular unrest into account as they mediate conflicts among political participants." "The Soviet System" (1977), p. 24.

25. On bureaucratic blocks to reform see, for example, Anders Aslund, *Gorbachev's Struggle for Economic Reform: The Soviet Reform Process, 1985–88* (Ithaca, N.Y.: Cornell University Press, 1989); Anthony Jones and William Moskoff, *Ko-ops: The Rebirth of Entrepreneurship in the Soviet Union* (Bloomington: Indiana University Press, 1991), esp. chap. 4.

26. Exceptions to this generalization can be found in Lapidus, "Social Trends" (1983); Hauslohner, "Gorbachev's Social Contract" (1987); and Seweryn Bialer, "Gorbachev's Move," *Foreign Policy,* no. 68, Fall 1987, pp. 59–87.

27. See, for example, Victor Zaslavsky, *The Neo-Stalinist State: Class, Ethnicity, and Consensus in Soviet Society* (Armonk, N.Y.: M. E. Sharpe, 1982); Andrew G. Walder, *Communist Neo-Traditionalism: Work and Authority in Chinese Industry* (Berkeley and Los Angeles: University of California Press, 1986).

28. Zaslavsky, *Neo-Stalinist State* (1982), p. 52.

29. Walder, *Neo-Traditionalism* (1986).

30. I am referring here to the work of scholars such as Peter Lange, Suzanne Berger, Philippe Schmitter, Charles Maier, John Goldthorpe, and others, as represented in Suzanne D. Berger, ed., *Organizing Interests in Western Europe: Pluralism, Corporatism, and the Transformation of Politics* (New York: Cambridge University Press, 1981); John H. Goldthorpe, ed., *Order and Conflict in Contemporary Capitalism* (London: Oxford University Press, 1984).

31. The term *corporatism,* to oversimplify somewhat, may be used to describe either a set of institutional relations or a system of interest representation and intermediation. I am using the term in the second sense.

32. See, for example, Charles S. Maier, " 'Fictitious Bonds . . . of Wealth and

Law': On the Theory and Practice of Interest Representation" (pp. 27–62), and Claus Offe, "The Attribution of Public Status to Interest Groups: Observations on the West German Case" (pp. 123–158), in Suzanne D. Berger, ed., *Organizing Interests in Western Europe: Pluralism, Corporatism, and the Transformation of Politics* (New York: Cambridge University Press, 1981); Charles S. Maier, "Preconditions for Corporatism" (pp. 39–59), and Gerhard Lehmbruch, "Concertation and the Structure of Corporatist Networks" (pp. 60–80), in John H. Goldthorpe, ed., *Order and Conflict in Contemporary Capitalism* (London: Oxford University Press, 1984).

33. For this critical perspective see, for example, Offe, "The Attribution of Public Status to Interest Groups," and Philippe C. Schmitter, "Interest Intermediation and Regime Governability in Contemporary Western Europe and North America" (pp. 287–330), in Berger, *Organizing Interests* (1981).

34. See, for example, Peter Lange, "Unions, Workers, and Wage Regulation: The Rational Bases of Consent" (pp. 98–123), in Goldthorpe, *Order and Conflict* (1984).

35. See Valerie Bunce and John Echols III, "Soviet Politics in the Brezhnev Era: Pluralism or Corporatism?" in Donald R. Kelley, ed., *Soviet Politics in the Brezhnev Era* (New York: Praeger, 1980), pp. 1–28; and for a critique of Bunce and Echols, along with another attempt to apply a corporatist model to Soviet trade unions, see Blair Ruble, "The Applicability of Corporatist Models to the Study of Soviet Politics: The Case of the Trade Unions" (paper no. 303, Carl Beck Papers in Russian and East European Studies, University of Pittsburgh, 1983).

36. Bunce and Echols, "Soviet Politics" (1980).

37. See Jurgen Kocka, "Class Formation, Interest Articulation, and Public Policy: The Origins of the German White-Collar Class in the Late Nineteenth and Early Twentieth Centuries" (pp. 63–82), and Suzanne D. Berger, "Regime and Interest Representation: The French Traditional Middle Classes" (pp. 83–102), in Berger, *Organizing Interests* (1981).

38. On corporatist arrangements limiting the responsiveness of trade union officials to their rank and file, see John T. S. Keeler, "Corporatism and Official Union Hegemony: The Case of French Agricultural Syndicalism" (pp. 185–208), and Schmitter, "Interest intermediation," in Berger, *Organizing Interests* (1981).

39. On disadvantaged challengers, see Keeler, "Corporatism" (1981).

40. See, for example, Lange, "Unions" (1984); Maier, "Fictitious Bonds" (1981).

41. Ruble, "Applicability of Corporatist Models" (1983), pp. 5–6.

42. This will hold whether or not deterioration was a direct and intended result of reform policies. We will see that unanticipated or dysfunctional effects of Gorbachev's policies did in fact undercut economic and price stability, often in spite of his intentions.

43. It might be argued that powerful ministerial bureaucracies had a direct interest in such policies, which provide benefits for their workers. I am assuming, however, that these bureaucracies had less interest in the funding of amorphous societal benefits than in direct allocations to their sectors.

44. For examples of this repudiation, see Gorbachev's speech to the media in

January 1988, in *Pravda,* Jan. 13, 1988, p. 2; and in May, *Pravda,* May 11, 1988, p. 2. The Gorbachev leadership's ideological and political assault on the Brezhnev welfare state and its conception of social justice will be discussed at some length in chapter 4.

2. Brezhnev's Welfare State

1. See Alfred B. Evans, "Economic Reward and Inequality in the 1986 Program of the Communist Party of the Soviet Union," in Donna Bahry and Joel Moses, eds., *Political Implications of Economic Reform in Communist Systems: Communist Dialectic* (New York: New York University Press, 1990), pp. 162–196. Evans's article, which contrasts the 1961 and 1986 party programs, first drew my attention to the significance of the Third Party Program in codifying the principles of the social contract.
2. The text of the Third Party Program is in Charlotte Saikowski and Leo Gruliow, eds., *Current Soviet Policies IV: The Documentary Record of the 22nd Congress of the Communist Party of the Soviet Union* (New York: Columbia University Press, 1962), pp. 1–33. Part II, which deals with domestic policy and is of central concern here, appears on pp. 14–33.
3. Robert C. Tucker, "The CPSU Draft Program: A Credo of Conservatism," *Problems of Communism,* vol. 10, Sept.-Oct. 1961, p. 3. For a similarly skeptical view see, "First Impressions of the Draft Program of CPSU," *Radio Free Europe: Background Information, USSR,* Aug. 1, 1961, pp. i–xi.
4. This point is also made by Rudolph Schlesinger, "The CPSU Programme: The Conception of Communism," *Soviet Studies,* vol. 13, Apr. 1962, pp. 383–406. Schlesinger wrote, "Where the programme deals with economic prospects, a careful though far-seeing formulation of practical aims is combined with a preservation of traditional formulae" (p. 395).
5. For a thorough review of the state of social welfare at this time, with available data, see Alec Nove, "Toward a 'Communist Welfare State'? Social Welfare in the U.S.S.R.," *Problems of Communism,* vol. 9, Jan.-Feb. 1960, pp. 1–10.
6. *Current Soviet Policies IV, 22nd Congress,* esp. pp. 21–28.
7. *Current Soviet Policies IV, 22nd Congress,* p. 21.
8. See Schlesinger, "CPSU Programme"; Nove, "Social Welfare"; Robert A. Feldmesser, "Equality and Inequality under Khrushchev," *Problems of Communism,* vol. 9, Mar.-Apr. 1960, pp. 31–39; Alec Nove, *An Economic History of the USSR* (New York: Penguin, 1969), pp. 347–354.
9. See George Breslauer, *Khrushchev and Brezhnev as Leaders: Building Authority in Soviet Politics* (Winchester, Mass.: Allen and Unwin, 1982), pp. 89–92, on Khrushchev's budgetary priorities at the 22nd Congress; see also Rush V. Greenslade, "Forward to Communism?" *Problems of Communism,* vol. 11, Jan.-Feb. 1962, pp. 36–42. Greenslade also makes the critical point that free provision of services may not increase equality because, "There is no guarantee . . . that the services promised in the plan will be unlimited in supply or equally distributed. Free housing, for example, is . . . rationed

and assigned . . . Rationing systems are . . . notoriously amenable to the provision of special privilege to a favored minority" (p. 41).

10. The program's radicalism was, however, limited to the realm of distributive relations; the political and institutional system was to change very little, the party maintaining its leading role, but now as paternalistic ensurer of "rising well-being of the working people." On political aspects of the program see Schlesinger, "CPSU Programme," pp. 396–406.

11. See Breslauer, *Building Authority,* pp. 93–95. Breslauer makes it clear that after 1962 Khrushchev avoided further retail price increases. See also "Khrushchev Explains Wage Pause," *Radio Liberty Research Bulletin,* 463/82, Nov. 24, 1982, pp. 1–12.

12. *Current Soviet Policies V, The Documentary Record of the 23rd Congress of the Communist Party of the Soviet Union* (Columbus, Ohio: American Association for the Advancement of Slavic Studies [AAASS], 1973), p. 153. In the same speech, Brezhnev also remarked on the repudiation of several of Khrushchev's policies. *Current Soviet Policies VI, The Documentary Record of the 24th Congress of the Communist Party of the Soviet Union* (Columbus, Ohio: AAASS, 1973), p. 117. There are many other explicit references to the Third Party Program at the Brezhnev-era CPSU congresses. See, for example, *Current Soviet Policies VII, The Documentary Record of the 25th Congress of the Communist Party of the Soviet Union,* (Columbus, Ohio: AAASS, 1976), p. 16; *Current Soviet Policies V, 23rd Congress,* p. 155.

13. *Current Soviet Policies V, 23rd Congress,* p. 20 (emphasis added). Formulations from the program such as "creation of the material and technical base of communism," and "overcoming disparities in living and cultural conditions between city and countryside," for example, were referred to constantly as both goals and justifications of policy.

14. *Current Soviet Policies V, 23rd Congress,* p. 106. On reductions in manual labor, see *Current Soviet Policies VI, 24th Congress,* pp. 24–25; on improvements in labor safety, see *Current Soviet Policies VIII, The Documentary Record of the 26th Congress of the Communist Party of the Soviet Union* (Columbus, Ohio: Current Digest of the Soviet Press, 1981), p. 110.

15. See *Current Soviet Policies V, 23rd Congress,* pp. 20, 107; *Current Soviet Policies VI, 24th Congress,* pp. 22, 129–132; *Current Soviet Policies VII, 25th Congress,* pp. 16, 72–75; *Current Soviet Policies VIII, 26th Congress,* p. 39.

16. On uses of social consumption funds, see *Current Soviet Policies V, 23rd Congress,* pp. 20–21, 106; *Current Soviet Policies VI, 24th Congress,* pp. 16–19, 116–117, 132–133; *Current Soviet Policies VII, 25th Congress,* pp. 15–16, 72–75.

17. *Current Soviet Policies VIII, 26th Congress,* p. 22.

18. *Current Soviet Policies VIII, 26th Congress,* p. 16.

19. See, for example, David Granick, *Job Rights in the Soviet Union: Their Consequences* (New York: Cambridge University Press, 1987), pp. 70–84; Ed A. Hewett, *Reforming the Soviet Economy: Equality versus Efficiency* (Washington, D.C.: Brookings Institution, 1988) pp. 39–42; David Lane, *Soviet Labour and the Ethic of Communism: Full Employment and the Labour Process in*

the USSR (Boulder, Colo.: Westview, 1987), esp. chaps. 2, 4, 9. The one important exception is Central Asia, which was broadly recognized to have growing unemployment, estimated at 4 percent in 1979; see Anna Jutta Pietsch, "Shortage of Labor and Motivation Problems of Soviet Workers," in David Lane, ed., *Labour and Employment in the USSR* (New York: New York University Press, 1986), pp. 176–190, esp. p. 185. Qualifications to the claim of full employment in Slavic regions, the central concern here, will be discussed further.

20. Granick, *Job Rights* (1987), p. 76; see also the discussion on pp. 76–84. Granick's conclusion that most job seekers found employment within a month is confirmed by numerous other studies. See, for example, Murray Feshbach, "Manpower in the USSR: A Survey of Recent Trends and Prospects," in *New Directions in the Soviet Economy: Studies Prepared for the Subcommittee on Foreign Economic Policy of the Joint Economic Committee, Congress of the United States* (Washington, D.C.: U.S. GPO, 1966), p. 733; J. L. Porket, *Work, Employment, and Unemployment in the Soviet Union* (New York: St. Martin's Press, 1989), p. 94. Porket reports that Soviet sources published in 1978–1983 put the average period between jobs at 20–30 days. (Repeat references to papers for the Joint Economic Committee will be designated JEC.)

21. Feshbach, "Manpower," (JEC, 1966), pp. 734–735, reports that 80 percent of those displaced in the early 1960s were reabsorbed by their own organizations, the remaining 20 percent made redundant. Similar results were reported for dismissals during the Shchekino experiment.

22. Blair Ruble, "Full Employment Legislation in the USSR," *Comparative Labor Law,* vol. 2, Fall 1977, p. 177. Ruble refers particularly, though not exclusively, to the 1970 *Fundamental Principles of Labor Legislation,* which codified the reinforcement of workers' rights to full and secure employment.

23. Mark Harrison, "Lessons of Soviet Planning for Full Employment," in Lane, *Labour and Employment* (1986), p. 70.

24. Murray Feshbach and Stephen Rapawy, "Labor Constraints in the Five-Year Plan," in *Soviet Economic Prospects for the Seventies: A Compendium of Papers Submitted to the Joint Economic Committee, Congress of the United States* (Washington, D.C.: U.S. GPO, 1973), p. 533; Stephen Rapawy, "Regional Employment Trends in the U.S.S.R.: 1950 to 1975," in *The Soviet Economy in a Time of Change: A Compendium of Papers Submitted to the Joint Economic Committee, Congress of the United States* (Washington, D.C.: U.S. GPO, 1979), p. 602; Murray Feshbach and Stephen Rapawy, "Soviet Population and Manpower Trends and Policies," in *Soviet Economy in a New Perspective: A Compendium of Papers Submitted to the Joint Economic Committee, Congress of the United States* (Washington, D.C.: U.S. GPO, 1976), quote from p. 131. The average of 88 percent labor force participation is for 1970–1979 and excludes private subsidiary agriculture; see Murray Feshbach, "Population and Labor Force," in Abram Bergson and Herbert Levine, eds., *The Soviet Economy: Toward the Year 2000* (Boston: Allen and Unwin, 1983), pp. 79–111. For comparative labor participation rates in France, West Germany, and Hungary in 1981, see Lane, *Soviet Labour* (1987), p. 34. The

major distinction of the Soviet case is the high full-time employment rate for women.

25. Gregory Grossman, "An Economy at Middle Age," *Problems of Communism,* vol. 25, Mar.-Apr. 1976, pp. 18–33. On problems with labor supply anticipated to begin with the 1971–1975 plan, see Gosplan Chair N. K. Baibakov, *Ekonomicheskaia Gazeta,* no. 21, May 1968, pp. 3–10, esp. p. 5.

26. See the statement of the Deputy Chair of the RSFSR State Committee for Utilization of Labor Resources in *Sotsialisticheskaia Industriia,* Aug. 18, 1970, p. 3.

27. Feshbach and Rapawy, "Soviet Population" (JEC, 1976), p. 128. The Brezhnev leadership's policy responses to the labor shortage also included: tightening of labor discipline and manipulation of incentives to ensure that priority sectors had workers; stress on productivity increases as the key to growth; and, eventually, pronatalist legislation.

28. Granick, *Job Rights* (1987), p. 81; Lane, *Soviet Labour* (1987), p. 66; this frictional-unemployment figure covers estimates for the 1960s through early 1980s. See also Hewett, *Reforming* (1988), pp. 40–42; *Izvestiia,* Oct. 7, 1965, p. 3, reports on results of a survey of recent hires at large enterprises in Gorky.

29. Feshbach and Rapawy, "Labor Constraints," (JEC, 1973), p. 536; Granick, *Job Rights* (1987), p. 84; Porket, *Work* (1989), pp. 101–102; E. Manevich, "Vseobshchnost' Truda i Problemy Ratsional'nogo Ispol'zovaniia Rabochei Sily v SSSR" *Voprosy Ekonomiki,* no. 6, 1965, pp. 27–28, which refers to lack of vacancies for women in Siberia. See also *Trud,* Mar. 26, 1967, p. 2, for figures on the extent of juvenile unemployment, including in Slavic regions; Porket, *Work* (1989), pp. 106–110.

30. For a detailed study of such dismissals, see Nicholas Lampert, *Whistleblowing in the Soviet Union: A Study of Complaints and Abuses under State Socialism* (New York: Schocken Books, 1985), esp. chap. 5.

31. Hewett, *Reforming* (1988), p. 42, puts the overall Soviet rate at under 2 percent; Peter Wiles puts the Soviet estimate according to U.S. definitions and procedures at 1.3–1.8 percent; see P. J. D. Wiles, "A Note on Soviet Unemployment by U.S. Definitions," *Soviet Studies,* vol. 23, Apr. 1972, p. 626.

32. See, for example, Porket, *Work* (1989), esp. chap. 2.

33. For a discussion of these pressures and incentives see Linda J. Cook, "Gorbachev's Reforms: The Implications of Restructuring for Workers' Employment Security," in Donna Bahry and Joel Moses, eds., *Political Implications of Economic Reform in Communist Systems* (New York: New York University Press, 1990), pp. 198–200; Porket, *Work* (1989), pp. 36–37; for evidence on levels of overstaffing, see Manevich, "Vseobshchnost' Truda," esp. p. 28.

34. Peter Hauslohner, "The Incapable State: The Curious Case of the Labor Ministry," in David Cameron and Peter Hauslohner, eds., *Political Control of the Soviet Economy* (New York: Cambridge University Press, forthcoming); Hauslohner, "Managing the Soviet Labor Market: Politics and Policymaking under Brezhnev" (Ph.D. diss., University of Michigan, 1984); Philip Hanson, "The Serendipitous Soviet Achievement of Full Employment: Labour Short-

age and Labour Hoarding in the Soviet Economy," in David Lane, ed., *Labour and Employment in the USSR* (New York: New York University Press, 1986), pp. 83–111.

35. See Lane, *Soviet Labour* (1987), p. 45 (Table 3.1), on sources of work force recruitment in the RSFSR and Ukraine in 1975 and 1980. Granick, *Job Rights* (1987), p. 22 (Table 2.2), shows that hiring by enterprises through labor offices in the RSFSR increased only from 3.5 percent in 1970 to 9.7 percent in 1980. On retraining, see Feshbach, "Manpower" (JEC, 1966), pp. 734–735.

36. For the concept of hard and soft budget constraints, see Janos Kornai, *Economics of Shortage* (New York: North Holland Publishing Company, 1980); it should be noted that Kornai himself considers the wage fund, once set by bureaucratic bargaining between enterprise management and the state, to be a hard constraint.

37. Hanson, "Soviet Achievement of Full Employment" (1986), p. 88.

38. On these protections, see the discussion by a consultant to USSR Gossnab's legal department on laws governing worker layoff procedures, in "Poriadok Uvol'neniia Rabotnikov pri Sokrashchenii Chislennoste ili Shtatov Predpriiatii i Organizatsii," *Material'no-Tekhnicheskoe Snabzhenie,* no. 1, Jan. 1986, pp. 75–79; *Labor Legislation in the USSR* (Moscow: Novosti Press Agency, 1972), pp. 10–19, 43–53.

39. For the resolution on the quota increase, see *Izvestiia,* Feb. 6, 1966, pp. 1, 3; for discussion of its significance, see "Labor Exchanges to be Established Throughout USSR," *Radio Free Europe Research Report,* Feb. 9, 1966, pp. 1–4.

40. See Blair Ruble, *Soviet Trade Unions: Their Development in the 1970s* (New York: Cambridge University Press, 1981), pp. 64–89.

41. See Lampert, *Whistleblowing* (1985); the discussion of letters and protests against illegal dismissals in Alex Pravda, "Spontaneous Workers' Activities in the Soviet Union," in Arcadius Kahan and Blair Ruble, eds., *Industrial Labor in the USSR* (New York: Pergamon, 1979), pp. 343–366. On large-scale illegal layoffs during the initial Shchekino experiments, see Karl Ryavec, *Implementation of Soviet Economic Reforms: Political, Economic, and Social Processes* (New York: Praeger, 1975), p. 194.

42. Granick, *Job Rights* (1987), p. 89 (Table 3.2); estimated from a range of sources presented in Table 3.2, on disciplinary dismissals affecting 1–2 percent of the industrial labor force annually in 1965–1980. On court reinstatements, see Ruble, "Full Employment" (1977).

43. See Hauslohner, "Managing" (1984). On the abortive efforts of the Brezhnev leadership to establish employment agencies which could effectively allocate labor, see Andreas Tenson, "The Curtailment of the Powers of Public Employment Agencies," *Radio Liberty Report,* July 9, 1973, pp. 1–4.

44. Boris Rumer, "Structural Imbalance in the Soviet Economy," *Problems of Communism,* vol. 33, July-Aug. 1984, pp. 28–29; "Sotsial'nyi Progress i Programma Povysheniia Narodnogo Blagosostoianiia," *Ekonomika i organizatsiia promyshlonnogo proizvodstva,* no. 5, 1981, p. 13.

45. On the multiple obstacles to technological modernization of Soviet industry in general, see the excellent article by Gertrude E. Schroeder, "Soviet Technology: The System vs. Progress," *Problems of Communism,* vol. 19, Sept.-Oct. 1970, pp. 19–30.

46. Alastair McAuley, *Economic Welfare in the Soviet Union: Poverty, Living Standards, and Inequality* (Madison: University of Wisconsin Press, 1979), pp. 197–206.

47. Janet G. Chapman, "Earnings Distribution in the USSR, 1968–76: Comments on the Notes of Nove and McAuley," *Soviet Studies,* vol. 35, July 1983, pp. 410–413.

48. Leonard Joel Kirsch, *Soviet Wages: Changes in Structure and Administration since 1956* (Cambridge: M.I.T. Press, 1972), pp. 122–123. The 1971–1975 reorganization is sometimes referred to as the second wage reform, following the first Khrushchev wage reform of 1956–1960.

49. See Daniel L. Bond and Herbert S. Levine, "The 11th Five-Year Plan, 1981–85," in Seweryn Bialer and Thane Gustafson, eds., *Russia at the Crossroads: The 26th Congress of the CPSU* (Boston: Allen and Unwin, 1982), p. 91; the draft plan called for "gradual increase in the minimum wage," but gave no specific figure; the figure of 80 rubles per month, for 1985, was announced at the Congress.

50. McAuley, *Economic Welfare* (1979), p. 226, estimates that as few as 3 percent of industrial workers fell below the minimum in 1968.

51. Janet C. Chapman, "Recent Trends in the Soviet Industrial Wage Structure," in Arcadius Kahan and Blair Ruble, eds., *Industrial Labor in the USSR* (New York: Pergamon, 1979), p. 168.

52. See Chapman, "Recent Trends" (1979), for a parallel wage index deflated by the Schroeder and Severin price index, which will be discussed later.

53. Ibid., pp. 151–183; Gertrude E. Schroeder, "Consumption," in Abram Bergson and Herbert S. Levine, eds., *The Soviet Economy: Toward the Year 2000* (Boston: Allen and Unwin, 1983), pp. 336–346.

54. Chapman, "Recent Trends" (1979), p. 159.

55. McAuley, *Economic Welfare* (1979), pp. 218–231. Inter-republic differentials, by contrast, increased somewhat; see Schroeder, "Consumption" (1983), pp. 336–346.

56. Alec Nove, "Income Distribution in the USSR: A Possible Explanation of Some Recent Data," *Soviet Studies,* vol. 34, April 1982, p. 286–288.

57. See the discussion of this issue in Michael Ellman, "A Note on the Distribution of Earnings in the USSR under Brezhnev," *Slavic Review,* vol. 39, December 1980, pp. 669–671; Nove, "Income" (1982), pp. 286–288; and in the comments on Nove's article by McAuley in *Soviet Studies,* vol. 34, July 1982, pp. 443–447; and by Chapman in *Soviet Studies,* vol. 35, July 1983, pp. 410–413.

58. Schroeder, "Consumption" (1983), p. 337 (Table 10.9).

59. Murray Yanowitch, *Social and Economic Inequality in the Soviet Union* (White Plains, N.Y.: M. E. Sharpe, 1977), pp. 29–33.

60. Lane, *Soviet Labour* (1987), p. 177. The establishment of relative uniformity

of pay for similar jobs and skill levels was considered necessary to reduce turnover which, though average by international standards, was thought much too high by Soviet labor experts.

61. On the safety net which protected enterprises from failure during the Brezhnev period, see Hewett, *Reforming* (1988), pp. 207–210; on workers' income security, see Hewett, pp. 39–43.

62. Gertrude E. Schroeder, "Soviet Economic Reform at an Impasse," *Problems of Communism,* vol. 20, July-Aug. 1971, pp. 36–46. Schroeder presents a case in which managers were given some freedom to determine wages and incentives, but central authorities soon became concerned that wages were increasing more rapidly than productivity and that white-collar workers were benefiting disproportionately from bonus payments, and imposed new restrictions and limits. She also reports that, in a survey of plant managers in 1970, more than three-fourths singled out wages as the area in which greater leeway was most needed.

63. McAuley, *Economic Welfare* (1979), pp. 206–210.

64. Ibid., pp. 209–211.

65. Ibid., chap. 9.

66. See, for example, Lane, *Soviet Labour* (1987), pp. 116–120.

67. See, for example, Chapman "Recent Trends" (1979); Schroeder, "Consumption" (1983).

68. The point about continuity between Khrushchev and Brezhnev in these policy areas is made by Jerry Hough, "The Brezhnev Era: The Man and the System," *Problems of Communism,* vol. 25, March-April 1976, pp. 11–13.

69. The concept of anticipatory response is adopted from Seweryn Bialer, *Stalin's Successors: Leadership, Stability, and Change in the Soviet Union* (New York: Cambridge University Press, 1980), p. 161. On the initial motivations of post-Stalinist social policies, including the need to rely on incentives (versus Stalinist compulsion) for labor, popular expectations, and considerations of political stability and international competition, see Nove, "Toward a 'Communist Welfare State'?" (1960), pp. 1–10.

70. Granick, *Job Rights* (1987), p. 76.

71. Morris Bornstein, "Soviet Price Policies," *Soviet Economy,* vol. 3, April-June 1987, p. 119.

72. Morris Bornstein, "Soviet Price Theory and Policy," in *New Directions in the Soviet Economy, Part I,* (JEC, 1966), pp. 65–98.

73. See also Morris Bornstein, "Soviet Price Policy in the 1970s," in *Soviet Economy in a New Perspective* (JEC, 1976), pp. 47–51.

74. Michael Kaser, "Economic Policy," in Archie Brown and Michael Kaser, eds., *Soviet Policy for the 1980s* (Bloomington: Indiana University Press, 1982), p. 211.

75. Bornstein, "Soviet Price Policies" (1987), p. 123. The prices of two-thirds of these goods were raised up to 10 percent, because increases to this level could be made with minimal oversight by state authorities.

76. Gregory Grossman, "A Note on Soviet Inflation," in *Soviet Economy in the 1980's: Problems and Prospects, Part I: Selected Papers Submitted to the Joint*

Economic Committee, Congress of the United States (Washington: U.S. GPO, 1983), pp. 267–286; Gregory Grossman, "An Economy at Middle Age," *Problems of Communism,* vol. 25, March-Apr. 1976, pp. 18–33; Fyodor I. Kushnirsky, "Inflation Soviet Style," *Problems of Communism,* vol. 33, Jan.-Feb. 1984, pp. 48–53.

77. Bornstein, "Soviet Price Policy in the 1970s" (JEC, 1976), p. 49; Bornstein, "Soviet Price Policies" (1987), p. 117. Beginning in 1983, additional price surcharges for weak farms were added to the subsidies, producing subsidy totals of R54.6 billion for 1983, R54.7 billion for 1984, and R58.8 billion for 1985.

78. Bornstein, "Soviet Price Policies" (1987), pp. 124–125.

79. The 1979 figure is from Gertrude Schroeder, "Consumption" (1983), pp. 330; and N. N. Glushkov, "Khoziastvennyi Mekhanizm i Praktika Planovogo Tsenoobrazovaniia," *Kommunist,* no. 8, 1980, pp. 57–59; and includes both food and housing subsidies. The figure for 1985, for food subsidies only, is from Bornstein, "Soviet Price Policies" (1987), p. 116–117. Because the 1985 figure excludes housing subsidies, the increase in subsidies for food alone was significantly steeper than the figures in the text indicate.

80. Subsidies for children's clothing and furniture, for example, were more than R1 billion per year in the mid-1980s; see Bornstein, "Soviet Price Policies" (1987), p. 125.

81. See, for example, David W. Bronson and Barbara S. Severin, "Recent Trends in Consumption and Disposable Money Income in the U.S.S.R.," in *New Directions in the Soviet Economy, Part II-B* (JEC, 1966), pp. 495–529; Schroeder, "Consumption" (1983).

82. Trevor Buck and John Cole, *Modern Soviet Economic Performance* (New York: Basil Blackwell, 1987), pp. 93–94; these figures are presented by Buck and Cole as a "guesstimate" of Soviet inflation.

83. Gertrude E. Schroeder, "Soviet Living Standards: Achievements and Prospects," in *Soviet Economy in the 1980's, Part 2* (JEC, 1983), pp. 367–387.

84. M. Elizabeth Denton, "Soviet Consumer Policy: Trends and Prospects," in *Soviet Economy in a Time of Change: A Compendium of Papers Submitted to the Joint Economic Committee, Congress of the United States,* vol. 1 (Washington, D.C.: U.S. GPO, 1979), esp. pp. 783–784. Of course, special access to scarce goods had long been available to Soviet state and party elites. According to Denton, after the meat shortages of the late 1970s, additional closed distribution systems developed which widened the circle of those with such access beyond the "traditionally" privileged. When I lived in Moscow during 1981 and 1982 a variety of foodstuffs, especially meat and produce, were regularly sold to employees at the Academy of Social Sciences library and the Lenin Library, and to students and other residents at the main Moscow State University dormitory.

85. Bornstein, "Soviet Price Theory" (JEC, 1966), pp. 65–98; Bornstein, "Soviet Price Policy in the 1970s" (JEC, 1976); Bornstein, "Soviet Price Policies" (1987); Schroeder, "Soviet Living Standards" (JEC, 1983).

86. Data for 1960–1970 are from David W. Bronson and Barbara S. Severin,

"Soviet Consumer Welfare: The Brezhnev Era," in *Soviet Economic Prospects for the Seventies* (JEC, 1973), p. 381; and for 1979, from Schroeder, "Consumption" (1983), p. 330.

87. Schroeder, "Consumption" (1983), p. 330.

88. Bronson and Severin, "Recent Trends" (JEC, 1966), p. 514.

89. Gertrude E. Schroeder and Barbara S. Severin, "Soviet Consumption and Income Policies in Perspective," *Soviet Economy in a New Perspective* (JEC, 1976), pp. 620–660; statistics are from p. 636.

90. *PlanEcon Report: Developments in the Economies of the Soviet Union and Eastern Europe,* vol. 4, Jan. 29, 1988, p. 25 (Table 9). The data show that savings deposits increased from R13.7 billion in 1977 to R15.1 billion in 1979, then declined.

91. See, for example, Zev Katz, "Insights from Emigrés and Sociological Studies on the Soviet Economy," in *Soviet Economic Prospects for the Seventies* (JEC, 1973), pp. 89–94; Gregory Grossman, "Notes on the Illegal Private Economy and Corruption," *Soviet Economy in a Time of Change,* vol. 1 (JEC, 1979), pp. 834–855.

92. Some services (e.g., medical care) may be legally provided to private individuals for a fee, after registration with the state; any proceeds are, however, taxed heavily. For further discussion of this topic see chapter 5.

93. Grossman, "Private Economy and Corruption" (JEC, 1979), p. 840.

94. Ibid., pp. 834–855.

95. Chapman, "Recent Trends" (1979), p. 166.

96. Schroeder and Severin, "Soviet Consumption" (JEC, 1976), p. 631; *PlanEcon Report,* July 13, 1990, p. 5 (Table 1).

97. Schroeder, "Soviet Living Standards" (JEC, 1982), p. 369.

98. Though, as McAuley, Madison, and others point out, eligibility for several categories of social consumption funds (i.e., pensions) is tied to work and income level, and is therefore not redistributive—it is even regressive in its effect on overall income distribution; see, for example, McAuley, *Economic Welfare* (1979), p. 291.

99. Alastair McAuley, "Social Policy," in Archie Brown and Michael Kaser, eds., *Soviet Policy for the 1980s* (Bloomington: Indiana University Press, 1982), pp. 152 (Table 6.2), 165.

100. Ibid., pp. 146–169.

101. Bornstein, "Soviet Price Policies" (1987), p. 125; McAuley, *Economic Welfare* (1979), p. 289.

102. McAuley, "Social Policy" (1982), p. 153.

103. Christopher M. Davis, "The Organization and Performance of the Contemporary Soviet Health Service," in Gail Lapidus and Guy Swanson, eds., *State and Welfare USA/USSR: Contemporary Policy and Practice* (Berkeley and Los Angeles: University of California Press, 1988), pp. 116–120.

104. Gur Ofer and Aaron Vinocur, "The Distributive Effects of the Social Consumption Fund in the Soviet Union," in Gail Lapidus and Guy Swanson, eds., *State and Welfare USA/USSR: Contemporary Policy and Practice* (Berkeley and Los Angeles: University of California Press, 1988), p. 251.

105. *USSR: Measures of Economic Growth and Development, 1950–1980,* U.S. Congress, Joint Economic Committee (Washington, D.C.: U.S. GPO, 1982), pp. 72–74, (Table A-9).

106. Feshbach and Rapawy, "Labor Constraints" (JEC, 1973), pp. 495–496; the 1975 figure is as planned.

107. Bronson and Severin, "Soviet Consumer Welfare" (JEC, 1973), p. 385.

108. Bernice Madison, "Social Services for Families and Children in the Soviet Union Since 1967," *Slavic Review,* vol. 31, December 1972, pp. 831–852; see statistics on p. 832; Stephen Sternheimer, "The Vanishing *Babushka:* A Roleless Role for Older Soviet Women?," in Horst Herleman, ed., *Quality of Life in the Soviet Union* (Boulder, Colo.: Westview, 1987), pp. 133–149.

109. Richard B. Dobson, "Higher Education in the Soviet Union: Problems of Access, Equity, and Public Policy," in Gail Lapidus and Guy Swanson, eds., *State and Welfare USA/USSR: Contemporary Policy and Practice* (Berkeley and Los Angeles: University of California Press, 1988), pp. 17–60; see statistics on p. 22.

110. Friedrich Kuebart, "Aspects of Soviet Secondary Education: School Performance and Teacher Accountability," in Horst Herleman, ed., *Quality of Life in the Soviet Union* (Boulder, Colo.: Westview, 1987), pp. 83–94. As Kuebart notes, no official Soviet data were published regularly on drop-out rates.

111. Dobson, "Higher Education" (1988), presents data on aspirations for higher education exceeding achievement and on the much greater likelihood (2.5–3.5 times greater) that children of the urban intelligentsia would enter college after high school completion, versus blue-collar offspring; see esp. pp. 34–50.

112. On the scale and effects of the second economy, see especially Gregory Grossman, "The 'Second Economy' of the USSR," in *Problems of Communism,* vol. 26, Sept.-Oct. 1977, pp. 25–40.

3. Full Employment, Price Stability, and Labor Quiescence under Brezhnev

1. David W. Carey, "Developments in Soviet Education," in *Soviet Economic Prospects for the Seventies: A Compendium of Papers Submitted to the Joint Economic Committee, Congress of the United States* (Washington, D.C.: U.S. GPO, 1973), pp. 603–608. The share of working youth who participated in evening and correspondence study programs, and were entitled to some paid leave time in association with their studies, had also been increasing since 1958.

2. E. Manevich, "Vseobshchnost' Truda i Problemy Ratsional'nogo Ispol'zovaniia Rabochei Sily v SSSR," *Voprosy Ekonomiki,* no. 6, 1965, pp. 23–30; V. Shubkin, "O Konkretnykh Issledovanniiakh Sotsial'nykh Protsessov," *Kommunist,* no. 3, 1965, pp. 48–57; Carey, "Soviet Education" (JEC, 1973). Carey reports that, as a consequence of the postwar baby boom, full-time enrollments in general education schools had increased by 3.4 percent per year in 1955–1960 and by 5.4 percent per year in 1960–1965 (p. 610).

3. Seymour M. Rosen, "Changing Guideposts in Soviet Education," in *New Directions in the Soviet Economy: Studies Prepared for the Subcommittee on Foreign Economic Policy of the Joint Economic Committee, Congress of the United States* (Washington, D.C.: U.S. GPO, 1966), p. 820; *Komsomolskaia Pravda,* Apr. 14, 1966, p. 2.
4. "Labor Exchanges to be Established Throughout USSR," *Radio Free Europe: USSR* (hereafter, *RFE:USSR*), Feb. 9, 1966, p. 2.
5. Carey, "Soviet Education" (JEC, 1973), p. 603; E. Manevich reported a surplus of manpower, in part because of "a natural increase in the number of working youth," in Leningrad, Moscow, Odessa, Belorussia, and the Central Black-Earth and Southwestern regions, as well as in some non-Slavic regions; *Voprosy Ekonomiki,* no. 6, 1965, p. 27; *Trud,* March 26, 1967, p. 2, recounted a report by a senior Gosplan official on significant levels of youth unemployment in both Tula and Kemerovo Oblasts.
6. Peter Hauslohner, "Managing the Soviet Labor Market: Politics and Policy-Making under Brezhnev," (Ph.D., diss., University of Michigan, 1984), esp. chap. 3, pp. 178–261; Abraham Katz, *The Politics of Economic Reform in the Soviet Union* (New York: Praeger, 1972), esp. pp. 127–179.
7. J. L. Porket, *Work, Employment and Unemployment in the Soviet Union* (New York: St. Martin's Press, 1989), pp. 37–38, reports that, from the early 1960s, labor experts in the Soviet Union and Eastern Europe recognized the irrationality of the attained high employment levels.
8. For the text of the resolution see *Izvestiia,* Feb. 6, 1966, pp. 1, 3; quote from p. 3. The resolution directed the Councils of Ministers of the fifteen republics to prepare concrete measures for the allocation of school graduates to jobs for every city and district, and to establish a proportion of young workers, ranging from 0.5 to 10 percent, for every enterprise and establishment.
9. Compulsory youth quotas were first introduced in 1957, but the maximum quota to this point had been 5 percent of the labor force; see "Labor Exchanges," *RFE:USSR,* Feb. 9, 1966, pp. 1–4. Hiring in excess of the quota was to be allowed "as an exception" in 1966; see clause 10 of the resolution in *Izvestiia,* Feb. 6, 1966, p. 3. The resolution also made provision for expanding educational opportunities at the upper levels of secondary school.
10. *Izvestiia,* Feb. 6, 1966, p. 1, 3; Hauslohner, "Managing" (1984), pp. 190; 245; Edmund Nash, "Recent Changes in Labor Controls in the Soviet Union," in *New Directions in the Soviet Economy* (JEC, 1966), pp. 849–971.
11. *Komsomolskaia Pravda,* Apr. 14, 1966, p. 2; *Trud,* June 26, 1966, p. 2; *Pravda,* July 5, 1967, p. 3 "Inspection raids" were carried out by the Komsomol to check on the reservation of jobs for adolescents.
12. On quotas for disabled workers see *Pravda,* Mar. 25, 1965, p. 1; Murray Feshbach and Steven Rapawy, "Labor Constraints in the Five-Year Plan," in *Soviet Economic Prospects for the Seventies* (JEC, 1973), p. 496.
13. For discussion of the labor shortage, see chapter 2.
14. On labor legislation and pronatalist motives, see Lotta Lennon, "Women in the USSR," *Problems of Communism,* vol. 20, July-Aug., 1971, pp. 47–58.
15. See the discussion in Hauslohner, "Managing" (1984), pp. 193–201.

16. For a discussion of unemployment in small towns and cities see chapter 2, of this text; for unemployment in Central Asia, see Anna-Jutta Pietsch, "Shortage of Labor and Motivation Problems of Soviet Workers," in David Lane, ed., *Labour and Employment in the USSR* (New York: New York University Press, 1986), pp. 182–186.

17. Alec Nove, "Agriculture," in Archie Brown and Michael Kaser, *Soviet Policy for the 1980s* (Bloomington: Indiana University Press, 1982), p. 171. In comparative terms, the Soviet subsidy on meat and dairy products alone in 1986 (approximately R50 billion, or $70 billion at the official exchange rate) was more than double the European Community total or the U.S. farm subsidy, though the exchange rate complicates the comparison; see Elizabeth Teague, *Solidarity and the Soviet Worker: The Impact of the Polish Events of 1980 on Soviet Internal Politics* (London: Croom Helm, 1988), p. 345.

18. Vladimir G. Treml, "Subsidies in Soviet Agriculture: Record and Prospects," *The Soviet Economy in the 1980's: Problems and Prospects, Part 2: Selected Papers Submitted to the Joint Economic Committee, Congress of the United States* (Washington, D.C.: U.S. GPO, 1983), p. 172. (For the percent of the total budget, see Chapter 2, note 79 above.)

19. David W. Bronson and Barbara S. Severin, "Recent Trends in Consumption and Disposable Money Income in the U.S.S.R.," in *New Directions in the Soviet Economy,* (JEC, 1966), pp. 495–508; for example, the rate of increase in per capita availability of animal products declined by more than one-half during 1959–1963 (p. 502).

20. Keith Bush, "Agricultural Reforms since Khrushchev," in *New Directions in the Soviet Economy, Part II-B* (JEC, 1966), p. 458.

21. Werner G. Hahn, *The Politics of Soviet Agriculture, 1960–1970* (Baltimore: Johns Hopkins University Press, 1972), pp. 168–171.

22. *Pravda,* Apr. 11, 1965, p. 1.

23. See "Brezhnev the Agrarian—II," *RFE:USSR,* Mar. 27, 1965, esp. p. 2; *Pravda,* Apr. 15, 1965, p. 1.

24. *Pravda,* Apr. 11, 1965, p. 1.

25. *Pravda,* Apr. 20, 1965, p. 1.

26. See Bush, "Agricultural Reforms" (JEC, 1966), p. 461, citing Brezhnev's speech in *Pravda,* Mar. 27, 1965, pp. 2–4.

27. Hahn, *Politics of Agriculture* (1972), pp. 168–171. According to Hahn, "From all appearances, the leaders were in substantial agreement on the need for more aid to agriculture, with even those less enthusiastic than Brezhnev and Polyansky voicing approval" (p. 170).

28. For accounts of the 1962 unrest see the *New York Times,* Oct. 8, 1962, p. 1; *Radio Liberty Research Bulletin (RLRB)* 311/88, July 20, 1988, p. 11, which recounts the first official Soviet commentary on the 1962 events; Albert Boiter, "When the Kettle Boils Over . . ." *Problems of Communism,* vol. 13, Jan.-Feb. 1964, pp. 33–43.

29. Hahn, *Politics of Agriculture* (1972), pp. 189–206. For Brezhnev's speech at the October 1968 Central Committee Plenum, see *Pravda,* Oct. 31, 1968, pp. 1–3; discussion of cutbacks is on p. 2.

30. Jerzy F. Karcz, "Seven Years on the Farm: Retrospect and Prospects," in *New Directions in the Soviet Economy* (JEC, 1966), pp. 383–450, esp. the appendix, "Note on Soviet Income Elasticities of Demand," pp. 436–439.

31. Douglas B. Diamond and Constance B. Krueger, "Recent Developments in Output and Productivity in Soviet Agriculture," in *Soviet Economic Prospects for the Seventies* (JEC, 1973), p. 319.

32. Hahn, *Politics of Agriculture* (1972), pp. 225–235.

33. *Pravda,* July 3, 1970, p. 2.

34. *Pravda,* July 21, 1970, pp. 1–2.

35. David M. Schoonover, "Soviet Agricultural Policies," in *The Soviet Economy in a Time of Change: A Compendium of Papers Submitted to the Joint Economic Committee, Congress of the United States,* vol. 2 (Washington, D.C.: U.S. GPO, 1979), pp. 87–115; esp. pp. 99–107.

36. "Brezhnev the Agrarian: Agricultural Development for the 1971–75 Plan," *RFE:USSR,* July 7, 1970, p. 4.; this figure includes large-scale new investment in rural housing and cultural construction.

37. Hahn, *Politics of Agriculture* (1972), pp. 225–227, provides evidence that some agriculture officials, including RSFSR premier Voronov and Estonian leaders, favored more efficient livestock-raising techniques rather than price increases and large-scale central investment in livestock complexes (another element of Brezhnev's 1970 program).

38. Hahn, *Politics of Agriculture* (1972), p. 240.

39. *Pravda,* July 3, 1970, pp. 1–2; quote from p. 2.

40. Boris Rumer, "Structural Imbalance in the Soviet Economy," *Problems of Communism,* vol. 33, July-Aug. 1984, p. 29.

41. Schoonover, "Soviet Agricultural Policies" (JEC, 1979), pp. 103–113.

42. Nove, "Agriculture" (1982), p. 171.

43. Milk prices were raised an average of 8 percent in April 1975; prices for a range of products were raised again beginning January 1979; see Schoonover, "Soviet Agricultural Policies" (JEC, 1979), pp. 107, 110.

44. Teague, *Solidarity,* (1988), esp. pp. 73–138.

45. See chapter 2 of this text; Teague, *Solidarity* (1988), pp. 119–125. The number or percentage of factories affected is indeterminate.

46. For a summary of the full 1982 agricultural program, see "Party Session Approves Food Program," *Current Digest of the Soviet Press,* June 23, 1982, pp. 1–8.

47. See the text of Brezhnev's speech to the May 1982 Central Committee Plenum in *Pravda,* May 25, 1982, pp. 1–2; quote from p. 1.

48. *Pravda,* May 28, 1982, pp. 1–2.

49. Teague, *Solidarity* (1988), pp. 113, 115.

50. It should be emphasized, however, that Teague's research provides only qualified support for this argument, as she concludes that, by the beginning of 1982 (well before adoption of the food program) the Soviet leadership had become less anxious about popular discontent and was more inclined toward tough measures; see Teague, *Solidarity* (1988), esp. pp. 125–133.

51. During a research trip to Moscow in June 1991, I discussed the interpretations and conclusions presented here with Soviet labor experts, including

Dr. Nikolai Popov of the All-Union Center for the Study of Public Opinion and Dr. Vladimir Kosmarsky of the Institute for the Study of Employment Problems, who expressed general agreement with them. More information on the causes and extent of labor unrest under Brezhnev may, however, become available in the postcommunist period.

52. On problems of unrepresentativeness and sample bias in the surveys I have used, see Zvi Gitelman, "Soviet Political Culture: Insights from Jewish Emigres," *Soviet Studies,* vol. 29, Oct. 1977, pp. 546–548; Brian Silver, "Political Beliefs of the Soviet Citizen: Sources of Support for Regime Norms," in James Millar, ed., *Politics, Work, and Daily Life: A Survey of Former Soviet Citizens* (New York: Cambridge University Press, 1987), pp. 103–105.

53. Alex Inkeles and Raymond A. Bauer, *The Soviet Citizen: Daily Life in a Totalitarian Society,* (Cambridge: Harvard University Press, 1961), pp. 233–254; esp. p. 238. When asked what should be kept if the Bolshevik regime were replaced, the respondents gave by far the strongest support to the system of public education and socialized health care.

54. Quotes are from Inkeles and Bauer, *Soviet Citizen* (1961), pp. 236 and 242.

55. Gitelman, "Soviet Political Culture" (1977). Gitelman's respondents emigrated between 1969–72, and were interviewed in 1972; all were men with at least secondary education.

56. Ibid., pp. 553, 558.

57. Ibid., p. 562; the other positively evaluated aspects of Soviet life were interpersonal relations and some aspects of culture.

58. Silver, "Political Beliefs" (1987), pp. 100–141; esp. pp. 110–111, 116–122.

59. Ibid., p. 132.

60. Quote is from *Pravda,* Jan. 13, 1988, p. 1.

61. *Izvestiia,* Apr. 16, 1988, p. 3.

62. Alex Pravda, "Spontaneous Workers' Activities in the Soviet Union," in Arcadius Kahan and Blair Ruble, eds., *Industrial Labor in the USSR* (New York: Pergamon, 1979), pp. 348–349.

63. Betsy Gidwitz, "Labor Unrest in the Soviet Union," *Problems of Communism,* vol. 31, Nov.-Dec. 1982, p. 32; Ludmilla Alexeyeva, *Soviet Dissent: Contemporary Movements for National, Religious, and Human Rights* (Middletown, Conn.: Wesleyan University Press, 1985), p. 402. Unrest at this time was also reported in Ivanovo.

64. Teague, *Solidarity* (1988), p. 39.

65. Pravda, "Spontaneous Workers' Activities" (1979), p. 354.

66. These generalizations are based on the data and sources in Table 3.3.

67. For a somewhat different list of strikes and commentary, see Walter Connor, *The Accidental Proletariat: Workers, Politics, and Crisis in Gorbachev's Russia* (Princeton: Princeton University Press, 1982), pp. 213–225, 249–257.

68. "An Organized Truck Drivers' Strike," *RLRB* 194/78, Sept. 4, 1978, pp. 1–2.

69. For examples of strikes over food shortages and housing conditions during these years, see Gidwitz, "Labor Unrest" (1982), pp. 32–34.

70. See, for example, Pravda, "Spontaneous Workers' Activities" (1979), pp. 351–52.

71. For reports on these strikes, see: *RLRB* 219/80, June 16, 1980, p. 4, citing

a report in the *Financial Times,* June 13, of a two-day strike at Togliatti Motor Works which idled 170,000 people; *RLRB* 196/81, May 12, 1981, pp. 3–4, citing a samizdat report; Gidwitz, "Labor Unrest" (1982), pp. 33–34; Blair Ruble, "Soviet Trade Unions and Labor Relations after 'Solidarity,'" *Soviet Economy in the 1980s: Problems and Prospects, Part 2: Selected Papers Submitted to the Joint Economic Committee, Congress of the United States* (Washington, D.C.: U.S. GPO, 1983), pp. 364–365. The official Soviet press denied these reports; see, for example, *Pravda,* June 19, 1980, p. 5; June 21, 1980, p. 4.

72. Gidwitz, "Labor Unrest" (1982), pp. 33–35. On the strikes in Kiev, see *"Samizdat* Report on Strikes in Kiev," *RLRB* 267/81, July 6, 1981, pp. 1–3; *"Samizdat* Report on Strike in Kiev and Food Supply Problems," *RLRB* 477/81, Dec. 1, 1981, pp. 1–2.

73. On Solidarity and Soviet labor politics, see especially the excellent study by Teague, *Solidarity* (1988).

74. On sources of workers' grievances in the strikes of the early 1980s, see *RLRB* 230/80, June 23, 1980, pp. 1, 10; "Labor Problems in the Ukraine," *RLRB* 389/81, Sept. 29, 1981, pp. 1–3; *"Samizdat* Report," *RLRB* 267/81, July 6, 1981, pp. 1–3; *"Samizdat* Report," *RLRB* 477/81, Dec. 1, 1981, pp. 1–2; "Fun and Games on Soviet Construction Sites," *RLRB* 247/82, June 18, 1982, pp. 1–4; *RLRB* 293/82, July 20, 1982, pp. 1–3.

75. For a parallel discussion of these efforts with broadly similar conclusions, see Connor, *Accidental Proletariat* (1991), pp. 225–235.

76. On Klebanov and the origins of his organization, see John C. Michael, "The Independent Trade-Union Movement in the Soviet Union," *RLRB* 304/79, Oct. 11, 1979; pp. 1–18; Alexeyeva, *Soviet Dissent* (1985), pp. 406–416.

77. Elizabeth C. Scheetz, "Disaffected Workers Publicly Defend Their Rights," *RLRB* 47/78, Feb. 28, 1978, pp. 1–6; quote on p. 4.

78. Alexeyeva, *Soviet Dissent* (1985), pp. 408–409.

79. Michael, "Independent Trade-Union Movement" (1979), pp. 3–4.

80. See "An Interview with Vladimir Borisov, Founding Member of the Soviet Independent Trade Union SMOT," *RLRB* 372/81, Sept. 18, 1981, pp. 1–8, on SMOT's aims, structure, and scope of activities.

81. For SMOT's publication of materials on Solidarity, which were omitted from official Soviet media, see *RLRB* 113/82, Mar. 9, 1982, p. 2.

82. See *RLRB* 229/82, June 8, 1982, pp. 1–3; *RLRB* 419/82, Oct. 20, 1982, pp. 1–4; Alexeyeva, *Soviet Dissent* (1985), p. 411.

83. For example Klebanov had been a mining foreman, Kuvakin was a specialist in labor law, and Nikitin, another prominent activist in the workers' movement, was an electromechanical engineer from Donetsk, though many others were blue-collar workers by occupation; see also Connor, *Accidental Proletariat* (1991), pp. 225–235.

84. See "Russian Group Issues Proclamation of Support for Polish Workers," *RLRB* 291/81, July 24, 1981, pp. 1–4.

85. See, for example, the report on settlement of the Togliatti strike, in which workers' demands for pay were met and the department head and chief

accountant dismissed, in *RLRB* 196/81, May 12, 1981, pp. 3–4. For other cases of strikes which were quickly settled in the workers' favor, see "*Samizdat* Report," *RLRB* 477/81, Dec. 1, 1981. pp. 1–2; *RLRB* 293/82, July 20, 1982, pp. 1–3.

86. For a report on these strikes, see "*Samizdat* Report," *RLRB* 267/81, July 6, 1981, pp. 1–3.

87. See the reports in *RLRB* 219/80, June 16, 1980, pp. 1–6; *RLRB* 230/80, June 23, 1980, pp. 1, 10; "*Samizdat* Report," *RLRB* 477/81, Dec. 1, 1981, pp. 1–3.

88. Gidwitz, "Labor Unrest" (1982); Connor, *Accidental Proletariat* (1991), p. 222, notes that executions were also rumored.

89. See Michael, "Independent Trade-Union Movement" (1979), pp. 1-18, for specifics on harassment, charges, arrests, and incarceration of AFTU members.

90. See *RLRB* 105/79, March 21, 1979, pp. 1–4; *RLRB* 154/79, "Persecution of Independent Soviet Trade Unionists," May 18, 1979, pp. 1–3; *RLRB* 190/79, June 18, 1979, p. 2; *RLRB* 320/79, Oct. 22, 1979, p. 6; *RLRB* 326/79, Oct. 29, 1979, p. 2; and many similar reports through 1980.

91. See, for example, *Pravda,* Aug. 24, 1980, p. 4; Sept. 1, 1980, p. 5.

92. See, for example, *Izvestiia,* Nov. 25, 1980, p. 4; Jan. 28, 1981, p. 4; *Pravda,* Nov. 26, 1980, p. 5; Jan. 25, 1981, p. 5.

93. See, for example, the appeal of Leningrad workers to their Polish "class brothers" to remember their common struggle and victory in WWII and to oppose Solidarity's irresponsible actions and efforts to restore capitalism, in *Pravda,* Sept. 13, 1981, p. 4.

94. Up to this point, most Soviet commentary had maintained the distinction between the "antisocialist, extremist elements in Solidarity's leadership," and the rank and file which might still be brought back into the socialist fold. See "Press Attacks on Solidarity," *Current Digest of the Soviet Press,* vol. 33, no. 49, Jan. 6, 1982.

95. Elizabeth Teague, "Workers' Protests in the Soviet Union," *RLRB* 474/82, Nov. 29, 1982, p. 14–15; Table 3, on p. 14, compares the results of the internal poll with the Soviet Area Audience and Opinion Research results in Teague.

96. Teague, "Workers' Protests" (1982), p. 15.

97. Teague, *Solidarity* (1988), p. 153.

98. See Boris Meissner, "The 26th Party Congress and Soviet Domestic Politics." *Problems of Communism,* vol. 30, May-June 1981, pp. 15–22; "The Twenty-Sixth Congress of the CPSU: Brezhnev and Shibaev on Soviet Trade Unions," *RLRB* 93/81, Mar. 2, 1981, pp. 1–3. This constituted a marked shift from Brezhnev's position at the 25th Congress in February 1976, when he stressed the unions' role in raising production.

99. See, for example, "Local Trade-Union Chief on Working Conditions in Donetsk," *RLRB* 131/81, Mar. 25, 1981, pp. 1–3; "Twenty-Sixth Congress," *RLRB* (1981), p. 2.

100. See, for example, the reports in *Pravda,* Mar. 9, 1982, p. 2; *Pravda,* Mar. 22, 1982, p. 1; and the report on an open letter day at the Belgorod Asbestos-Cement Products Combine, in *Pravda,* Apr. 25, 1982, p. 3.

101. See Ruble, "Soviet Trade Unions" (JEC, 1983), quote is from p. 353; see also Meissner, "26th Congress" (1981); Teague, *Solidarity* (1988).

102. Connor, *Accidental Proletariat* (1991), p. 221. Connor's major study of Soviet labor supports the contract thesis. However, he adds the important argument that the greater maturity of the Brezhnev-era (versus Khrushchev-era) working class, in terms of education, urban origins, and hereditary worker status, helps account for the stronger organization of later strikes as well as for the state's efforts to manage them without resorting to violence; see esp. pp. 217–220.

103. David Lane, *Soviet Labour and the Ethic of Communism: Full Employment and the Labour Process in the USSR* (Boulder, Colo.: Westview, 1987), pp. 229–230.

4. Gorbachev's Reforms

1. See Gorbachev's address to the June 1987 Central Committee Plenum, "O zadachakh partii po korennoy perestroike upravleniya ekonomikoy," *Pravda,* 26 June 1987, pp. 1–5; quote is from p. 1.

2. On these points see also Alfred B. Evans, "Economic Reward and Inequality in the 1986 Program of the Communist Party of the Soviet Union," in Donna L. Bahry and Joel C. Moses, eds. *Political Implications of Economic Reform in Communist Systems: Communist Dialectic* (New York: New York University Press, 1990), pp. 162–196; Peter Hauslohner, "Gorbachev's Social Contract," *Soviet Economy,* vol. 3, Jan.-Mar. 1987, pp. 54–89; Hans Aage, "Popular Attitudes and Perestroika," *Soviet Studies,* vol. 43, Jan. 1991, pp. 3–25.

3. See, for example, Gorbachev's report to the April 1985 Central Committee Plenum, in which he listed as one of the cardinal tasks of scientific and technical progress, "[the need to] raise the role and prestige of masters, engineers, designers, and technology experts and raise the material and moral incentives for their labor," in *Foreign Broadcast Information Service, Daily Report: Soviet Union (FBIS:SU),* Apr. 24, 1985, p. R7 citing *Pravda,* Apr. 24, 1985; the interview with V. Gavrilov, Vice-Chair of the State Committee on Labor and Social Questions, in *Izvestiia,* Sept. 26, 1986, p. 2; the article by the academic economist N. Rimashevskaia, "Raspredeleniie i Spravedli-vost'" *Ekonomicheskaia Gazeta (Ek. Gaz.),* no. 40, Oct. 1986, pp. 6–7.

4. See Rimashevskaia, "Raspredeleniie" (1986).

5. See the articles by E. Antosenkov, Director of the Labor Research Institute, in *Izvestiia,* Apr. 26, 1985,. p. 2; and by the prominent labor specialist L. Gordon (with E. Klopov) in *Pravda,* Oct. 24, 1986, pp. 2–3.

6. Tatyana Zaslavskaya, "Chelovecheskii faktor razvitiia ekonomiki i sotsial'-naia spravedlivost'," *Kommunist,* no. 13, Sept. 1986, pp. 61–73; quote is from p. 66.

7. Quote is from Leonid Abalkin, "The Core of Economic Life," in *Current Digest of the Soviet Press (CDSP),* vol. 38, Jan. 21, 1987, p. 13, trans. from *Ekonomika i organizatsiia promyshlennogo proizvodstva,* no. 9, 1986, pp. 3–16.

8. See Slyunkov's report to the June 1987 Central Committee Conference, in *Pravda,* June 13, 1987, p. 2.
9. They disagreed, however, over the likely or necessary extent of bankruptcies: Abalkin and Ryzhkov suggested that there would be few; Aganbegyan, that eventually many thousands of enterprises should be closed; see the discussion in chapter 5 on the politics of enterprise insolvency.
10. Zaslavskaya, "Chelovecheskii faktor" (1986), p. 70; V. Kostakov, "Zaniatost': Defitsit ili Izbytok?" *Kommunist,* no. 2, Jan. 1987, pp. 78–89.
11. See Nikoali Shmelev, "Avansy i Dolgi," *Novyi Mir,* no. 6, June 1987, pp. 142–158; quote is from p. 149. Gorbachev praised the article but took exception to its approval of unemployment. He insisted that, while reform would temporarily displace workers, it would not create structural unemployment in the Soviet economy.
12. *FBIS:SU,* Mar. 7, 1985, p. S3, citing TASS, Mar. 4, 1985.
13. Gorbachev, "O zadachakh partii" (1987), p. 2.
14. Zaslavskaya, "Chelovecheskii faktor" (1986); Zaslavskaya's argument was more complicated than the reformers' standard claim of excessive egalitarianism; she claimed that the distribution system was neither egalitarian nor meritocratic, and argued that it should be reorganized according to the principles of basic provision for those in need, and distribution according to labor for all others.
15. Quote is from an interview with Zaslavskaya, "Personality of a Scholar and Restructuring," in *CDSP,* vol. 39, May 20, 1987, p. 7, translated from *Argumenty i Fakty,* March 21–27, 1987, pp. 1–2.
16. See Gorbachev's speech in *Pravda,* Oct. 2, 1987, p. 2.
17. V. Kryazhev, "Public Consumption Funds and Social Justice," in *CDSP,* vol. 38, Jan. 29, 1987, p. 6, trans. from *Ek. Gaz.,* no. 52, Dec. 1986, p. 2; see also T. Serebrennikova, "Ekonomicheskie i Sotsialnye Funktsii Raspredeleniia," *Ek. Gaz.,* no. 41, 1986, p. 8.
18. See Gorbachev's remarks during his visits to Vladivostok, *Pravda,* July 27, 1986, pp. 1–2; and Khabarovsk, *Pravda,* Aug. 2, 1986, pp. 1–2.
19. For the best statement of this argument, with supporting data, see M. N. Rutkevich, "Ravenstvo i Spravedlivost'—Tseli Sotsial'noi Politiki KPSS," *Voprosy istorii KPSS,* no. 1, Jan. 1986, pp. 37–52.
20. Zaslavskaya, "Chelovecheskii faktor" (1986).
21. See *Pravda,* Dec. 19, 1985; quote is from p. 3; Rutgaizer argued that extensive state provision had been necessary in the past, to protect poorer strata of the population, but was no longer necessary, because of "greater social homogeneity" and increased wages.
22. See, for example, A. Galaeva's interview with E. Chazov, "Vrach na Poroge Tysiacheletiia," *Literaturnaiia Gazeta,* Apr. 29, 1987, p. 11.
23. Zaslavskaya, "Chelovecheskii faktor" (1986); see also Rutkevich, "Ravenstvo i Spravedlivost'" (1986); Evans, "Economic Reward" (1990), esp. pp. 164, 182.
24. On Ligachev's opposition to markets and privatization as bearers of social injustice and inequality and as a threat to political stability, see Anders As-

lund, *Gorbachev's Struggle for Economic Reform: The Soviet Reform Process, 1985–88* (Ithaca, N.Y.: Cornell University Press, 1989), pp. 48–55.

25. A. Bim and A. Shokhin, "Sistema Raspredeleniia: Na Putiakh Perestroiki," *Kommunist,* no. 15, Oct. 1986, pp. 64–73.

26. Aslund, *Gorbachev's Struggle* (1989), esp. p. 5; Aslund also includes here the conservative nationalist literary journals, such as *Nash Sovremmenik.* Also notable is Eric Goldhagen's trenchant remark on the weakness of the old system's intellectual defenders, who have "Nina Andreeva as their spokesperson." (Comments on presentation, "The Soviet Social Contract," Russian Research Center, Harvard University, December 1990.)

27. Hauslohner, "Gorbachev's Social Contract" (1987), p. 61.

28. On the reliability and representativeness of the center's surveys, see David S. Mason and Svetlana Sydorenko, *"Perestroyka,* Social Justice, and Soviet Public Opinion," *Problems of Communism,* vol. 39, Nov.-Dec. 1990, esp. note 40, p. 40.

29. For survey results indicating strong support of egalitarian norms see, for example, Mason and Sydorenko, *"Perestroyka"* (1990), pp. 34–43. While Mason and Sydorenko do find some ambivalence on social contract issues, particularly on state intervention in income distribution (p. 41), they agree that "especially on the issue of social justice, the public mood runs counter to the interests of the reformers" (p. 39). For a review of some rather scattered and uneven data which suggest less coherent opinion patterns, see Hans Aage, "Popular Attitudes and Perestroika," *Soviet Studies,* vol. 43, no. 1, 1991, pp. 3–25.

30. The text of Gorbachev's speech is in *Pravda,* May 8, 1988, p. 2; commentary from the economics department is in *Pravda,* Mar. 4, 1988, p. 2.

31. M. N. Sidorov, "Structural Shifts in the National Economy Examined," in *Izvestiia Akademii Nauk SSSR, Seriia Ekonomicheskaia,* no. 2, Mar.-Apr. 1986, trans. in *Joint Publications Research Service: USSR: Economic Affairs* (hereafter referred to as *JPRS:USSR:Economic Affairs*), July 24, 1986, pp. 1–19; Sidorov's data show that the share of Soviet workers employed in material production declined 1.7 percent in the Ninth Five-Year Plan, 1.3 percent in the Tenth, and 0.7 percent in the Eleventh (statistics partly calculated from text).

32. Ibid. A combination of lack of incentives for technical innovation in the planning mechanism, direction of investment to new construction rather than to retooling of obsolete plants, and insufficient investment in the machine-building sector which is critical to technical modernization throughout industry largely explains the continuing heavy reliance on manual labor.

33. Total for manual workers is from S. Ivanov, "Sokrashchat' Ruchnoi Trud," in *Ek. Gaz.,* no. 5, Jan. 1986, p. 7; total for labor force (including worker, white-collar, and kolkhoznik groups) is from V. Trunin and A. Markosian, "Ekonomicheskie Osnovy Sotsial'noi Spravedlivosti," in *Ek. Gaz.,* no. 4, Jan. 1987, p. 16.

34. Gorbachev, "O Piatiletnem Plane Ekonomicheskogo i Sotsial'nogo Razvitiia

SSSR na 1986–1990 gody," in *Kommunist,* no. 10, July 10, 1986, pp. 9–12; "Builders in the Beginning of the Five-Year Plan," in *Ekonomika Stroitel'-stva,* no. 1, Jan. 1986, pp. 3–11, trans. in *JPRS:USSR:Economic Affairs,* May 30, 1986, p. 19.

35. V. Mart'ianov and V. Tambovtsev, "Tselevaia kompleksnaia programma sokrashcheniia ruchnogo truda," *Sotsialisticheskii Trud,* no. 10, Oct. 1985, pp. 12–17.

36. V. Kulakov, "Planirovanie ispol'zovaniia trudovykh resursov" *Planovoe Khoziaistvo,* no. 11, Nov. 1988, pp. 110-116; *FBIS:SU,* Feb. 14, 1989, pp. 75–76, trans. from *Trud,* Feb. 10, 1989, p. 34.

37. See *FBIS:SU,* July 17, 1987, p. S1, citing Tokyo (English), July 11, 1987.

38. Kostakov, "Zaniatost'" (1987). Kostakov proposed increases in transfer payments, including pensions, student stipends, and benefits to mothers of young children, in order to ease out of the labor force the youngest, oldest, and most overburdened workers who tended to be marginally productive, and to allow them a livable income without jobs.

39. Gorbachev, "O Piatiletnem" (1986).

40. Kostakov, "Zaniatost'" (1987), p. 86.

41. Zaslavskaya, "Chelovecheskii factor" (1986), pp. 70–71.

42. See the text of the law in *Pravda,* July 1, 1987, pp. 1, 4.

43. For more extensive discussion of the Brezhnev-era system of cross-subsidization and causes of overstaffing, see Linda J. Cook, "Gorbachev's Reforms: The Implications of Restructuring for Workers' Employment Security," in Donna L. Bahry and Joel C. Moses, eds., *Political Implications of Economic Reform in Communist Systems: Communist Dialectic* (New York: New York University Press, 1990), pp. 197–223.

44. *Pravda,* July 1, 1987, pp. 1, 4.

45. See Ed A. Hewett, "The June 1987 Plenum and Economic Reform," *PlanEcon Report,* vol. 3, no. 30, July 23, 1987, pp. 1–8.

46. See the text of Article 23 of the Law on the State Enterprise in *Pravda,* July 1, 1987, p. 4; its significance and implications will be discussed further in chapter 5.

47. The quote is from *Sotsialisticheskaia Industriia* (hereafter, *Sots. Indust.*), Dec. 5, 1987, p. 2.

48. Kostakov, "Zaniatost'" (1987). See also Vladimir G. Kostakov with Abram Bergson and Jerry Hough, "Labor Problems in Light of *Perestroyka,*" *Soviet Economy,* vol. 4, Jan.-Mar. 1988, esp. pp. 100–101, on the old system of employers' responsibility and intentions of reformist legislation; on employers' obligations for placement under the Brezhnev system, see chapter 2 of this text.

49. The text of the resolution is in *Sots. Indust,* Jan. 19, 1988, pp. 1–2; quote is from p. 2.

50. See the commentary by Viktor Buynovskii, deputy chairman of the USSR State Committee for Labor and Social Issues, in *FBIS:SU,* Jan. 21, 1988, p. 49, citing TASS, Jan. 20, 1988; and by I. Prostiakov, deputy chairman of

the USSR Council of Ministers' Bureau for Social Development, in *Pravda,* Jan. 21, 1988, p. 2. The considerable significance of this point will become clear in the discussion of the reform's effects.

51. Quotes are from the text of the resolution in *Sots. Indust.,* Jan. 19, 1988, pp. 1–2.

52. Ibid.; see also *Pravda,* Jan. 21, 1988, p. 2; "Prokhorov on 'Job Placement' Resolution," in *FBIS:SU,* Jan. 22, 1988, p. 46, citing TASS, Jan. 22, 1988.

53. Since the 1950s, workers had enjoyed not only job security but also the right to quit jobs and seek new ones at their own initiative, a right which afforded real leverage to skilled workers in labor-short production sectors, and which was preserved throughout the Brezhnev period, even in the face of perceived excessive labor turnover and severe regional labor shortages. See Hauslohner, "Managing the Soviet Labor Market: Politics and Policymaking Under Brezhnev" (Ph.D. diss., University of Michigan, 1984), esp. chaps. 6–8. V. Zaslavsky argues that workers' rights to personal mobility within the labor sphere were critical for the maintenance of political stability, because the possibility of quitting provided a 'safety valve' for discontent, directing it into individual (versus potentially collective) acts. See Victor Zaslavsky, *Neo-Stalinist State: Class, Ethnicity, and Consensus in Soviet Society* (Armonk, N.Y.: M. E. Sharpe, 1982).

54. For discussion of this resolution see Janet G. Chapman, "Gorbachev's Wage Reform," *Soviet Economy,* vol. 4, no. 4, Oct.-Dec. 1988, p. 338–365.

55. See the interview with B. N. Gavrilov, vice-chair of the USSR State Committee on Labor and Social Issues, in *Izvestiia,* Sept. 26, 1986, p. 2; Chapman, "Gorbachev's Wage Reform" (1988).

56. On problems and inconsistencies, see Chapman, "Gorbachev's Wage Reform" (1988), pp. 355–359; Aslund, *Gorbachev's Struggle* (1989), pp. 81–84.

57. For the text of the resolution, see *Pravda,* July 2, 1986, pp. 1–2; state acceptance was intended to raise the technological level as well as the quality of output.

58. See Aslund, *Gorbachev's Struggle* (1989), pp. 76–80.

59. *Pravda,* July 2, 1986, p. 2.

60. At both the April 1985 Plenum and the 27th CPSU Congress, Gorbachev had spoken of the need for a "more flexible price system." See Aslund, *Gorbachev's Struggle* (1989), p. 28. For background on the price reform see Morris Bornstein, "Soviet Price Policies," *Soviet Economy,* vol. 3, Apr.-June 1987, pp. 96–134.

61. Aslund, *Gorbachev's Struggle* (1989), pp. 128–136.

62. Retail price reform was finally enacted in April 1991, after many months of inflation and deterioration of supplies in consumer markets, and was accompanied by both unrest and compensation policies (see chapter 7 of this text).

63. Quote is from Gorbachev, "O zadachakh partii po korennoy perestroyke upravleniya ekonomikoy," *Pravda,* 26 June 1987, p. 2.

64. Ibid.

65. For a discussion of the Law on Individual Labor Activity, see Aslund, *Gorbachev's Struggle* (1989), pp. 159–163; Roger Blough, Jennifer Muratore, and

Steve Berk, "Gorbachev's Policy on the Private Sector: Two Steps Forward, One Step Backward," in *Gorbachev's Economic Plans, Vol. 2: Study Papers Submitted to the Joint Economic Committee, Congress of the United States* (Washington, D.C.: U.S. GPO, 1987), pp. 261–271.

66. For a discussion of the Law on Cooperatives, see Aslund, *Gorbachev's Struggle* (1989), pp. 163–174.

67. Cooperative incomes were, of course, taxed, and their rate of taxation became a major source of policy controversy; see Anthony Jones and William Moskoff, *Ko-ops: The Rebirth of Entrepreneurship in the Soviet Union* (Bloomington: Indiana University Press, 1991), esp. chaps. 4 and 7.

68. On increased benefits for the genuinely underprivileged in Soviet society under Gorbachev, including pensioners and children, see Mervyn Matthews, *Patterns of Deprivation in the Soviet Union Under Brezhnev and Gorbachev* (Stanford, Calif.: Hoover Institution Press, 1989), pp. 26–29.

69. Abalkin quote is from *FBIS:SU,* July 10, 1987, p. S4, trans. from *Der Spiegel,* July 6, 1987, pp. 98–103. Burlatsky quote is from *FBIS:SU,* July 23, 1987, p. R23, trans. from *Pravda,* July 18, 1987, p. 3.

70. Quote is from *FBIS:SU,* June 24, 1987, p. S4, trans. from *Literaturnaia Gazeta,* June 3, 1987, p. 10.

71. Seweryn Bialer, "Gorbachev's Move," *Foreign Policy,* no. 68, Fall 1987, p. 87.

72. For Goskomstat figures, see *Pravda,* Oct. 25, 1988, p. 3; Oct. 31, 1989, p. 2.

73. For VTsSPS figures, see the statements by Deputy Chair G. Yanaev in *Trud,* Dec. 5, 1989, p. 2.

74. See *FBIS:SU,* Oct. 31, 1988, pp. 72–73, citing TASS, Oct. 28, 1988. For quarterly statistics on changes in both total and industrial employment, 1987 through early 1989, see *PlanEcon Report,* vol. 5, no. 17, Apr. 28, 1989, p. 4. These statistics show slow but steady decline in industrial employment, and are thus compatible with my argument.

75. See "RSFSR Council of Ministers on Economic Reform," in *FBIS:SU,* Feb. 3, 1989, pp. 60–61, citing TASS, Jan. 30, 1989.

76. I. E. Zaslavsky, "Problemy vysvobozhdeniia, perepodgotovki, i trudoustroistva kadrov v novykh usloviiakh khoziaistvovaniia," *Ekonomicheskiie Nauki,* 6, 1988, pp. 29–34; *Izvestiia,* April 18, 1988, p. 1.

77. I. A. Vedernikov, "Trade Unions and Social Aspects of Job Placement for Released Workers," *Mashinostroitel',* 3, 1988, pp. 1–4; trans. in *JPRS: USSR:Economic Affairs,* July 14, 1988, pp. 49–53; statistics cited are on p. 49.

78. On the predominance of redistribution within enterprises, see I. E. Zaslavsky, "Problemy vysvobozhdeniia" (1988).

79. On the percentage of those released who retired on pensions, see the report of Goskomstat in *Pravda,* Oct. 25, 1988, pp. 3–4.

80. F. R. Filippov, "Sotsial'niye garantii effektivnoi zaniatosti," *Sotsiologicheskie Issledovaniia,* 5, Sept.-Oct., 1988, pp. 25–33; for trade union claims that these were the groups mainly affected by dismissals, see Stepan Shalayev's report

to the sixth All-Union Central Council of Trade Unions (VTsSPS) Plenum, in *Trud,* Sept. 6, 1989, pp. 1–3; and VTsSPS deputy chairman Genrady Yanayev's speech, *Trud,* Dec. 5, 1989, pp. 2. Public opinion data provide further confirmation that these groups suffered the brunt of layoffs; when asked in a 1990 All-Union Center for the Study of Public Opinion (VTsIOM) survey, "Whom, in your opinion, does unemployment threaten more than others today?" respondents gave the following replies: youth, 42 percent; women with young children, 40 percent; workers with low qualifications, 29 percent; people of pension age, 25 percent; responses for all other groups were much lower. Figures are all-union averages. See *Obshchestvennoe mnenie v tsifrakh,* VTsIOM, vyp. 12(19), April 1990, p. 14.

81. For a discussion of localized unemployment as a result of lack of jobs in small towns even before the reform period, see I. Adirim, "A Note on the Current Level, Pattern, and Trends of Unemployment in the USSR," *Soviet Studies,* vol. 41, 1989, pp. 455–457.

82. V. V. Scherbitskii, *Izvestiia,* Dec. 13, 1987, p. 4; John Tedstrom, "Soviet Economic Performance in 1987: Stumbling Along the Path of Reform," *RLRB* 60/88, no. 7, Feb. 17, 1988, pp. 2–3. On the "massive failure of the regime to redirect investment resources to machinery and equipment," as the Twelfth Five-Year Plan directed, see *PlanEcon Report,* vol. 4, nos. 3–4, Jan. 29, 1988, pp. 18–21.

83. Peter Rutland's study of the Shchekino experiment, for example, concluded that more than two-thirds of released workers were ultimately moved to other jobs at the same enterprise; Peter Rutland, "The Shchekino Method and the Struggle to Raise Labour Productivity in Soviet Industry," *Soviet Studies,* vol. 36, July 1984, p. 349.

84. See, for example, Gorbachev, "O Piatiletnem" (1986), pp. 9–12; the commentary on the Resolution on Employment by the deputy chairman of the USSR Council of Ministers Bureau for Social Development, I. Prostiakov, *Pravda,* Jan. 21, 1988, p. 2.

85. See, for example, VTsSPS deputy chair G. Yanaev in *Trud,* Dec. 5, 1989, p. 2–3.

86. Chapman, "Gorbachev's Wage Reform" (1988), pp. 354–362; though the percentage varied greatly among republics.

87. Chapman, "Gorbachev's Wage Reform" (1988), pp. 354–362; Aslund, *Gorbachev's Struggle* (1989), pp. 81–84; Aslund's assessment is somewhat more negative than Chapman's, but both find positive effects in the early stages of the reform's implementation.

88. *Trud,* June 9, 1987, pp. 1–2; the state product-acceptance system reportedly monitored more than 20 percent of industrial output by mid-1987; see *FBIS:SU,* July 20, 1987, p. S9, citing TASS, July 18, 1987. (Note, however, *PlanEcon* claims that while quality control had a serious impact in the first quarter of 1987 and led to significant increases in the share of products refused because of low quality, the standards were relaxed in the second quarter of 1987; see *PlanEcon Report,* vol. 3, Aug. 13, 1987, pp. 1, 8; vol. 4, Jan. 29, 1988, pp. 1, 16.)

89. *Trud,* July 21, 1987, p. 1.
90. See, for example, "State Quality Control Rejects Substandard Items," *FBIS:SU,* Oct. 27, 1988, p. 87, citing TASS, Oct. 26, 1988.
91. Chapman, "Gorbachev's Wage Reform" (1988), p. 361.
92. See the January-February 1988 Industrial Performance Report, "O Rabote Promyshlennosti v Ianvare-Fevrale 1988 goda," *Ek. Gaz.* 12, 1988, p. 8.
93. See the interview with V. Omelianchuk, in *FBIS:SU,* Oct. 27, 1988, pp. 87–88, citing TASS, Oct. 26, 1988.
94. A list and a more thorough characterization of these strikes can be found in chapter 6.
95. For a discussion of inflation and other problems in the Soviet consumer economy in 1988–1989, and their impact on workers' real wages as well as wage policy, see chapter 5.
96. See, for example, the account of a bus plant strike, "An Emergency," in *Moscow News* (English ed.), no. 42, Oct. 25–Nov. 1, 1987, pp. 8–9.
97. On the Council of Ministers' meeting and accompanying discussions, see *FBIS:SU,* July 27, 1988, pp. 54–61, citing Moscow Television Service, July 25, 1988; *FBIS,* July 28, 1988, pp. 66–68, trans. from *Izvestiia,* July 24, 1988, p. 4; *FBIS:SU,* July 29, 1988, pp. 65–69, trans. from *Sots. Indust.,* July 26, 1988, p. 2.
98. John Tedstrom, "Recent Trends in the Soviet Economy: A Balance Sheet on the Reforms," *Radio Liberty: Report on the USSR,* vol. 1, no. 5, Feb. 3, 1989, p. 12.
99. *PlanEcon Report,* vol. 6, nos. 46–47, Nov. 23, 1990, p. 8, for statistics on average cooperative pay.
100. For a listing of all cooperatives on Jan. 1, 1990, with breakdown by type of activity (that is, product or service provided), see *Narodnoe khoziaistvo SSSR v 1989 g.: Statisticheskii ezhegodnik* (Moscow: Goskomstat, 1990), p. 268.
101. See the case study on restricting privatization of medical care in chapter 5.
102. Evans, "Economic Reward" (1990), p. 164.

5. *Job Security, Medical Services, and Price Stability under Gorbachev*

1. The Kosygin reform (which was discussed in the chapter 3 case study on youth employment) constitutes something of an exception here. However, it was much less comprehensive than Gorbachev's reform program, and Brezhnev's commitment to it remains somewhat questionable.
2. Gorbachev, "Korennoi vopros perestroika," address at the June 8–9 Economic Conference at the CPSU Central Committee, *Pravda,* June 13, 1987, pp. 1–3.
3. Gorbachev, "O zadachakh partii po korennoi perestroike upravleniia ekonomikoi," report to the June 25, 1987, Plenum of the CPSU Central Committee, *Pravda,* June 26, 1987, pp. 1–5; quote from p. 3.
4. N. I. Ryzhkov, "O perestroike upravleniia narodnym khoziaistvom na sovremennom etape ekonomicheskogo razvitiia strany," report delivered at

the June 29, 1987, session of the USSR Supreme Soviet, *Pravda,* June 30, 1987, pp. 2–4.

5. The text of the law, "Zakon Soiuza Sovetskikh Sotsialisticheskikh Respublik O gosudarstvennom predpriiatii (ob"edinenii)" is in *Pravda,* July 1, 1987, pp. 1–4; quote is from p. 4.

6. The text of the "Basic Provisions," "Osnovnie polozhenii korennoi perestroiki upravleniia ekonomikoi," is in *Pravda,* June 27, 1987, pp. 2–3.

7. See B. I. Gostev, "O gosudarstvennom biudzhete SSSR na 1988 god i ob ispolnenii Gosudarstvennogo biudzheta za 1987 god," in *Pravda,* Oct. 20, 1987, pp. 3–4; and the interview with Gostev in *Foreign Broadcast Information Service, Daily Report: Soviet Union (FBIS:SU),* Dec. 30, 1987, esp. pp. 65–68, citing Moscow Television Service (MosTel), Dec. 25, 1987.

8. Gostev, "O gosudarstvennom biudzhete" (1987).

9. Ryzhkov, "O perestroike upravleniia" (1987); quote is from p. 3.

10. Anders Aslund, *Gorbachev's Struggle for Economic Reform: The Soviet Reform Process, 1985–1988* (Ithaca, N.Y.: Cornell University Press, 1989), pp. 134–135.

11. Ibid.

12. Ibid., pp. 128–134.

13. Aslund, *Gorbachev's Struggle* (1989).

14. Ed A. Hewett, "The June 1987 Plenum and Economic Reform," *PlanEcon Report,* vol. 3, July 23, 1987, pp. 1–8.

15. N. V. Talyzin, "O gosudarstvennom plane ekonomicheskogo i sotsialnogo razvitiia SSSR na 1988 god i o khode vypolneniia plana v 1987 gody," *Pravda,* Oct. 20, 1987, pp. 1–3.

16. Nikolai Viktorovich Garetovsky, "Perestroika Bankovskoi Sistemy" *Ekonomicheskaia Gazeta (Ek. Gaz.),* no. 50, Dec. 1987, pp. 4–9; quote is from p. 9.

17. S. A. Shalayev, "Vystuplenie predsedatelia VTsSPS," *Izvestiia,* Oct. 20, 1987, pp. 5–6; quote is from p. 5. Shalayev was speaking at a session of the USSR Supreme Soviet.

18. See, for example, the session of the USSR Supreme Soviet Debate on the Report of the State Plan for Social and Economic Development of the USSR for 1988, at which speakers addressing the problems their districts would face under self-financing included the Kazakh, Armenian, and Uzbek premiers, the deputy premier of the RSFSR, and party secretaries from the Altai Krai and Tbilisi Gorkom; speeches are in *Izvestiia,* Oct. 22, 1987, pp. 2–5; Oct. 23, 1987, p. 2. For an example of lobbying by a local party official, see Moscow party secretary L. N. Zaikov's report in *Pravda,* Nov. 28, 1987, p. 2; Ukrainian party secretary Shcherbitsky was also quite active in the campaign.

19. See Nazarbayev's address in *FBIS:SU,* Nov. 18, 1987, pp. 70–73, quote is from p. 72; translated from *Kazakhstanskaia Pravda* (in Russian), Oct. 22, 1987, p. 2.

20. See, for example, Zaikov's report in *Pravda* (1987).

21. Ed A. Hewett, *Reforming the Soviet Economy: Equality versus Efficiency* (Washington, D.C.: Brookings Institution, 1988), p. 28.

22. On regional lobbying in the Soviet polity, see Donna Bahry, *Outside Moscow: Power, Politics, and Budgetary Policy in the Soviet Republics* (New York: Columbia University Press, 1987).

23. On problems in the fuel complex see the remarks of the first deputy chairman of the USSR State Pricing Committee A. Komin, "Perestroika Ekonomiki: Kompetentnost i Glasnost," *Ek. Gaz.*, no. 43, Oct. 1988, pp. 4–5; production of gas, by contrast, was profitable. For plans to revise wholesale prices only after full transition to self-financing see Aslund, *Gorbachev's Struggle* (1989), pp. 128–136.

24. Komin, "Perestroika Ekonomiki" (1988), p. 3.

25. See the discussion of obstacles to retail price reform in the case study on price reform later in this chapter.

26. See the discussion of obsolete mining facilities, especially in the Donbass, in chapter 6.

27. See V. Androsenko's report to the Magaden Obkom Plenum on the anticipated effects of economic accountability, "Poka ne grianul khozrashet: S plenuma Magadanskogo obkoma KPSS," *Sotsialisticheskaia Industriia (Sots. Indust.)*, Dec. 22, 1987, p. 5.

28. Most of these reports came from ministries or central planning agencies, which might well be suspected of antireform bias. It is significant that the reformers had to rely on these sources, and the claims and conclusions of their reports (which typically emphasized dire warnings of threats and risks) as a central basis for decision making. This was one of the critical points of antireform influence available to the conservative Brezhnevite establishment.

29. V. A. Balakin, "Restructuring of the Economic Mechanism in Construction Needs New Acceleration," *Promyshlennoe Stroitelstvo*, no. 6, 1988, pp. 2–3, trans. in *Joint Publications Research Service USSR: Economic Affairs (JPRS:USSR: Economic Affairs)*, Oct. 4, 1988, pp. 38–40.

30. B. Smirnov, S. Sinel'nikov, and A. Vissarinnov, "Illyuzii i real'nost khozrascheta," report by staffers at USSR Gosplan Scientific Research Economics Institute, *Sots. Indust.*, June 10, 1988, p. 2.

31. The figure for construction is from Balakin, "Restructuring" (1988); the figure for machine building is from *Sots. Indust.* Jan. 30–31, 1988, p. 1, with data from a preliminary analysis; in February 1988, the Ministry of Light Industry reported that one-third of its enterprises had not fulfilled their profit plan for the past year, and that the number of loss-makers had increased; see *Pravda*, Feb. 22, 1988, p. 2.

32. See the Goskomstat figures in *Izvestiia*, Dec. 9, 1988, p. 2.

33. On continuing ministerial redistribution of profits, see, for example, Komin, "Perestroika Ekonomiki" (1988). For a cogent explanation of the problems and inconsistencies which helped to undermine the effectiveness of the Law on the State Enterprise, see Aslund, *Gorbachev's Struggle* (1989), pp. 61–62; 113–126.

34. Several industrial workers and managers who addressed the 19th Conference protested that continuing recentralization of much of their enterprises' earnings undermined efforts to achieve profitability and demoralized those

genuinely trying to improve performance. Delegates also accused the ministries of continuing interference in their enterprises' planning and production through the notorious "state order," and continuing central control over allocations of supplies. See *Current Soviet Policies X: The Documentary Record of the 19th Conference of the Communist Party of the Soviet Union* (Columbus, Ohio: Current Digest of the Soviet Press, 1988), esp. speeches by V. V. Bakatin (pp. 26–27), I. K. Polozhkov (pp. 50–51), V. M. Platonov (p. 65).

35. For the report on the closing of a sewn-goods factory in Lvov Oblast see G. Nekrasova and E. Savinova, "Esli predpriiatie obankrotilos," in *Sots. Indust.*, Aug. 18, 1988, p. 2; on the agricultural machine-building enterprises in Saratov Oblast, see A. Baranov, E. Leont'eva, and V. Lifanov, "Lomat stereotipy proshlogo," *Sots. Indust.*, July 19, 1988, pp. 1–2.

36. See Gorbachev's report to the July 29, 1988, CPSU Central Committee Plenum, *Pravda,* July 30, 1988, pp. 1–3.

37. See the report of the Sept. 10 Council of Ministers' meeting in *FBIS:SU,* Oct. 5, 1988, p. 68, trans. from *Izvestiia,* Oct. 3, 1988, p. 2.

38. Gostev, "O gosudarstvennom biudzhete," *Pravda,* Oct. 28, 1988, p. 4; *FBIS:SU,* Oct. 27, 1988, p. 51, citing TASS, Oct. 27, 1988.

39. "V sovete ministrov SSSR," *Pravda,* Sept. 11, 1988, p. 2.

40. See the article by Iu. Krasopol'sky in *Trud,* Sept. 16, 1988, p. 2; the interview with the chairman of the USSR Bank for Industrial Construction M. Zotov, "Bankrotami ne nazoveshch, a platit'nechem," in *Sots. Indust.,* Sept. 20, 1988, p. 2; N. Lemayev in *Pravda,* Sept. 22, 1988, p. 2, on bankruptcies and reorganizations proposed by the USSR Ministry of Petroleum Refining and Petrochemical Industry; the interview with I. S. Silayev, chairman of the Council of Ministers Bureau of Machine-Building, in *Izvestiia,* Oct. 13, 1988, p. 2; the *Wochenpresse* interview with V. Golovachev, editor-in-chief of *Trud,* reported in *FBIS:SU,* Feb. 14, 1989, pp. 75–76.

41. Baranov, Leonteva, and Lifanov, "Lomat stereotipy" (1988).

42. See, for example, the reports in *FBIS:SU,* May 19, 1989, pp. 107–108, citing *Sovetskaia Rossia,* May 14, 1989, p. 2; Zotov, "Bankrotami ne nazoveshch" (1988).

43. See the discussion with V. I. Gostev in *Izvestiia,* Mar. 30, 1989, p. 2; the targets are given in a report on a Council of Ministers' meeting in *FBIS:SU,* Jan. 19, 1989, p. 41, citing MosTel, Jan. 17, 1989; this meeting also reported that approximately 15 percent of enterprises in "the main branch of the National Economy" were loss-making, and that over the past three years they had registered losses of about R11 billion each year.

44. See the report on the Supreme Soviet's fall Planning and Budget meetings in *Pravda,* Oct. 28, 1988, pp. 2–4; on options for reorganization, see also *FBIS:SU,* Jan. 31, 1989, pp. 81–82, citing *Morning Star,* Jan. 30, 1989, p. 6.

45. Figures are from *PlanEcon Report,* vol. 7, nos. 11–12, March 27, 1991, p. 20. I have found no series of figures on subsidies to enterprises overall, only the single figure of R12 billion from Goskomstat, cited in the text, and the comparable figure of about R11 billion yearly cited at the January 1989

Council of Ministers' meeting. Presumably this is the total for subsidies to both heavy and light industry, while the PlanEcon figures are for heavy industry only.

46. Quote is from an interview with Leonid Abalkin, director of the USSR Academy of Sciences Institute of Economics, in *FBIS:SU,* Jan. 27, 1989, p. 84, trans. from *Selskaia Zhizn,* Jan. 24, 1989, p. 1.

47. See the interviews with Chazov in *Pravda,* Apr. 13, 1987, p. 3; *Literaturnaia Gazeta,* Apr. 29, 1987, p. 11; and *Sovetskaia Rossiia,* July 5, 1987, p. 1, trans. in *Current Digest of the Soviet Press (CDSP),* vol. 39, no. 27, Aug. 5, 1987, p. 22. See also Mark G. Field, "Soviet Health Problems and the Convergence Hypothesis," in Anthony Jones, Walter D. Connor, and David E. Powell, eds., *Soviet Social Problems* (Boulder, Colo.: Westview, 1991), pp. 78–93. Chazov acknowledged that pollution and other environmental factors also contributed to health problems.

48. See, for example, the discussion of extortion and bribe taking by medical workers, by the USSR prosecutor general in *Izvestiia,* June 2, 1986, p. 3; the report from the USSR Congress of Physicians, in *Pravda,* Oct. 18, 1988, pp. 1, 3.

49. For the reformist critique of the welfare state, including universal state provision of social services, see the discussion in chapter 4.

50. Christopher Mark Davis, "Developments in the Health Sector of the Soviet Economy, 1970–1990," in *Gorbachev's Economic Plans, Vol. 2: Study Papers Submitted to the Joint Economic Committee, Congress of the United States* (Washington, D.C.: U.S. GPO, 1987), pp. 312–335.

51. For a summary of this decision see Margot Jacobs, "Are the Restrictions on Medical Cooperatives Justified?" *Radio Liberty: Report on the USSR (RL:USSR),* vol. 1, no. 13, Mar. 31, 1989, pp. 9–12.

52. This figure is cited by V. Treskunov, deputy director of the USSR Ministry of Public Health's Chief Administration for Therapeutic and Preventive Assistance, in *Izvestiia,* July 11, 1986, p. 3; see also the report on financial and other restrictions placed on fee-charging polyclinics in Moscow, *Izvestiia,* Jan. 21, 1986, p. 3.

53. See *CDSP,* vol. 38, no. 28, Aug. 13, 1986, pp. 7–8, citing *Izvestiia,* July 11, 1986, p. 3; see also *CDSP,* vol. 38, no. 3, Feb. 19, 1986, p. 21, citing *Izvestiia,* Jan. 21, 1986, p. 3.

54. For a draft of the "Basic Guidelines" see *Pravda,* Aug. 15, 1987, pp. 1–3; the final version followed this draft closely. The guidelines also made reference to "economically accountable" medical facilities; the meaning of this term, and its relationship to fee-charging services, is unclear. Medical professionals correctly charged that the guidelines were vague on the privatization issue.

55. Davis, "Developments" (JEC, 1987), pp. 331–332.

56. See the discussion of this resolution in *Izvestiia,* Oct. 22, 1986, p. 3.

57. *Pravda,* Aug. 15, 1987, pp. 1–3. Chazov stated that overall spending on capital investment in medicine would increase from R9 to R25 billion; see *Izvestiia,* July 7, 1988, p. 6.

58. *Izvestiia,* Sept. 29, 1987, p. 2.

59. The text of the law, passed by the Supreme Soviet on Nov. 19, 1986, is in *Pravda,* Nov. 21, 1986, pp. 1, 3; the specific provisions for medical activity are in Articles 18 and 19.

60. See the restrictions on private medical practice listed by L. E. Kunelsky, member of the collegium of the USSR State Committee on Labor and Social Issues, in *Izvestiia,* Apr. 30, 1987, p. 6.

61. The text of the law is in *Pravda,* June 8, 1988, pp. 2–5; quote is from p. 2. Cooperatives' rights were subject to a number of limitations and stipulations; for medical cooperatives, the most important in practice would prove to be the stipulation, in Article 27, that a cooperative was entitled to lease from state and other organizations *unused* machinery and equipment (my emphasis). For a very good discussion of development and restriction of medical cooperatives see also Anthony Jones and William Moskoff, *Ko-ops: The Rebirth of Entrepreneurship in the Soviet Union* (Bloomington: Indiana University Press, 1991), pp. 57–61.

62. *Izvestiia,* Sept. 10, 1987, p. 3. According to data from the USSR Ministry of Finance, slightly more than 200,000 people were registered as engaged in individual labor activity; of these, 109,000 were in handicrafts, 64,000 in consumer services, and 2,500 in medical services.

63. *Meditsinskaia Gazeta,* Dec. 30, 1988, p. 4.

64. See Jacobs, "Restrictions" (1989), p. 11; David E. Powell, "The Entrepreneurial Spirit and Soviet Medicine," in B. Dallago, G. Ajani, and B. Grancelli, eds., *Privatization and Entrepreneurship in Post-Socialist Countries: Economy, Law, and Society* (New York: St. Martin's, 1992), pp. 215–244; Jones and Moskoff, *Ko-ops* (1991), p. 58. Jones and Moskoff report, on the basis of an interview with Yuri Vorontsov, an official of the Cooperative Union, that some doctors working in co-ops earned four to five times what they had earned in state hospitals.

65. *Izvestiia,* Nov. 17, 1988, p. 3; *Moscow News,* no. 35, Sept. 6–13, 1987, p. 14.

66. On the various difficulties faced by Soviet cooperatives, see Anthony Jones and William Moskoff, "New Cooperatives in the USSR," *Problems of Communism,* vol. 38, Nov.-Dec. 1989, pp. 27–39.

67. Evidence of public support in principle for the availability of paid medical services was provided in an interview with Dr. Nikolai Popov, VTsIOM, Moscow, May 4, 1991. Popov reported that, when asked whether Soviets had a right to paid medical services as a supplement to free state medical services, 58 percent of respondents answered positively, 37 percent negatively. Respondents (all RSFSR residents) were more "liberal" on this issue than on rights for private education and other aspects of state provision.

68. *Moscow News,* no. 44, Nov. 8–15, 1987, p. 10; Article 42 of the 1977 Soviet constitution states, "Citizens of the USSR have the right to health protection." See also Christopher Mark Davis, "The Organization and Performance of the Contemporary Soviet Health Service," in Gail W. Lapidus and Guy E. Swanson, eds., *State and Welfare USA/USSR: Contemporary Policy and Practice* (Berkeley and Los Angeles: University of California Press,

1988), p. 115. For citizens' claims that paid medical treatment violated their rights, see, for example, *Izvestiia,* July 11, 1986, p. 3.

69. Powell, "Entrepreneurial Spirit" (1992).

70. See Chazov's charges to this effect (among his justifications for prohibiting diagnostic cooperatives), *Izvestiia,* Dec. 23, 1988, p. 3; *Meditsinskaia Gazeta,* Dec. 30, 1988, p. 2.

71. On the Union of Moscow Health Cooperatives and its goals, see the article in *Meditsinskaia Gazeta,* Aug. 19, 1988, p. 1; Jones and Moskoff, *Ko-ops* (1991), p. 58.

72. The vote on regulating medical cooperatives at the congress was 4,861 for, 12 against; Jacobs, "Restrictions" (1989), p. 10.

73. For the text of Order 785, see *Izvestiia,* Nov. 17, 1988, p. 3; for discussion, see Jacobs, "Restrictions" (1989), pp. 9–12.

74. *Izvestiia,* Dec. 23, 1988, p. 3.

75. Ibid. Chazov stressed that the Law on Cooperatives gave state organizations the right to lease only equipment which was not in use, and asserted that chief physicians were leasing out, for their personal profit and in violation of the Law on Cooperatives, equipment very much needed for use in state clinics.

76. See the text of the resolution, which was issued on Dec. 29, 1988, in *Izvestiia,* Dec. 31, 1988, p. 2.

77. On the need to protect society in areas of medicine where cooperative members' mistakes "could have irreparable social consequences," see *Trud,* Jan. 4, 1989, p. 1; on justifications for the restrictions, see the interview with an assistant minister of health in *Meditsinskaia Gazeta,* Jan. 6, 1989, p. 1.

78. Cited in Jacobs, "Restrictions" (1989), p. 9.

79. On closings, see *CDSP,* vol. 40, no. 46, Dec. 14, 1988, p. 23; on the emergency session see Jones and Moskoff, *Ko-ops* (1991), p. 59.

80. See Ryzhkov on continuing co-op violations, in *Pravda,* Oct. 26, 1989, p. 3.

81. *Izvestiia,* Dec. 31, 1988, p. 2.

82. *Narkhoz SSSR v 1989,* p. 612. While Soviet health care spending continued to grow in terms of rubles, it declined as a percent of GNP from 6.6 percent in 1965 to 4.1 percent in 1970 and 4 percent in 1987; in most industrial nations the share is 6 to 12 percent. See Field, "Soviet Health Problems" (1991), p. 83.

83. Retail price reform finally went into effect on April 2, 1992. As it had promised from the outset, the government provided compensation. For further discussion of price reform, see chapter 7.

84. A. Bim and A. Shokhin, "Sistema Raspredeleniia: Na Putiakh Perestroiki," *Kommunist,* no. 15, Oct. 1986, pp. 64–73; quote is from pp. 69–70.

85. For discussion of the Novocherkassk strikes, see chapter 3.

86. See the interview with Pavlov in *Trud,* Sept. 9, 1988; quote is from p. 2.

87. See *Literaturnaia Gazeta,* Jan. 20, 1988, p. 10. According to the editors' commentary, "very many" letters, which were often from pensioners, expressed alarm and panic over the prospect of retail price increases.

88. *Nedelia,* no. 19, May 9–15, 1988, p. 7, trans. in *FBIS:SU,* May 19, 1988, pp.

61–62. See also Hans Aage, "Attitudes towards Reform of Retail Prices," *Radio Liberty Research Bulletin, (RLRB)* 523/88, Nov. 23, 1988, esp. pp. 4–6.

89. *Moscow News,* Oct. 2–9, 1988, p. 13.

90. The cited figures are estimates from *PlanEcon Report,* vol. 5, nos. 6–7, Feb. 17, 1989, p. 9; vol. 7, nos. 11–12, March 27, 1991, p. 10. The lower official figures given in these years were universally considered, and later admitted, to be seriously underestimated; see Anders Aslund, "Gorbachev, Perestroyka, and Economic Crisis," *Problems of Communism,* vol. 40, Jan.-Apr. 1991, p. 20.

91. See *Izvestiia,* Sept. 10, 1988, p. 1; *Trud,* Sept. 29, 1988, p. 2; On causes of inflation and shortages see also *PlanEcon Report,* vol. 5, Feb. 17, 1989, pp. 8–9.

92. See *Izvestiia,* Sept. 10, 1988, p. 1.

93. On the erosion of the range of cheap consumer goods at this time see *Sots. Indust.,* Sept. 15, 1988, p. 3; *Izvestiia,* Sept. 10, 1988; p. 1; *Sovetskaia Rossiia,* Oct. 15, 1988, p. 1, trans. in *FBIS:SU,* Oct. 21, 1988, pp. 81–82; quote is from p. 82.

94. See the report of the Supreme Soviet Commission on Labor, Prices, and Social Policy, *Pravda,* Sept. 23, 1989, p. 2.

95. See Jones and Moskoff, *Ko-ops* (1991), esp. chap. 4.

96. *PlanEcon Report,* vol. 6, Nov. 23, 1990, p. 20; vol. 7, Mar. 27, 1991, p. 25.

97. *Sovetskaia Rossiia,* Oct. 15, 1988, p. 1, trans. in *FBIS:SU,* Oct. 21, 1988, pp. 81–82.

98. In early October the Planning and Budget Commissions of the Supreme Soviet recommended administrative measures to control price increases; see *Trud,* Sept. 29, 1988, p. 2; *Ek. Gaz.,* no. 43, Oct. 1988, pp. 4–5; the quoted phrase, on p. 5, is from A. Komin, first deputy chair of Goskomtsen.

99. See the interview with Shmelev in *Moscow News,* no. 50, Dec. 18–25, 1988, p. 10.

100. *Pravda,* Jan. 6, 1989, p. 1.

101. See "Official Interviewed on Price Setting Measures," *FBIS:SU,* Jan. 9, 1989, p. 89.

102. See *FBIS:SU,* Jan. 24, 1989, p. 55, citing MosTel, June 23 News Conference on Nonfood Goods. Local soviets were also given direct control over some cooperative prices.

103. The text of the resolution is in *Pravda,* Feb. 4, 1989, pp. 1–2; quote is from p. 2.

104. For lists of demands made by the striking miners see, for example, *Izvestiia,* July 18, 1989, p. 6; July 14, 1989, p. 3. For further discussion, see chapter 6.

105. For a report on one such demonstration in Kiev, see *Pravda Ukrainy,* Oct. 15, 1989, p. 1; for further discussion see chapter 6.

106. On these measures, see *FBIS:SU,* Nov. 21, 1989, p. 54, citing TASS's review of the Nov. 20 Supreme Soviet Session.

107. *FBIS:SU,* Dec. 1, 1989, pp. 45–46, citing *Pravda,* Nov. 26, 1989, pp. 1, 3.

6. Soviet Workers and Their Discontents

1. For statements of this commonly held view, see Timothy J. Colton, "Approaches to the Politics of Systemic Economic Reform in the Soviet Union," *Soviet Economy,* vol. 3, Apr.-June 1987, pp. 166–169; Gail W. Lapidus, "Social Trends," in Robert F. Byrnes, ed., *After Brezhnev: Sources of Soviet Conduct in the 1980s* (Bloomington: Indiana University Press, 1983), pp. 188–190.

2. See, for example, Blair A. Ruble, "The Social Dimensions of *Perestroyka,*" *Soviet Economy,* vol. 3, Apr.-June 1987, pp. 171–179.

3. For reports on reform experiments on the Belorussian Railroad, see: *Moscow News,* no. 23, June 15–22, 1986, pp. 8–9; no. 10, Mar. 15–22, 1987, p. 11.

4. See *Trud,* Dec. 16, 1987, p. 4; *Sotsialisticheskaia Industriia (Sots. Indust.),* Dec. 29, 1987, p. 1.

5. See Pukhova's speech in *Pravda,* July 2, 1988, p. 11, in which she also asserted that the reform's pressures for more efficient labor organization "have jeopardized the most vulnerable part of the labor collective—women with children."

6. *Sots. Indust.,* Dec. 5, 1987, p. 2; *Izvestiia,* Feb. 13, 1988, p. 3.

7. See, for example, *Trud,* Dec. 29, 1987, p. 2.

8. These strikes, and the sources reporting them, are as follows: A strike at the Likino Bus Manufacturing Plant, reported in *Moscow News,* no. 42, Oct. 25–Nov. 1, 1987, pp. 8–9; a bus drivers' strike in Chekhov, reported in *Moscow News,* no. 38, Sept. 27–Oct. 4, 1987, p. 9; a strike by drivers in Ufa, reported in *Soviet Labor Review (SLR),* vol. 5, no. 3, Oct. 1987, p. 1, citing *Komsomolskaia Pravda,* Sept. 23, 1987; a week-long dispute at the Yaroslavl Motor Works reported in "USSR this Week," p. 1, *Radio Liberty Research Bulletin (RLRB)* 6/88, no. 1, Jan. 6, 1988; a work stoppage by Omsk delivery drivers, reported in *Sots. Indust.,* Feb. 24, 1988, p. 2; a bus drivers' strike in Saratov, reported in *Pravda,* Apr. 13, 1988, p. 2; a drivers' strike in Severodvinsk and a strike at the Kuibyshev Textile Factory, both reported in *SLR,* vol. 6, no. 4, Dec. 1988, p. 2; a strike by Arkhangelsk bus drivers, reported in *SLR,* vol. 6, no. 3, Oct. 1988, p. 4; a series of three strikes in Kamensk-Uralsky, reported in *SLR,* vol. 6, no. 3, Oct. 1988, p. 2, citing *Uralskii Rabochii,* Aug. 14, 1988; two strikes at the Leningrad Shipbuilding Plant, reported in *Pravda,* Apr. 25, 1988, pp. 1–2; a strike at a Moscow housing construction company, reported in "USSR this Week," p. 7, *RLRB* 139/88, no. 14, Apr. 6, 1988, citing *Pravda,* Mar. 30, 1988; a strike by bus drivers in Chernovtsky, reported in "USSR this Week," pp. 5–6, *RLRB* 323/88, no. 30, Part II, July 27, 1988, citing *Pravda,* July 18, 1988.

9. "Bus Plant Strike Causes Explored," *Foreign Broadcast Information Service, Daily Report: Soviet Union (FBIS:SU),* Oct. 21, 1987, pp. 64–66, trans. from *Moskovskiie Novosti,* no. 42, Oct. 18, 1987, pp. 8–9; quote is from p. 64.

10. "Bus Plant Strike" *(FBIS:SU,* 1987), pp. 64–65.

11. See *Pravda,* July 18, 1988, p. 4.

12. See, for example, Sergei Voronitsyn, "Lessons of the Dispute at the Yaro-

slavl Motor Works," *RLRB,* no. 9, Mar. 2, 1988, Part I; the report on the Omsk delivery drivers' strike in *Sots. Indust.,* Feb. 24, 1988, p. 2; the report on the Lipetsk bus drivers' protest in "USSR this Week," p. 10, in *RLRB* 412/88, no. 38, Sept. 21, 1988.

13. Quote is from "Bus Plant Strike" (*FBIS:SU,* 1987), p. 64.

14. Ibid.

15. For statistics on the increase in average wages and salaries beginning in 1988, which reportedly averaged more than 8 percent per quarter through most of 1989 and 1990, see *PlanEcon Report,* vol. 6, nos. 46–47, Nov. 23, 1990, p. 8 (Table 2). For the relationship between average wages and overall labor productivity during the same period, which shows labor productivity consistently to be well below wage increases, and to be steady or declining through most of the period, see *PlanEcon Report,* vol. 6, no. 16, Apr. 20, 1990, p. 3.

16. See the report in *Trud,* July 16, 1989, p. 1.

17. On the scale and course of the miners' strike see Walter D. Connor, *The Accidental Proletariat: Workers, Politics, and Crisis in Gorbachev's Russia* (Princeton: Princeton University Press, 1991), pp. 276–280.

18. See *FBIS:SU,* Oct. 17, 1988, p. 34, trans. from *Pravda Ukrainy (Pr. Uk.),* Oct. 6, 1988, pp. 1–3; *FBIS:SU,* Dec. 29, 1988, p. 53, trans. from *Pr. Uk.,* Dec. 21, 1988, p. 4. *Izvestiia,* Jan. 6, 1989. p. 1.

19. See *FBIS:SU,* Oct. 25, 1988, pp. 76–77, trans. from *Pr. Uk.,* Oct. 12, 1988, p. 3; *FBIS:SU,* Dec. 14, 1988, pp. 65–66; trans. from *Pr. Uk.,* Dec. 3, 1988, p. 3; *FBIS:SU,* Feb. 7, 1989, pp. 55–56, trans. from *Pr. Uk.,* Jan. 24, 1989, p. 1.

20. See, for example, the report on conditions in the Kuzbass in *Sots. Indust.,* Mar. 28, 1989, p. 2.

21. See, for example, the report in *Trud,* Mar. 10, 1989, p. 2.

22. See David Marples, "Will a New Order Revitalize the Ukrainian Coalfields?" *RLRB* 173/88, no. 17, Apr. 27, 1988, pp. 1–4.

23. This series of six articles by V. Andreianov and G. Dorofeev was published in *Sots. Indust.* on July 26, 27, 29, 31, and Aug. 2, 3, 1988; see also David Marples, "Working Conditions in Ukrainian Coal Mines Criticized," *RLRB* 437/88, no. 41, Oct. 12, 1988, pp. 1–3.

24. See the article by V. S. Shatalov in *Ekonomicheskaia Gazeta (Ek. Gaz.),* no. 7, Feb. 1989, pp. 17–18; See also David Marples, "New Revelations Underline Seriousness of Problems in Ukrainian Coal Mines," *Report on the USSR* (a publication of Radio Liberty), vol. 1, no. 14, Apr. 7, 1989, pp. 23–25.

25. On election defeats of party secretaries in mining districts, see Jerry F. Hough, "The Politics of Successful Economic Reform," *Soviet Economy,* vol. 5, Jan.-Mar. 1989, pp. 14–15.

26. For the text of the draft law see *FBIS:SU,* May 9, 1989, pp. 48–58, trans. from *Trud,* Apr. 29, 1989, pp. 2–3.

27. See the interview with M. A. Srebny, chairman of the Coal Industry Trade Union, in *FBIS:SU,* May 11, 1989, pp. 46–47, trans. from *Trud,* May 5, 1989,

p. 2; and on the strikes, see *Izvestiia,* Mar. 20, 1989, p. 2; *Pravda,* Apr. 13, 1989, p. 6; *Trud,* Apr. 20, 1989, p. 2.

28. See *FBIS:SU,* Apr. 10, 1989, pp. 53–54, trans. from *Sovetskaia Rossia,* Apr. 9, 1989, p. 2; *Trud,* Apr. 25, 1989, p. 2.

29. See *FBIS:SU,* May 11, 1989, pp. 46–47, trans. from *Trud,* May 5, 1989, p. 2.

30. For reports on the strike and its early development see *FBIS:SU,* July 18, 1989, pp. 67–81, citing various sources; *Trud,* July 16, 1989, p. 1.

31. See *Trud,* July 18, 1989, p. 1.

32. See *Pravda,* July 19, 1989, p. 2, on commissions sent from Moscow to bargain with the miners; *Izvestiia,* July 20, 1989, p. 3.

33. See *Izvestiia,* July 20, 1989, p. 3; *FBIS:SU,* July 20, 1989, pp. 55–59, citing Moscow Domestic Service (Russian), July 19, 1989.

34. See *FBIS:SU,* July 25, 1989, p. 57, trans. from *Trud,* July 16, 1989, p. 1; Connor, *Accidental Proletariat* (1991), pp. 279–289.

35. For the text of the draft Law on Labor Disputes, see *FBIS:SU,* Aug. 16, 1989, pp. 35–36, trans. from *Izvestiia,* Aug. 16, 1989, p. 1.

36. Quote is from *FBIS:SU,* July 27, 1989, p. 61, citing Moscow Television Service, Vremia Newscast, July 26, 1989.

37. For lists of miners' demands see, for example, *Izvestiia,* July 19, 1989, p. 6; *Trud,* July 12, 1989, p. 1.

38. See, for example, *Izvestiia,* July 17, 1989, p. 6.

39. Quote is from a report on strikes in the Kuzbass, *FBIS:SU,* July 17, 1989, p. 34, citing Moscow Domestic Service (Russian), July 15, 1989.

40. Quote is from *Izvestiia,* July 17, 1989, p. 6.

41. This is the figure given by the prime minister in *FBIS:SU,* Aug. 7, 1989, p. 68, citing TASS, Aug. 4, 1989.

42. For a different interpretation, which gives more weight to the leadership role of educated specialists in the miners' strikes, see Peter Rutland, "Labor Unrest and Movements in 1989 and 1990," *Soviet Economy,* vol. 6, no. 4, 1990, pp. 345–384.

43. Quotes are from: *Trud,* July 23, 1989, p. 1; *FBIS:SU,* July 25, 1989, p. 55, trans. from *Izvestiia,* July 23, 1989, p. 1.

44. Quote is from an interview with A. Melnikov, first secretary of the Kemerovo Oblast Pasrty Organization, in *Sovetskaia Rossia,* Aug. 6, 1989, p. 2, translated in *FBIS:SU,* Aug. 24, 1989, p. 60. See also the statements by AUCCTU chair Shalayev in *FBIS:SU,* July 24, 1989, p. 53; Central Committee secretary N. Slyunkov in *FBIS:SU,* July 19, 1989, p. 65, citing TASS, July 18, 1989.

45. See the report by David Marples, "Why the Donbass Miners Went on Strike" in *Report on the USSR,* vol. 1, no. 36, Sept. 8, 1989, pp. 30–32; statistics are on p. 31.

46. Mervyn Matthews, *Patterns of Deprivation in the Soviet Union under Brezhnev and Gorbachev* (Stanford, Calif.: Hoover Institution Press, 1989), pp. 80–89.

47. Thane Gustafson, *Crisis amid Plenty: The Politics of Soviet Energy under Brezhnev and Gorbachev* (Princeton: Princeton University Press, 1989), pp.

258–261; John Tedstrom, "The Importance of the Soviet Coal Industry," *Report on the USSR,* vol. 1, no. 31, Aug. 4, 1989, pp. 13–14; David Marples, "Emergence of a Coal-Mining Crisis in the Donetsk Basin: Planning and Investment Decisions," *Report on the USSR,* vol. 1, no. 32, Aug. 11, 1989, pp. 10–12.

48. See David Marples, "Increased Militancy in the Donetsk Coal Basin," *Report on the USSR,* vol. 1, no. 49, Dec. 8, 1989, p. 10–11; *Izvestiia,* Sept. 5, 1989, p. 3; *Sots. Indust.,* Sept. 2, 1989, p. 2; *Trud,* July 26, 1989, p. 1; Theodore Friedgut and Lewis Siegelbaum, "Perestroika from Below: The Soviet Miners' Strike and Its Aftermath," *New Left Review,* vol. 18, no. 1, May-June 1990, pp. 26–32.

49. See the interview with Riabev in *Pravda,* Nov. 12, 1989, p. 3; and on negotiations with the miners, *Izvestiia,* Oct. 23, 1989, p. 3; May 23, 1990, p. 6; *Trud,* Dec. 30, 1989, p. 1.

50. See *Moscow News,* no. 13, Apr. 8–15, 1990, pp. 8–9; *Pravda,* June 16, 1990, p. 2.

51. For reports on these strikes, see *Trud,* July 26, 1989, p. 3; Aug. 22, 1989, p. 1.

52. For reports on dockers' strikes, see *FBIS:SU,* Mar. 7, 1990, p. 109, citing Maritime Press Service (Leningrad), Mar. 1, 1990; and among drivers and fitters, *FBIS:SU,* Apr. 9, 1990, pp. 44–45, trans. from *Komsomolskaia Pravda,* Apr. 5, 1990, p. 1. For discussion of continuing transport strikes, see chapter 7.

53. For the text of the resolution "On Procedures for Settling Collective Labor Disputes," see *Pravda,* Oct. 14, 1989, pp. 1–2; and for a good discussion of its implications, see D. J. Peterson, "The Supreme Soviet Passes Strike Legislation," *Report on the USSR,* vol. 1, no. 44, Nov. 3, 1989, pp. 11–13.

54. On Gorbachev's effort to get a strike ban passed, see *FBIS:SU,* Oct. 3, 1989, pp. 57–61, esp. pp. 60–61, citing TASS and Moscow World Service, both for Oct. 3, 1990. Gorbachev lost in part because the liberal Interregional Group of Deputies considered the legislation too restrictive.

55. See *FBIS:SU,* Oct. 30, 1989, p. 61, citing TASS, Oct. 29, 1989.

56. On the formation of the United Front, see *FBIS:SU,* Aug. 25, 1989, p. 82, trans. from *Leningradskaia Pravda,* July 18, 1989, p. 3; *FBIS:SU,* Oct. 20, 1989, pp. 71–73, trans. from *Trud,* Oct. 15, p. 2; Yitzhak M. Brudny, "The Heralds of Opposition to Perestroika," *Soviet Economy,* vol. 5, Apr.-June 1989, esp. pp. 192–196.

57. See M. Steven Fish, "The Emergence of Independent Associations and the Transformation of Russian Political Society since 1985" (paper presented at the 1990 American Political Science Association Annual Meeting, San Francisco, Aug. 30–Sept. 2, 1990), pp. 11–13.

58. Quotes are from *Leningradskaia Pravda,* July 18, 1989, p. 3, trans. in *FBIS:SU,* Aug. 25, 1989, p. 82; *Moskovskaia Pravda,* Sept. 19, 1989, p. 2, trans. in *FBIS:SU,* Oct. 17, 1989, p. 93.

59. Vera Tolz, "Politics in Leningrad and the Creation of Two Popular Fronts,"

Report on the USSR, vol. 1, no. 29, July 21, 1989, pp. 38–40; Brudny, "Heralds" (1989), pp. 192–196.

60. Quote is from *FBIS:SU,* Sept. 18, 1989, p. 75, citing Moscow Television Service, Sept. 17, 1989.

61. Tolz, "Politics in Leningrad" (1989), pp. 38–40; *Sovetskaia Kultura,* Sept. 16, 1989, p. 1, trans. in *FBIS:SU,* Oct. 6, 1989, pp. 63–65.

62. Quotes are from *Moskovskaia Pravda,* Sept. 19, 1989, p. 2, trans. in *FBIS:SU,* Oct. 17, 1989, p. 93; see also *Sovetskaia Rossia,* Sept. 13, 1989, p. 2, trans. in *FBIS:SU,* Oct. 16, 1989, pp. 81–83; Vera Tolz, "The United Front of Workers of Russia: Further Consolidation of Antireform Forces," *Report on the USSR,* vol. 1, no. 39, Sept. 29, 1989, pp. 11–13.

63. See, for example, *Trud,* June 24, 1988, p. 2; Oct. 15, 1989, p. 2; *Trud,* Oct. 15, 1989, p. 2, trans. in *FBIS:SU,* Oct. 20, 1989, pp. 71–73; *Moskovskaia Pravda,* Sept. 19, 1989, p. 2, trans. from *FBIS,* Oct. 17, 1989, pp. 92–95; quote is from p. 93.

64. For further discussion of the OFT, see Connor, *Accidental Proletariat* (1991), pp. 293–302.

65. See Shalayev's report to the Dec. 1987 AUCCTU Plenum, "On the Work of Primary Trade Union Organizations in the New Economic and Self-Management Conditions," in *FBIS:SU,* Mar. 1, 1988, pp. 52–71, trans. from *Trud,* Dec. 13, 1987, pp. 2–4.

66. For the trade union program, see *Trud,* June 7, 1989, p. 1.

67. Quotes are from *Trud,* July 23, 1989, p. 1.

68. See the report on the Presidium in *FBIS:SU,* Aug. 4, 1989, pp. 63–64; quotes are from p. 63, trans. from *Trud,* July 30, 1989, p. 1.

69. Quote is from *FBIS:SU,* Sept. 13, 1989, p. 41, trans. from *Trud,* Sept. 6, 1989, pp. 1–3. See, also *FBIS:SU,* Sept. 6, 1989, pp. 66–68, trans. from *Trud,* Aug. 25, 1989, p. 1.

70. See Shalayev's address in *FBIS:SU,* Sept. 13, 1989, pp. 39–50; trans. from *Trud,* Sept. 6, 1989, pp. 1–3; quotes on p. 40, 42.

71. See *FBIS:SU,* Sept. 13, 1989, pp. 38–39, trans. from *Trud,* Sept. 7, 1989, p. 1.

72. See *Izvestiia,* Oct. 4, 1989, p. 1, on a rally in Moscow; *FBIS:SU,* Oct. 27, 1989, p. 63, citing TASS, Oct. 26, 1989, on one in Leningrad; *FBIS:SU,* Nov. 16, 1989, pp. 103–104, trans. from *Pr. Uk.,* Oct. 15, 1989, p. 1, on a mass meeting in Kiev to support AUCCTU policies.

73. See sources cited in note 72; for a skeptical comment on the authenticity of these rallies, see Connor, *Accidental Proletariat* (1991), pp. 291–292.

74. See, for example, Shalayev's endorsement of a price control resolution in *Trud,* Nov. 26, 1989, pp. 1–2.

75. See *Trud,* Jan. 24, 1990, p. 1; *Pravda,* Feb. 11, 1990, p. 2.

76. Gorbachev appointed one of the OFT's leaders, V. A. Yarin, to his short-lived Presidential Council in early 1990.

77. See Vera Tolz, "Informal Political Groups Prepare for Elections in RSFSR," *Report on the USSR,* vol. 2, Feb. 23, 1990, p. 27, which reports on two independent polls showing similar results.

78. This poll result was reported in *Russkaia Mysl,* Feb. 2, 1990, cited in Tolz, "Informal Political Groups" (1990), p. 2.

79. See the report on election results in *Moscow News,* no. 10, Mar. 18–25, 1990, pp. 4–5; John B. Dunlop, "Moscow Voters Reject Conservative Coalition," *Report on the USSR,* vol. 2, no. 16, Apr. 20, 1990, pp. 15–17.

80. See the discussion in chapter 1 of Andrew Walder, *Communist Neo-Traditionalism: Work and Authority in Chinese Industry* (Berkeley and Los Angeles: University of California Press, 1986); Victor Zaslavsky, *The Neo-Stalinist State: Class, Ethnicity, and Consensus in Soviet Society* (Armonk, N.Y.: M. E. Sharpe, 1982).

7. Failure of the Social Contract

1. For estimates of unemployment, see D. J. Peterson, "New Data Published on Employment and Unemployment in the USSR," *Report on the USSR,* (Radio Liberty Publication), vol. 2, no. 1, Jan. 5, 1990, pp. 3–4; "International: Unemployment Provision in the Former Communist Countries," *Radio Free Europe/Radio Liberty (RFE/RL) Research Report,* vol. 1, no. 2, Jan. 10, 1992, pp. 27–29; *Izvestiia,* Jan. 5, 1990, p. 2; Apr. 7, 1990, p. 1. For the impact on women, see Sarah Ashwin, "Development of Feminism in the Perestroika Era," *Report on the USSR,* vol. 3, no. 35, Aug. 30, 1991, pp. 21–25; and on youth, *Izvestiia,* Apr. 7, 1990, p. 1.

2. On projected numbers of unemployed, see *Trud,* Oct. 12, 1990, p. 1; Feb. 5, 1991, p. 2; for reports of opinion polls showing widespread popular fears of unemployment, see *Foreign Broadcast Information Service: Daily Report: Soviet Union (FBIS: SU),* July 2, 1991, p. 79, citing Moscow Russian Television Network, June 29, 1991; William Moskoff, "The Soviet Economy: The Slide to the Abyss," in Anthony Jones and David E. Powell, eds., *Soviet Update: 1989–1990* (Boulder, Colo.: Westview, 1991), p. 32.

3. On the employment law see *Pravda,* Jan. 25, 1991, p. 1; and on the GCTU's draft, see *Trud,* July 19, p. 2; Oct. 24, pp. 2–3, 1990.

4. See Elizabeth Teague, "Tackling the Problem of Unemployment," *Report on the USSR,* vol. 3, no. 45, Nov. 8, 1991, pp. 1–7; *Pravda,* Jan. 25, 1991, p. 1.

5. See Teague, "Tackling" (1991); *FBIS:SU,* June 17, 1991, pp. 94–95, citing Moscow Radio, Rossii Network, June 15, 1991.

6. See "International: Unemployment Provision" (*RFE/RL,* 1992); International Monetary Fund (IMF), *Economic Review: The Economy of the Former USSR in 1991* (Washington, D.C.: IMF, April 1992), p. 9.

7. See Teague, "Tackling" (1991), p. 3, reporting on an interview with Minister of Labor A. Shokhin of the RSFSR in October 1991; also based on my interview with Margarita Garcia-Tser, research associate at the Institute for Employment Problems, Moscow, July 15, 1992.

8. IMF, *Economic Review* (1992), p. 4; Teague, "Tackling" (1991), pp. 3–7.

9. IMF, *Economic Review* (1992), p. 65 (Table 25). Moskoff reports that, in mid-1990, there were 210,000 cooperatives employing 5.2 million people;

and that by the end of 1990, 2,400 enterprises had converted to leasing; Moskoff, "The Soviet Economy" (1991), pp. 43–44.

10. Teague, "Tackling" (1991), p. 3.

11. IMF, *Economic Review* (1992), pp. 16, 70.

12. The unions, for example, demanded that enterprises be closed only with their consent; see *Trud,* Oct. 24, 1990, pp. 2–3.

13. See Mark Rhodes, "Food Supply in the USSR," *Report on the USSR,* vol. 3, no. 41, Oct. 11, 1991, pp. 11–16; Moskoff, "The Soviet Economy" (1991), pp. 29–34.

14. Gertrude Schroeder, "*Perestroyka* in the Aftermath of 1990," *Soviet Economy,* vol. 7, Jan.-March 1991, p. 4.

15. See Philip Hanson, "Pavlov's Price Increases," *Report on the USSR,* vol. 3, no. 12, Mar. 22, 1991, pp. 8–10.

16. For the text of the decree see *Pravda,* Mar. 20, 1991, pp. 1–2; and for Senchagov's breakdown, *FBIS:SU,* Mar. 21, 1991, p. 29, citing TASS, Mar. 20, 1991.

17. On compensation levels, see *Izvestiia,* Feb. 16, 1991, p. 1; on April 1991 price increase and its effect on wages, see IMF, *Economic Review* (1992), pp. 8, 60 (Table 20); on increases for light industrial goods and foodstuffs, see *FBIS:SU,* Apr. 3, 1991, p. 39, citing TASS, Apr. 2, 1991.

18. Quote is from *Izvestiia,* Apr. 14, 1991, p. 2.

19. See *FBIS:SU,* Mar. 22, 1991, p. 45, citing Moscow Radio Rossii, Mar. 18, 1991; the interview with the economist S. Shatalin in *FBIS:SU,* Apr. 5, 1991, p. 43–44, citing TASS, Apr. 4, 1991.

20. On the strike movement in Belorussia, see *Rabochaia Tribuna,* Apr. 24, 1991, pp. 1–2; Kathleen Mihalisko, "The Workers' Rebellion in Belorussia," *Report on the USSR,* vol. 3, no. 17, Apr. 26, 1991, pp. 21–25; on tensions and strikes in Ukraine, see *FBIS:SU,* Apr. 16, 1991, pp. 52–53, citing TASS, Apr. 15, 1991; Apr. 18, 1991, pp. 44–46, citing various sources. On overall numbers of strikes in this period, see IMF, *Economic Review* (1992), p. 9.

21. See IMF, *Economic Review* (1992), p. 8.

22. See *Pravda,* Mar. 20, 1991, p. 2; *Izvestiia,* Apr. 29, 1991, pp. 1–2.

23. See, for example, *Pravda,* July 9, 1991, p. 1.

24. See *Izvestiia,* Jan. 3, 1991, p. 4; Feb. 9, 1991, p. 2; *FBIS:SU,* Nov. 14, 1991, p. 27, citing *Pravda,* Nov. 13, 1991, p. 2.

25. See, for example, *FBIS:SU,* Apr. 8, 1991, p. 49, citing *Trud,* Apr. 5, 1991, p. 1.

26. See *Trud,* Oct. 24, 1990, pp. 2–3; Oct. 27, 1990, p. 1.

27. *Izvestiia,* Sept. 19, 1990, p. 2.

28. *Rabochaia Tribuna,* Nov. 16, 1990, p. 1; *Trud,* May 27, 1990, pp. 1, 2; Jan. 30, 1991, p. 1; Feb. 5, 1991, p. 2.

29. *Trud,* Oct. 19, 1990, pp. 1–2; Sept. 19, 1990, pp. 1–2.

30. *FBIS:SU,* Apr. 24, 1990, p. 63, citing TASS, Mar. 22, 1990.

31. See *Trud,* Oct. 26, 1990, p. 2.

32. In a 1990 poll on attitudes toward the reformed trade unions, 42 percent of respondents agreed that "everything remains as before in the work of the

trade unions," while 22 percent agreed that the new unions had "changed for the better." *Trud,* Oct. 26, 1990, p. 2.

33. *Trud,* Jan. 4, 1991, p. 2.

34. *FBIS:SU,* Oct. 25, 1990, pp. 44–48, citing TASS, Oct. 24, 1990; *Trud,* Feb. 21, 1991, p. 1.

35. *FBIS:SU,* Sept. 13, 1990, pp. 90–91, citing TASS, Moscow Television Service (MosTel), Sept. 12, 1990; *FBIS:SU,* Sept. 11, 1990, p. 75, citing *Sovetskaia Rossia,* Sept. 7, 1990, p. 1.

36. *Izvestiia,* Apr. 19, 1991, p. 2.

37. Ibid.

38. For data on attitudes see, for example, *Trud,* Oct. 26, 1990, p. 2.

39. See *Pravda,* Nov. 19, 1989, p. 2; *Rabochaia Tribuna,* Mar. 8, 1990, p. 2.

40. Quotes are from *Izvestiia,* July 11, 1990, p. 3.

41. See *FBIS:SU,* July 27, 1990. p. 83; citing Moscow World Service, July 27, 1990.

42. See *FBIS:SU,* Mar. 7, 1990, p. 109, citing Leningrad Maritime Press Service, Mar. 1, 1990; *FBIS:SU,* Apr. 9, 1990, pp. 44–45, citing *Komsomolskaia Pravda,* Apr. 5, 1990, p. 1; *FBIS:SU,* Apr. 12, 1990, p. 59, citing Moscow World Service, Apr. 11, 1990; *FBIS:SU,* July 27, 1990, p. 86, citing MosTel, July 24, 1990.

43. See *Gudok,* Oct. 7, 1990, p. 1, cited in *FBIS:SU,* Oct. 24, 1990, pp. 72–73; *Gudok,* Oct. 13, 1990, p. 1; Oct. 16, 1990, p. 1, cited in *FBIS:SU,* Oct. 23, 1990, pp. 61–62.

44. *FBIS:SU,* Mar. 15, 1991, pp. 23–24, citing Moscow Radio 1, Mar. 14, 1991; *FBIS:SU,* Mar. 26, 1991, pp. 31–32, citing *Izvestiia,* Mar. 22, 1991, p. 3; Walter D. Connor, *The Accidental Proletariat: Workers, Politics, and Crisis in Gorbachev's Russia* (Princeton: Princeton University Press, 1991), pp. 308–312.

45. *Izvestiia,* Mar. 15, 1991, p. 2. *Pravda,* claimed, not unfairly, that the miners put forth "a great patchwork of demands"; quote is trans. in *FBIS:SU,* Mar. 19, 1991, p. 44.

46. *Pravda,* Mar. 27, 1991, p. 2.

47. *Pravda,* Apr. 4, 1991, pp. 1–2.

48. Quote is from *FBIS:SU,* Apr. 12, 1991, p. 44, citing Radio 1 Network, Apr. 11, 1991.

49. *FBIS:SU,* Jan. 17, 1991, pp. 86–87, citing MosTel, Jan. 10, 1991; Jan. 25, 1991, p. 86, citing *Komsomolskaia Pravda,* Jan. 24, 1991, p. 2; March 1, 1991, pp. 28–29; March 12, 1991, pp. 64–65, citing various sources.

50. *Pravda,* May 1, 1991, p. 2; May 5, 1991, p. 3.

51. For arguments on this point, see Sarah Ashwin, "The 1991 Miners' Strike: New Departures in the Independent Workers' Movement," *Report on the USSR,* vol. 3, no. 33, 1991, Aug. 16, 1991, pp. 1–7.

52. *Trud,* Apr. 2, 1991, p. 1.

53. *Trud,* Mar. 23, 1991, p. 1; Apr. 3, 1991, p. 2; Apr. 19, 1991, p. 1.

54. The text is in *Trud,* Apr. 26, 1991, pp. 1–2.

55. See *FBIS:SU,* May 24, 1991, p. 29, citing TASS, May 23, 1991; May 29, 1991, pp. 37–38, citing TASS, May 28, 1991.

56. *FBIS:SU,* Apr. 23, 1991, p. 48; May 14, 1991, pp. 28–29; May 16, 1991, p. 38; May 17, 1991, p. 25; May 20, 1991, p. 27.
57. *FBIS:SU,* May 21, 1991, p. 32; May 23, 1991, p. 34.
58. *PlanEcon Report,* May 16, 1991, p. 15; John Tedstrom, "Economic Crisis Deepens," *RFE/RL Research Report,* vol. 1, no. 1, 1992, pp. 23–24.
59. Connor, *Accidental Proletariat,* pp. 298, 301.
60. *PlanEcon Report,* vol. 7, nos. 43–44, Dec. 9, 1991, p. 7.
61. Keith Bush, "Russia: Gaidar's Guidelines," *RFE/RL Research Report,* vol. 1, no. 15, Apr. 10, 1992, p. 23.
62. "Trade Unions," *Report on the USSR,* vol. 3, no. 41, Oct. 11, 1991, pp. 21–22; even the Independent Miners' Union enrolled only about 4 percent of all miners in mid-1991, though its influence clearly extended much further.
63. "Soviet Workers Find a Voice," *Report on the USSR,* July 13, 1990, p. 16.

8. Labor, Democracy, and Reform in the Post-Soviet Transition

1. See Peter Hauslohner, "Gorbachev's Social Contract," *Soviet Economy,* vol. 3, no. 1, 1987, pp. 54–89; Blair A. Ruble, "The Social Dimensions of *Perestroyka,*" *Soviet Economy,* vol. 3, no. 2, 1987, pp. 171–179.
2. One gets this impression, for example, in reading such commentaries as the following, from a July 1987 interview with the proreform Fedor Burlatsky: "We have repeatedly heard from the leaders of many enterprises that they are ready to reduce the number of workers by one-fourth or even by one- third on condition that the remaining wages fund the remuneration of workers who are left. On a nationwide scale, one-fourth means several tens of millions of people. What would one do with them?" *FBIS:SU,* July 23, 1987, p. R21, citing *Pravda,* July 18, 1987, p. 3.
3. See, for example, the reports in *Pravda,* Sept. 23, 1989, p. 3; Oct. 21, 1989, pp. 1–2; *Izvestiia,* Oct. 14, 1989, p. 2.
4. Charles Lindblom, *Politics and Markets: The World's Political-Economic Systems* (New York: Basic Books, 1977), p. 65.
5. Elizabeth Teague, "Russian Government Seeks 'Social Partnership,'" *RFE/RL Research Report,* vol. 1, no. 25, June 19, 1992, pp. 16–23.
6. Teague, "Russian Government" (1992), p. 23, citing the remarks of Gennadii Semigin, a representative of Russian businessmen on the tripartite commission.
7. From my interview with Pavel Kudiukin, deputy minister of labor of the Russian Federation, Moscow, July 15, 1992.
8. On the location of military production in isolated, closed cities see Julian Cooper, *The Soviet Defense Industry: Conversion and Reform* (New York: Council on Foreign Relations, 1991), pp. 19–29; for estimates of the effects of subsidy withdrawals and other reform measures on industry, see *Ekonomicheskaia Gazeta,* no. 47, November, 1992, p. 3.

Index

Abalkin, Leonid, 82, 84, 95, 105, 129, 241n9
AFTU. *See* Association of Free Trade Unions
Aganbegyan, Abel, 82, 110, 241n9
AIDS, 187
All-Union Center for the Study of Public Opinion (VTsIOM), 90, 190, 237n51, 246n80
All-Union Central Council of Trade Unions (AUCCTU; VTsSPS), 106, 120, 153, 172, 203, 210, 212; and Gorbachev reforms, 173, 174, 175, 176, 177, 180, 188, 207; and miners' strikes, 161, 163, 193
Andropov, Yuri, 220n12
Aslund, Anders, 90, 119, 242n26
Association of Free Trade Unions (AFTU), 73–74, 76
AUCCTU. *See* All-Union Central Council of Trade Unions
Authoritarianism, 3–4, 5, 205, 206, 210, 212, 213; attitude of intellectuals to, 4; of Brezhnev era, 202, 204; of Gorbachev, 206, 214; of Stalinist state, 69; and welfare state, 81, 83, 215
Avaliani, T., 161, 162

Balakin, V. A., 122
Baltics, 71, 171, 172, 176, 213, 214
Bank for Housing and Social Construction, 126
Banks, 119, 120, 123, 124, 125–126, 128, 183, 211

Bargaining, state-mediated, 12–13, 16, 17
Basic Law on Employment for the USSR and the Republics (1991), 181
Bialer, Seweryn, 1, 3, 105
Bim, A., 89, 139
Black markets, 44, 45, 46, 47, 52, 53, 134
Breslauer, George, 1
Brezhnev, Leonid, 1, 2, 7, 28, 161, 216; address to 23rd Congress, 22, 225n12; on agricultural policy, 63–64, 66; and corporatism, 13; 1982 Food Program of, 59, 64–66; and intellectuals, 220; and paternalism, 16, 17, 116; policies of, 3, 18, 21, 22, 32, 33, 38–40, 59, 67, 82, 83, 86, 116–117, 129; and the social contract, 6, 201, 205; speech to March 1965 Central Committee Plenum, 61; welfare state of, 19–53, 86–88, 89, 90, 91, 93, 104, 105, 116, 147, 167, 168, 178, 201, 224n44
Brezhnev era, 4, 5, 7, 8, 10, 15, 21; Economic Reforms (1965) of, 55, 56, 57; five-year plans of, 23, 33, 34, 48, 62, 63, 84; job security during, 26, 28, 29, 30, 31–32, 38, 201, 244n53; labor force in, 27, 39, 208, 240n102; labor policy in, 71, 84, 110, 152, 201, 202–203, 227n27; party congress reports of, 23, 25; prices in, 40–46, 86, 201; reaction to unrest in, 68–80; social policies and principles of, 22–25, 80, 110, 116, 140, 167, 201, 220n12; wage policies of, 33–40, 47, 83, 84, 100, 110, 155, 201, 204